Law and Society in Puritan Massachusetts

Studies in Legal History

Published by The University of North Carolina Press
in association with the
American Society for Legal History

EDITOR Morris S. Arnold

Editorial Advisory Board

John D. Cushing
Lawrence M. Friedman
Charles M. Gray
Thomas A. Green
Oscar Handlin
George L. Haskins
J. Willard Hurst
S. F. C. Milsom
Joseph H. Smith
L. Kinvin Wroth

Law and Society in Puritan Massachusetts

Essex County, 1629–1692

by DAVID THOMAS KONIG

The University of North Carolina Press
Chapel Hill

© 1979 The University of North Carolina Press
All rights reserved
Manufactured in the United States of America
Library of Congress Catalog Card Number 78-26685
ISBN 0-8078-1336-2

Library of Congress Cataloging in Publication Data

Konig, David Thomas, 1947–
　Law and society in Puritan Massachusetts.

　(Studies in legal history)
　Bibliography: p.
　Includes index.
　1. Law—Massachusetts—Essex Co.—History and
criticism.　2. Essex Co., Mass.—History.　I. Title.
II. Series.
KFM2999.E8K66　　340'.09744　　78-26685
ISBN 0-8078-1336-2

To the Memory of
MARGARET H. BAUM

Contents

Maps

Tables

Preface

I began this study to fill what I perceived to be a major gap in the literature of Early American history—the relationship of law and society. Legal scholars long have recognized the importance of the New England experience of the seventeenth century for the subsequent development of law and legal institutions in America. They have produced many fine studies from the perspective of their own discipline, examining with great diligence questions about doctrine, procedure, and institutional structure.[1] Nevertheless, scholars trained as historians have been remiss in asking questions of legal records as they pertain to the writing of history. Specifically, how did the legal system affect the lives of individuals in seventeenth-century New England? How did people in general—not just judges and lawyers—view the law, and what role did they assign to it in their society? Conversely, how was the law, like other institutions in early New England, affected by social, economic, and political change? That these questions have not been confronted in the vast literature on colonial New England is a serious oversight in view of the importance of legal institutions there.

This book examines law and society in Essex County, Massachusetts, from the granting of the first Bay Colony charter in 1629 to the arrival at Boston of its second charter in 1692. Litigation in Essex was so common that the county courts there heard literally thousands of cases during their existence under the colonial charter; in fact, between the last revision of the colony's legal code in 1672 and the final establishment of the Dominion of New England in 1686, Essex residents brought 2,942 cases before the courts. Despite the difficulties of travel during King Philip's War this one predominantly rural community—which never numbered more than 2,000 adult males during that period—managed to

---

1. Still most useful are George Lee Haskins, *Law and Authority in Early Massachusetts*, and Joseph H. Smith's introduction to his *Colonial Justice in Western Massachusetts (1639–1702)*. A useful collection of legal studies is David H. Flaherty, ed., *Essays in the History of Early American Law*.

bring an average of more than 200 cases a year to the county court.[2] This courtroom activity, moreover, was not the exclusive preserve of a small group of persistently litigious men. Of the 556 men listed on Salem's 1683 rate list (the best figures available for a control population) 62 were involved in court conflicts that year alone, while more than half of the others appeared in legal actions during the period between 1672 and 1692.[3] Whether as litigants, criminal defendants, or witnesses, these men were active parties to legal conflict. The commencement of a court action was not an inexpensive matter—court costs usually exceeded twenty shillings—nor was the journey to Salem or Ipswich, where the court met, an easy one in rural Essex. Yet it is safe to say that most men living there had some involvement with the court system and many of them appeared repeatedly.[4]

Curiously, historians have not attempted to explain precisely why that was so. Instead, they have rested on the assumption that the decline of piety and the pursuit of material goods by an increasingly acquisitive populace accounted for the high rate of legal conflict. Litigation is thus seen as merely another type of social pathology symptomatic of social divisiveness, unrestrained economic competition, or the total collapse of any coherent social ideology. The assumption, therefore, has been that the courts were a desperate last resort and served only to contain aggressiveness.[5]

By seventeenth-century standards, however, Essex was a remarkably stable society.[6] This book argues that legal institutions were to a large degree responsible for that stability and that litigation served a vital adaptive role in a period of growth and change. From the first arrival of

2. Evarts B. Greene and Virginia D. Harrington, *American Population before the Federal Census of 1790*, pp. xxiii, 20–21.

3. This does not include appearances at the witchcraft trials. Approximately 500 men voted in the election of selectmen in 1682. Salem Records, *EIHC*, 64:203. Rate lists for 1683 assessed 556 men for the two parishes and their ministers.

4. Court costs were set by law; they are enumerated in *Col. Laws 1672–86*, pp. 2, 130. Although written affidavits were permitted, any witness within ten miles of the courts at Salem or Ipswich had to be present "to be further Examined" (ibid., pp. 158–59). Inclusion of witnesses with plaintiffs and defendants derives from a characteristic of Essex litigation. Frequently a legal action was brought by one group of people against another, and the two principals named in the suit were chosen as a matter of convenience or because they were viewed as the leaders of the competing groups. These group actions might concern the location of a highway, a church matter, or a neighborhood quarrel.

5. The most recent and most prominent study to make litigation axiomatic with the decay of a once-harmonious social order is Kenneth A. Lockridge, *A New England Town, The First Hundred Years*, esp. pp. 145, 159.

6. For a general comment on the stability of seventeenth-century Massachusetts, see Timothy H. Breen and Stephen Foster, "The Puritans' Greatest Achievement," pp. 5–22.

colonists at Salem, a system of justices of the peace and quarterly courts was an indispensable support for the Puritan ideal of communalism that gave meaning to the Puritan colony. As is well known from many studies, this communal ideal soon faded in the New World environment, but existing interpretations leave the social and cultural development of Massachusetts at that point of collapse, or they view the rest of the seventeenth century as either a continued decline from orthodoxy or a drift with no direction. By contrast, this study sees the law and legal institutions as helping to create a new paradigm for the establishment of stable community life. Although early Puritan writers such as William Perkins had acknowledged the need for "wholesome lawes" in a godly society,[7] they had placed their main emphasis upon religion and the communal ideal for social stability. When these proved less than effective, legal institutions assumed a role of primary rather than only supplemental importance. Gradually, people came to recognize that litigation was a useful agent of orderly and desirable social change. Recourse to the law served, in James Willard Hurst's apt words, "to help create order and to choose among scarce satisfactions" as well as to achieve "acceptable balances of power in social relations."[8]

Anthropologists have identified and demonstrated the adaptive or "integrative" function of conflict,[9] but historians of seventeenth-century Massachusetts have viewed legal conflict only as harmful to social stability rather than supportive of it. They have seen it, in other words, only as destructive of community harmony rather than constructive of a new basis for harmony. I do not think that most residents of Essex County by the 1680s, for example, viewed litigation as serving only personal or purely material goals; the overwhelming weight of available evidence suggests, rather, that they recognized it as a constructive way to create and enforce what Charles M. Andrews defined as "standards of govern-

7. Perkins is cited by David B. Little in *Religion, Order, and Law*, p. 123. On the meaning and function of the paradigm, see Thomas S. Kuhn, *The Structure of Scientific Revolutions*.

8. J. Willard Hurst, "Legal Elements in United States History," pp. 67, 88, 91.

9. For a discussion of the "integrative" nature of conflict that is "based on a common acceptance of basic ends," see Lewis A. Coser, *The Functions of Social Conflict*, pp. 72–85. The functional interpretation of conflict draws upon a formulation made in the nineteenth century by Emile Durkheim in his *De la division du travail social* (1893), in which he demonstrated the process by which different and even competing individuals could become integrated into an "organic solidarity." On this point, see *Emile Durkheim on the Division of Labor in Society*, esp. pp. xxxix, 65, 113, 127. The functional school has come under attack in recent years, but its critics also recognize that conflict and "an ideology of community harmony" need not be incompatible. See, in this regard, Sally Falk Moore, "Selection for Failure in a Small Social Field," p. 109.

ment, conduct, and ways of living in order to meet the needs and obligations of their various and growing communities."[10] A "well-ordered"
society, they realized, required well-understood limits on behavior that
could not always be established by legislation or enforced by exhortation.
Though laws might set standards of dress, they could not set standards of
daily interpersonal activity, which had to be tested and established in
court. My concern in this book, therefore, is not only to examine the
internal development of legal doctrine and procedure, but also to discover the demands that social, economic, and political contingencies
placed on legal institutions and how those institutions changed in order
to become so important in society. As an examination of social, legal,
and institutional change, this study also is concerned with the position of
the legal system in a society with a multiplicity of institutional power
sources, ranging from town and congregation to a colony-wide assembly.
It is a subtheme of this book that the town and congregation—up to now
seen together as the most important focus of authority in early Massachusetts—were considerably less effective and thus less significant than
most historians are willing to admit. Instead, the county magistracy and
legal system must be viewed as serving many of the functions previously
identified with the town or congregation.

This responsibility for basic functions developed because the legal
system answered fundamental questions about the "well-ordered" community. Chapter 1 traces the transplantation of English legal institutions
to Massachusetts and suggests how important they were in providing
support for Puritan ideals of confraternity. Chapters 2 through 5 describe
the manner in which the questions of "community" and "acceptable
balances of power in social relations" were confronted and settled. How
was real property to be regulated when it was at first so plentiful that
people paid little attention to boundaries, fences, or deeds and records?
What constituted membership in a community,[11] and what were the privileges of outsiders? What type of behavior was acceptable and neighborly?

Because these questions were of baffling novelty and variety, answers
could be obtained only by testing and, in many cases, through overt
conflict. As the Reverend John Higginson of Salem acknowledged more
perceptively than many later historians, "the gift of Christ's peace" sometimes required litigation. Although it referred as much to a spiritual

10. Charles McLean Andrews, "On the Writing of Colonial History," pp. 37–38. For
comment on the meaning of litigation in premodern societies, see Keith Thomas, "History
and Anthropology," pp. 3–24.

11. A "community," according to anthropologist Raymond Firth, "involves a recognition, derived from experience or observation, that there must be minimum conditions of
agreement on common aims, and inevitably some common ways of behaving, thinking, and
feeling" (*Elements of Social Organization*, p. 27).

quest, his metaphor also reflected a social process at work, in which standards of neighborliness—the new community obligations and privileges—had to be demanded and asserted in court. Higginson counseled, "You must do as those that have a rich Legacy bequeathed to them; if they meet with any difficulty they put their case in Suit, they sue for their own at court."[12]

The resolution of social problems through legal conflict was not achieved simply or automatically, nor, for that matter, without challenge. For one thing, the benefits to be gained from litigation made Essex a contentious society. Through litigation, too, older values were attacked and newer ones elevated. With the aid of the county court system, a new basis of stability emerged by the end of the seventeenth century; but as chapter 6 explains, the new patterns of law and authority were subverted by an alienated minority who refused to accept them. Chapter 7 describes how peculiar circumstances drove many in Essex to apply drastic measures to preserve the new patterns. This struggle was intense, and one observer denounced its savagery: both the opponents and supporters of the new system, he remarked, were acting like "the Devill and the Turk . . . at war together."[13] His reference to the Devil was not coincidental; chapter 7 also reexamines the witchcraft prosecutions of 1692 to propose a new explanation for that peculiar course of events.

I would like to thank the many people who helped in the production of this work. The librarians and archivists of the Essex Institute in Salem, with their knowledge of Essex history and its abundant sources, were extremely helpful. Also of assistance were the staffs of the Yale University Sterling Law Library and Beinecke Rare Book Library, and of the Harvard University Houghton Library. Leo Flaherty of the Massachusetts Archives was as helpful to me as he has been to countless other scholars who have waded through the primary sources at the State House in Boston. I would also like to thank Donald Nutting of the Essex County Clerk's Office for his permission to use the irreplaceable manuscript records still on file at the county courthouse in Salem. Access to those records—for an uninterrupted period of nearly a year—was absolutely essential to this book. The Mark DeWolfe Howe Fund at Harvard University for studies in legal history contributed financial aid for part of the research, and for that support I am grateful.

Contributions to a work transcend the immediate or the direct, and

12. John Higginson, *Our Dying Saviour's Legacy of Peace to His Disciples in a Troublesome World*, p. 95. The same sentiment was expressed by William Hubbard of Ipswich in *The Benefit of a Well-Ordered Conversation*.
13. Wainwright v. Swan [1690], EP 48:88–99.

two people deserve particular acknowledgment. This study began as a doctoral dissertation under the guidance of Bernard Bailyn, whose high standards and consistently stimulating scholarship I have tried to make a model. To the same degree, I am indebted to William E. Nelson of the Yale Law School. His work in the field of legal history has brought to the subject the talent and attention it deserves and has been very influential in my thinking. My colleagues at Washington University—Rowland Berthoff, Richard Helmholz, Derek Hirst, and Michael Weinberg—have given me considerable guidance in refining my arguments. I have also benefited from helpful comments by Bruce Ackerman, Timothy H. Breen, Thomas Andrew Green, Edith Henderson, Stanley N. Katz, James H. Kettner, and Joseph H. Smith.

I am also indebted to the following for permission to reprint portions of this work that have appeared elsewhere: to the Wesleyan University Press, regarding portions of chapter 1 that appeared in B. C. Daniels, ed., *Town and County: Essays in the Structure of Local Government in the American Colonies*; to the *American Journal of Legal History* regarding part of chapter 2 that appeared in volume 18 (1974):137–77; and to the *Essex Institute Historical Collections*, where part of chapter 3 appeared in volume 110 (1974):167–80.

Finally, I am indebted to my wife, Judith Mann, for affording this author the Puritan ideal of "apt and cheerful conversation of man and woman, to comfort and refresh him against the solitary life."

Abbreviations

Acts and Resolves	*Acts and Resolves, Public and Private, of the Province of Massachusetts Bay*
Assts. Rec.	John Noble and John F. Cronin, eds., *Records of the Court of Assistants of the Colony of the Massachusetts Bay, 1630–1692*
CSP	W. N. Sainsbury and J. W. Fortescue, eds., *Calendar of State Papers, Colonial Series, America and West Indies*
Col. Laws 1660–72	William H. Whitmore, ed., *The Colonial Laws of Massachusetts. Reprinted from the Edition of 1660, with the Supplements to 1672, Containing Also the Body of Liberties of 1641*
Col. Laws 1672–86	William H. Whitmore, ed., *The Colonial Laws of Massachusetts. Reprinted from the Edition of 1672, with the Supplements through 1686*
Dalton Records	*Records of the Commissioners Court Held At Hampton, by Samuel Dalton, 1673–1680*
EMbk. 1638–48	Minutebook of the Essex Quarterly Court and County Court, terms held at Ipswich and Salem, 1638–1648
EMbk. 1655–66	Minutebook of the Essex County Court, terms held at Ipswich and Salem, 1655–1666
EP	File Papers of the Essex Quarterly Court and County Court, 1636–1692
IpMbk. 1646–66	Minutebook of the Essex County Court, terms held at Ipswich, 1646–1666
IpMbk. 1666–82	Minutebook of the Essex County Court, terms held at Ipswich, 1666–1682

IpMbk. 1682–92

Minutebook of the Essex County Court, terms held at Ipswich, 1682–1692

IpWbk.

Wastebook of material from the Essex County Court, terms held at Ipswich, 1682–1686

Marblehead Records, *EIHC*

William H. Bowden, comp., "Marblehead Town Records, 1648–1683," in Essex Institute Historical Collections

Mass. Arch.

Massachusetts Archives

Mass. Rec.

Nathaniel B. Shurtleff, ed., *Records of the Governor and Company of the Massachusetts Bay in New England*

NorMbk. 1648–78

Minutebook of the Norfolk County Court, terms held at Hampton and Salisbury, 1648–1678

NorMbk. 1672–81

Minutebook of the Norfolk County Court, terms held at Hampton and Salisbury, 1672–1681

NorWbk.

Wastebook of material from the Norfolk County Court, terms held at Hampton and Salisbury, 1650–1680

SaMbk. 1636–41

Minutebook of the Essex Quarterly Court, terms held at Salem, 1636–1641

SaMbk. 1667–79

Minutebook of the Essex County Court, terms held at Salem, 1667–1679

Salem Records, *EIHC*

Salem, Massachusetts, "Salem Town Records, 1638–1683," in Essex Institute Historical Collections

Salem Town Records, 1634–59

Salem, Massachusetts, *Town Records of Salem. October 1, 1634, to November 7, 1659*

Salisbury Records

Salisbury Town Records, 1638–1902

Saltonstall Papers

Robert E. Moody, ed., *The Saltonstall Papers, 1607–1815*

Saltonstall Records

Robert E. Moody, ed., "Records of the Magistrate's Court at Haverhill, Massachusetts, Kept by Nathaniel Saltonstall, 1682–1685"

SCJ   Records of the Massachusetts Bay
                             Superior Court of Judicature

Winthrop Letters   Winthrop Family, *Correspondence of
                             the Winthrop Family* published in
                             *Collections of the Massachusetts
                             Historical Society*, 4th ser.

Winthrop Papers   Winthrop Family, *The Winthrop
                             Papers*, vol. 1 (1498–1628).

WP   "Salem Witchcraft—1692." Verbatim
                             transcript compiled by A. N. Frost

WRec.   William E. Woodward, ed., *Records
                             of Salem Witchcraft*

Author's Note

Original forms of spelling, punctuation, and capitalization have been retained as completely as possible. For the purposes of clarity, several slight changes have been made in direct quotations: commas and periods have been added to excessively long sentences; abbreviations and contractions have been expanded; and the archaic usages of "u" for "v" and "y" for "th" have been modernized.

To avoid double dating, all dates are given in New Style; that is, the new year is assumed as beginning on 1 January, and all dates from then through 24 March are given as the new year.

Law and Society in Puritan Massachusetts

I English Law and Puritan Society

The Legal and Social
Foundations of Order, 1629–1640

When the Puritan settlers of Salem gathered to organize the first church of the newly chartered Massachusetts Bay Colony in August 1629, they signed a covenant that they hoped would be their guide "in all causes, as well Ecclesiasticall as Politicall." Drafted by John Endecott and their minister Samuel Skelton, it declared their goal of establishing a society based on Christian communalism—on mutual "watchfulness and tendernis"—and was typical of covenants to be written for virtually every town and congregation in the early years of the colony.[1] Yet no matter how fervently the Puritan founders wished and strove for a society ruled by such religious confraternity, they discovered that only thirty of the two hundred persons living at the Bay actually signed when it was presented to them. Church members were a minority of a population that included many people unsympathetic to reformed Congregationalism as well as others who had migrated to the New World to escape all types of authority. Among the latter, as Nathaniel Ward described those at Ipswich, were "ill and doubtfull persons" who not only refused to be bound by communal ideals, but who spent their time "in drinking and pilferinge."[2]

Communalism—whether drawn from ecclesiastical or secular sources—was thus an ideal of behavior and regulation to which Massachusetts society might aspire, but the colony's founders recognized that in Massachusetts, no less than in England, it was an ideal that required outside mechanisms of support if it was to assure the stability of their communities.[3] Wisely, therefore, they drew upon their English experience to create a system of local government that possessed the powers necessary to impose order and discipline. Their product closely resembled the oligarchical patterns of English county or borough government whose

1. Richard D. Pierce, ed., *Records of the First Church in Salem, Massachusetts, 1629–1736*, pp. 27–28. Lawrence Shaw Mayo, *John Endecott*, p. 29.
2. Ward to John Winthrop, Jr., Ipswich, 24 Dec. 1635, in *Winthrop Letters*, 7:24–25.
3. On the general subject of ideal and actual systems of law, see Leo Pospisil, "Legal Levels and the Multiplicity of Legal Systems in Human Societies," pp. 2–26.

justices of the peace and courts of quarter sessions were of proven effectiveness.

Effective governmental institutions were a preoccupation of early modern England, and especially so among Puritans. Although they opposed the crown's efforts to force an objectionable religious conformity upon them, they supported and encouraged efforts to bring stability to a disordered society.[4] To one contemporary observer, English communities seemed beset by thieves, drunkards, "common hedge-breakers, common peace-breakers, raylers, and sowers of discord between neighbours, keepers or haunters of baudy houses, common scolds," and the ubiquitous vagabond. The wandering poor were most worrisome, for the enclosure of common fields had dispossessed thousands and produced a population of menacing "sturdy Beggars" who streamed into London or wandered about the countryside. Many of these "night-walkers and day-sleepers" turned to crime as a way of life, and their numerous illegitimate offspring were a heavy drain on local institutions of relief. Seventeenth-century English thought was conditioned by these realities and was, not surprisingly, pervaded by fear of crime and anxiety about social instability.[5]

Vast economic and demographic changes had produced these symptoms, but Puritans attributed them to the innate depravity of the human personality. "We know," wrote Calvin, "that man is of so perverse and crooked a nature, that everyone would scratch out his neighbor's eyes if there were no bridle to hold them in."[6] The "bridle," such that it was translated into governmental institutions, was to be wielded by the elect —that is, by those who had been redeemed by God's grace. Indeed, the elect were under an obligation to impose restraint upon the unregenerate. John Winthrop, who had been named governor of the colony a few months before sailing to the New World in March 1630, was not self-serving when in mid-Atlantic he lectured his fellow emigrants on the "charity" involved in enforcing discipline among the unredeemed. Winthrop's subject was the "love" that bound a society together and through which man acted "to manifest the worke of [God's] Spirit." But the seventeenth-century Puritan concept of Christian love differed from the benign concept that would govern nineteenth-century democratic

4. An excellent recent study of Puritan efforts to impose stability is Keith E. Wrightson, "The Puritan Reformation of Manners, with special reference to the Counties of Lancashire and Essex, 1640–1660."

5. William Sheppard, The Court-keepers Guide, pp. 14–15. Christopher Hill, in explaining the pre-Civil War period, warns, "We shall often misinterpret men's thoughts and actions if we do not continually remind ourselves of this background of potential unrest" (The Century of Revolution, 1603–1714, p. 28).

6. Cited in Michael Walzer, The Revolution of the Saints, p. 33.

and egalitarian utopias. While many of the latter—products of a post-Enlightenment culture—presupposed man's equality and goodness, Winthrop and the Massachusetts Puritans distrusted man's nature. They saw the need, as an act of love, to rescue it from sinfulness. Winthrop was stating the generally accepted view of society when he said that there always would be people "highe and eminent in power and dignitie." It was these people, he submitted, who had an obligation to be the stewards of society, and one of their responsibilities—in fact, the one he listed first—was "upon the wicked in moderateing and restraineing them."[7]

The task of "moderateing and restraineing" the unregenerate would require every tool available to the Puritans. Ecclesiastical discipline was one method, but it was recognized that true reformation required that Puritans "adjoyne the sword to defend the word" of Scripture and reformation.[8] As one Lancashire minister said, directing his remarks to that county's justices of the peace, "Ministers are the mouth of the Church, [and] where we see abuses . . . we may ondly reprove and complaine. You have power to correct. A mutual help may worke a better reformation." It is noteworthy that this plea was directed to the justices of the peace, for it was upon them that the Puritan reformers placed their hopes for the reformation of society. Why was that so? The English legal system during the Tudor and Stuart periods was vast and complex, a system of overlapping and sometimes conflicting jurisdictions that ranged from the central courts at Westminster to the wide variety of manor and village courts. Similarly, the social and economic conditions of early-seventeenth-century England were heterogeneous and varied. Yet Puritan reformers—clerical and secular alike—emphasized the role of the justice of the peace, for it, above all other local legal institutions, had weathered the effects of social and political change and had demonstrated a power and a flexibility lacking in the others.[9] In spite of the symbolic value of the feudal and communal institutions, Puritan leaders placed great responsibility on the justice of the peace. The reasons for this increasing reliance are worth examining in detail.

Over the preceding centuries, many legal institutions that once had had the primary responsibility for resolving conflict or controlling disorder had sunk slowly into insignificance. The Tudors, for example, had sought to eliminate all vestiges of the feudal order that might challenge their control of the state, and they gradually reduced the power of the old sheriff's tourn. At one time the most important instrument of social

---

7. John Winthrop, "A Model of Christian Charity," p. 76.
8. Wrightson, "Puritan Reformation," p. 16.
9. Ministerial calls for reform are cited in ibid. On the varied character of just one region, see Clive Holmes, *The Eastern Association in the English Civil War.*

control and local administration, by the mid-fifteenth century the tourn had lost to the justices of the peace much of its power to hear and determine cases; by the end of the Tudor period it had declined still further, to the point that it was rarely the agent of "even the most elementary police tasks."[10]

But Tudor political opposition was hardly necessary to cause the decline of many other institutions, as the steady process of social change eroded the power of local courts that had been available for hundreds of years. These were the manorial courts leet and baron, as well as institutions of the village, hundred, and county. All were products of the Middle Ages and had relied on community pressures to be effective. Though Tudor policy did not destroy the local courts, social and economic change reduced the force of the pressures that had guaranteed their efficacy. To be sure, there were backwaters in the varied English social and legal geography where the relatively stable, interdependent community retained its full powers, but its greatest decline had occurred in areas where Puritanism—partly in reaction—was most influential. The strength of these courts had been the ideal of unanimity that governed the medieval manor. In conformity to the needs of common field husbandry, decisions had to be collective. Tenants had to decide which crops to plant in the field where their individual strips of land lay or which part of it should be left fallow; these were collective decisions that, once made, had to be recognized by all. Similarly, the tenants acted in a body to discharge their obligations to the lord, such as yoking their oxen together to plow his demesne. Repeatedly working in proximity with each other, they were neighbors who had known each other all their lives and were aware of whatever happened in their community.[11] Manorial institutions reflected this familiarity and collective effort in their procedures. Attendance at the manorial courts was mandatory for all tenants, both to confer legitimacy on their decisions and to bring forward all persons who could contribute information and guide them.

Theoretically, the courts leet and baron were distinct bodies, but in practice they were often combined. Leet jurisdiction was concerned with public nuisances and "evill members, and persons of ill behaviours that are dangerous to their neighbours." The lord's steward sat there as judge, presiding over a "presentment jury" elected from among those in attendance.[12] This body combined the functions of discovery, indictment,

10. Thomas G. Barnes, *Somerset, 1625–1640*, p. 124. G. C. F. Forster, *The East Riding Justices of the Peace in the Seventeenth Century*, p. 13.

11. H. S. Bennett, *Life on the English Manor*, pp. 44–49. See also W. O. Ault, *Open-Field Farming in Medieval England*, esp. pp. 20–34.

12. Sheppard, *Court-Keepers Guide*, p. 14. John Kitchin, *Jurisdictions; or, the Lawful Authority of Courts Leet, Courts Baron, Court of Marshalseyes, Court of Pypowder, and Antient Demesne*, pp. 16–21.

trial, and sentencing. Though some manors empaneled two juries—a grand jury for indictment and a petit or traverse jury for trial—most empowered a single group to perform all of these tasks. Once a presentment was made by a unanimous jury, explained a seventeenth-century treatise, "it is said to be as Gospell, and no Traverse lyeth to it, but in some speciall case, as when it doth concern freehold." After these jurors had accused and convicted, they then set the penalty. This amercement or fine was set by "afferers," who might be the entire jury or a few chosen from among them.[13]

Like the court leet, the court baron had been established to make justice available to villeins "at their own doors." Its purpose was not to "enquire of any offence against the State," but rather "to take care and inquire of causes concerning the Mannor," and it handled matters pertaining to the lord's own rights as well as to disputes among his tenants.[14] The court baron was truly an instrument of, by, and for a manor's residents, for the steward presided only on matters concerning the lord's rights or conveyance of freehold among copyholders. In all other cases, this court was conducted by twelve "suitors" chosen from the manor; they alone decided disputes over refusals to keep promises or pay debts, up to the value of forty shillings. When manorial management required it, they might make bylaws for the regulation of manorial business and set penalties for the violation of these laws.[15]

Although suitors of the court baron had little legal expertise and lacked the authority of the lord's steward to enforce their decisions, they possessed other strengths. For example, the weight of tradition was a guide to the rules that should be followed. In addition, their process of making decisions, like that of the leet, drew heavily upon the community's acquaintance with the parties. If, for instance, a man were accused of taking another's livestock as his own, he might bring to court a dozen neighbors to attest to his honesty; their "oath helping," or "wager of law," was sufficient to acquit him of the demand. This system worked well in a society in which a community trusted the knowledge a man's closest acquaintances had of him and in which patently false swearing would be uncovered sooner or later.[16]

13. For a description of the presentment jury, see Sheppard, *Court-Keepers Guide*, pp. 20–22; Kitchin, *Jurisdictions*, p. 83; and John P. Dawson, *A History of Lay Judges*, pp. 191–92.

14. Trespass by force and arms was not within its jurisdiction. For the court baron in general, see Sir Edward Coke, *The Fourth Part of the Institutes of the Laws of England*, chap. 57; Kitchin, *Jurisdictions*, pp. 344–69; and Sheppard, *Court-Keepers Guide*, pp. 3, 66.

15. Sidney Webb and Beatrice Webb, *English Local Government*, 2:13n, 18.

16. For a description of this procedure, see Bennett, *English Manor*, pp. 207–16; and W. S. Holdsworth, *A History of English Law*, 1:305–8, for the pleas in which wager of law

The medieval manorial courts therefore rested mainly, but not ex-clusively, on the community itself to be effective—for bringing actions, making decisions, and finally for enforcing their orders. Enforcement was the crucial element in the structure of local justice, and it was at that point that the ideal of unanimity was only as effective as the seigneurial power available to support it when challenged or defied. This was also true of the communal courts of the villages, which were instruments of regulation for social units that included more than one manor. Particu-larly in East Anglia, many "village communes" constituted their own juries or "jury-like bodies" from among the residents of the different manors to handle problems that concerned only the villagers and not the rights of the lord. Much like the court baron, they relied on local pres-sures to discover and punish offenders by distraining property to pay fines. However, the *villata*, the local unit of village authority, cannot be regarded as fully adequate to the needs and pressures of village life.[17] In practice, these communal bodies often had to enlist the aid of the lord's authority, for the village's power to fine was a limited and sometimes ineffective sanction and even neighborly pressures were ineffective before a recalcitrant offender.[18]

Villagers, therefore, had to secure aid when the legal weaknesses of their communities became apparent; and however much they sought to preserve the stability of their communities from within, support often had to come from without. Of course, to deny the full legal competency of the village to achieve order without external assistance is not at all to deny the importance of the village as an ideal. On the contrary, the village remained the focus of life in the early seventeenth century, and the fact that villagers sought outside aid to preserve community stability implies the high value they placed on the village ideal. Though the *legal* powers of the village may have been weakening, villagers were still active in trying to preserve their local community as a meaningful *social* unit.[19] To that end, recourse to outside legal authority might be necessary.

Other extramanorial courts suffered from the same problem. Courts of the hundred and county had been established to bring the king's justice to the shires. Conducted by twelve suitors, their jurisdiction was

---

was permitted. Oath-helpers were subject to penalty if a man's later behavior made it clear that their oath had been false swearing.

17. M. M. Postan, *The Medieval Economy and Society*, pp. 117–20.

18. J. Ambrose Raftis, *Tenure and Mobility*, p. 105.

19. Peter Laslett emphasizes that "living together in one township, isolated, spatially, from others of comparable size, of very much the same structure, inevitably means a communal sense and communal activity, even if that activity is trivial and symbolic, as it is in the *social club* which we treasure so much in our day" (*The World We Have Lost*, p. 60).

broad, ranging from debts and promises to the "chasing of hoggs with doggs" and other trespasses. While these courts relied less on the local community than did the others by not permitting wager of law, they were little less dependent ultimately on the pressures of the community for enforcement. This was so because these bodies were not "courts of record"; that is, their decisions had no standing with outside institutions such as the royal machinery of government. Also unable to obtain adequate support from the impotent sheriff, they had to draw upon the fact that their decisions had been made in the presence of numerous involved members of the community who, it was hoped, would assure compliance through local pressures.[20]

The ideal behind this entire system was described by Sir Thomas Smith in 1565 when he observed, "These courtes doe serve rather for men that can be content by their neighbors, and which love their quiet and profit in their husbandrie, more than to be busy in the law."[21] By the later sixteenth century, however, the problems of that ideal had become apparent —especially in Puritan areas—mainly because political, economic, and demographic change had weakened the all-inclusive nature of the medieval community. Quite simply, many people were no longer part of meaningful communities in the old sense. Uprooted by enclosure or the need to seek work in areas less severely affected by unemployment, they were unfamiliar with local customs and not well known by any "vicinage," or neighborhood. In sum, society was beginning to undergo what Christopher Hill calls the change "from a hierarchy of communities to the agglomeration of equal competing individuals depicted in *Leviathan*."[22] Without the habits of collective activities and the modes of thought endemic to communalism, the medieval local courts were shrinking to insignificance, doing little more than electing knights to Parliament (at the county courts) and managing the routine affairs of the manor. The latter was hardly a negligible concern, but when disputes involved difficult issues, these courts lacked the social foundation to function effectively. Typical of their limited capacity was the way in which the court of the manor near John Winthrop's in Suffolk could amerce only when "everyone in the village knew whether Samuel Ware let his trees 'over-

20. Coke, *The Fourth Part of the Institutes of the Laws of England*, chaps. 60 and 61. William Greenwood, *Curia Comitatus Rediviva, or the Pratique Part of the County-Court Revived*, pp. 108–55. Unless a writ of *justices* was obtained from the chancellor, moreover, the county court was limited to the recovery of only 40 shillings in damages, a sum that inflation was rendering insubstantial.

21. Smith is cited in Dawson, *Lay Judges*, p. 232.

22. Christopher Hill, *Society and Puritanism in Prerevolutionary England*, p. 487. For more on the high geographical mobility and instability of seventeenth-century England, see Philip J. Greven, Jr., *Four Generations*. pp. 267–68.

dreep' the highway or left his chimney in disrepair, and he could hardly deny the charge."[23]

The reason for this limited ability to respond was what Maitland aptly described as the "automatism of ancient agriculture and ancient government." Community practices had become so routinized over the course of generations that people could rely upon customary rules so generally accepted that they did not have to be committed to writing. But when unprecedented situations posed novel or difficult questions and consensus was impossible, contention made the community reluctant as well as unable to act. The Elizabethan justice of the peace William Lambarde was aware of the problems of applying traditional community procedures in a period of rapid and confusing change when he lectured a grand jury that people "vex and overcrow their neighbors . . . bastards be multiplied in parishes, [and] thieves and rogues do swarm the highways," but "scarcely any man [can be] found that will once move his finger" to promote order. William Sheppard, a law reformer critical of communal shortcomings, commented in 1657 that "there are many good Laws" against disorder, "but there is little execution of them: Not one Oath of a thousand that is sworn," he protested, "is punished."[24]

Punishment, of course, required officials and institutions capable of exercising adequate sanctions against offenders. Only the crown and the powerful country gentry, however, possessed such sanctions in the early seventeenth century. As a result, only those institutions able to draw upon these sources were able to function as effective instruments of social control or conflict resolution when the Puritan migration began. The court leet, for example, was able to continue even its "humble" existence mainly as a result of such external assistance. If its judgments were resisted, the justices of the peace were available for support because the leet was a court of record. As such, its decisions and orders were recognizable by the royal bureaucracy, while those of the court baron and county court, which were not courts of record, were not. Perhaps equally important was the interest of the manor lord in its continued existence for his personal gain: it was his personal franchise and its fees were a steady source of income.[25]

The central courts, because they were direct agents of royal authority and could draw upon the power and prestige of the sovereign, had an

23. Dawson describes Redgrave, near Bury St. Edmunds, in *Lay Judges*, pp. 191–92.

24. William Lambarde, *William Lambarde and Local Government*, pp. 73–74. William Sheppard, *England's Balme*, pp. 25–26.

25. For a theoretical discussion of the general issue of sanctions, see Harold Laswell and Richard Arens, "The Role of Sanction in Conflict Resolution," pp. 27–39. Holdsworth, *English Law*, 4:127–30.

enormous influence on English society. Tudor and Stuart monarchs employed the prerogative Star Chamber, while the archbishop of Canterbury controlled the ecclesiastical High Commission. But it was through the common law courts that central power was brought more regularly to bear on the general population when the assizes brought their circuit jurisdiction to the counties. Despite the antagonism between the common law and prerogative courts, both relied ultimately on the power of the crown, whose authority made the assizes formidable weapons against disorder. Puritan ministers recognized this fact, and their sermons at the opening of assize terms expressed their hope that Westminster would impose the order necessary for a reformed England. At the Hertford Assizes in 1619, for example, William Pemberton spoke of the judges there as the "masters and pilots in the ship of the commonwealth, who sit at the stern and guide it forward through their wisdom and fidelity . . . unto the desired haven of peace and prosperity."[26]

Though potent, the assizes were not always practicable as a ready or easily available agent of direct social regulation in local communities. The assizes visited the localities only semiannually and brought with them a relatively small staff. In addition, the assize courts were expensive ones in which to seek redress of civil grievances. In their *nisi prius* capacity[27] they dealt with a veritable storm of civil litigation during this period, but the benefits of royal authority came only at a high price. On the eve of the Civil War, Sir Edward Coke estimated that Englishmen were spending a million pounds every year on litigation before such courts, while Sir Matthew Hale later observed that costs were so outrageous that they were "often forty times more than the principall." Altogether, the costs of litigation were such that Winthrop listed them in 1624 as one of England's "common Greavances Groaninge for Reformation."[28]

Englishmen concerned about disorder, then, appreciated the authority of the assizes, but they had to look closer to home for less expensive and more accessible institutions capable of imposing order. In the seventeenth century, the parish was beginning to fill some of this need,

26. Cited in Walzer, *Revolution of the Saints*, p. 179. See also M. M. Knappen, *Tudor Puritanism*, pp. 174, 233.

27. *Nisi prius* civil jurisdiction was technically distinct from the gaol delivery authority of the assize courts. See Coke, *Fourth Institutes of the Laws of England*, chap. 56; and J. S. Cockburn, *A History of English Assizes, 1558–1714*, p. 70. Assizes were held only annually in the three most remote counties of the north. Ibid., p. 19.

28. Donald Veall, *The Popular Movement for Law Reform, 1640–1660*, pp. 37–38. Sir Matthew Hale, "Some Considerations touching the Amendment or Alteration of Lawes," p. 283. *Winthrop Papers*, 1:309–310. Figures on civil causes at *nisi prius* can be found in Cockburn, *Assizes*, p. 137.

because it was coming under the control of the "select vestry," a self-perpetuating oligarchy of the "chief men" of the parish whose prestige and financial weight helped promote efficient local government. Though the parish was an ecclesiastical division with no original basis in statute, royal decree, or commission, the Tudors had given it responsibilities far beyond its traditional duties of maintaining church property and punishing its parishioners' moral or religious transgressions. From its power to tax came a responsibility to repair highways, destroy pests, aid disabled soldiers and sailors, and build workhouses for the unemployed.[29]

Yet the parish, according to Sidney and Beatrice Webb, "was regarded by no one as an organ of autonomous self-government,"[30] and its capacity to cope with the broad spectrum of seventeenth-century disorder and community disruption was significantly limited by two factors. In the first place, its jurisdiction stopped sharply at the end of the list of duties specified by statute. The informal pressures that the locally eminent vestry may have been able to exert were considerable but were nevertheless limited to those affairs over which the parish had legal jurisdiction, such as the implementation of the poor laws.[31] Second, the vestry was forced to rely on the so-called customary parish officials to carry out its will—the constables, churchwardens, tithingmen, overseers of the poor, and surveyors of highways.[32] It was their lot, for example, actually to collect taxes, detect Sabbath violations, and set vagrants to work or warn them to another parish. Unfortunately, the men delegated to perform these unwelcome duties were in many cases hardly those who could do them well. Constables in particular were drawn from the lower ranks of society. Their low social standing weakened their efforts to command obedience, and if they did attempt to preserve the peace they might be sued or humiliated for their pains. Charged in the king's name to come to the aid of a beleaguered Middlesex constable in 1614, one Paul Jefferson embellished his refusal by ordering the officer, "I charge you in the Kinges name to kiss my tayle."[33] Left to its own devices, therefore, the parish was unable to overcome its legal shortcomings and to assume a greater role as an instrument of local control.

29. Holdsworth, *English Law*, 4:155–57.

30. Webb and Webb, *English Local Government*, 1:40.

31. Eleanor M. Trotter, *Seventeenth-Century Life in the Country Parish, with Special Reference to Local Government*, p. 23.

32. Ibid. Strictly speaking, the constable was an officer of the hundred, but his duties concerned parish affairs, and by a statute of 22 Henry VIII, c. 12, sec. 3, parishes were made liable to fine if he did not perform his duties. Holdsworth, *English Law*, 4:124, 158.

33. William LeHardy, ed., *County of Middlesex: Calendar to the Sessions Records*, 1:371. Barnes describes constables in Somerset as "lazy, disobedient, and negligent" (*Somerset*, p. 77).

Yet it must be emphasized that in the early Stuart period the parish was not the moribund institution that the manor was, nor was it as limited in its functions and legal powers as the village. Its effectiveness, however, was ultimately owing to the supervision and assistance of the justices of the peace, without whom the parish would have lacked much of its ability to act. It fell to the justices of Middlesex, for instance, to punish Paul Jefferson for his conduct toward a parish official trying to do his job. Indeed, much of the work of a county's justices was their supervision of local affairs.[34]

The county's justices met in a body once each quarter and, more frequently, they met in smaller groups as "petty sessions." The latter meetings were held at locations in different "divisions" of the county, but even the quarterly sessions might adjourn to meet at different towns "so that nobody," writes a historian of local government in Norfolk, "ever needed to travel outside his 'division' to attend quarter sessions." In addition, any one of the dozens of justices living in a county could act individually out of sessions at his residence.[35] Enforcing many statutes through summary conviction, he was utilizing what Lambarde called "the advantage and facilitie that they have to dispatch the affaire by meanes of their nearness and dwelling." As Tudor monarchs assumed more responsibility for establishing and maintaining civil order where local officials had failed, Tudor Parliaments delegated an ever greater share of this burden to the justice of the peace, sending him "not Loads, but Stacks of Statutes," as Lambarde described the situation.[36]

Unlike most other local officials, justices of the peace possessed the powers necessary to bear this burden and to perform their duties effectively. As members of the gentry, they could draw upon their wealth and social standing to command deference and compliance.[37] Among their most important assets, however, was a specific royal grant of power denied to the others—the "commission of the peace," issued by the chancellor under the Great Seal. The reformed commission of 1590 ordered justices to hold regular sessions where they were to enforce all statutes of the peace and try indicted offenses.[38] Given the authority to

34. Wrightson identifies the magistratical supervision of formerly negligent petty constables as one of the most important Puritan methods of effecting a social reformation ("Puritan Reformation," p. 135).

35. A. Hassell Smith, *County and Court*, p. 88. The authority of the justices acting individually, in petty sessions, or in quarter sessions, is distinguished in Holdsworth, *English Law*, 4:138–49.

36. William Lambarde, *Eirenarcha, or the Office of the Justices of Peace*, pp. 34, 246. See also, generally, Michael Dalton's handbook for justices, *Countrey Justice*.

37. G. M. Trevelyan, *English Social History*, p. 171, cited in J. H. Gleason, *The Justices of the Peace in England, 1558–1640*, p. 1.

38. The reformed commission of the peace can be found in G. R. Elton, *The Tudor*

order corporal punishment, commit offenders to gaol, or call upon the physical might of the crown if necessary, the justices possessed the legal powers required to bring peace to an unruly population. As a result, they did not have to rely on the sanctions of the community. They were not limited to imposing the dubious restraint of an oath, moreover, but could enforce any oath to keep the peace by further obtaining a surety bond. As Lambarde explained, "[O]ur Governours, knowing that evill men be more restrayned by losse of goods than by conscience of an oath, have used to take sure bonds, and that to the Prince, for the securitie of such as be in feare."[39]

The threat of forfeiting a sum of money was a considerable deterrent, and its effectiveness was increased by the procedures governing its application. To begin with, a justice need not have waited for a complaint in order to act. Lambarde pointed out that if a justice "see menne contending in hotte wordes, and threatning the one to hurte (or kill) the other, he may of discretion and ought of Duety (as I thinke) to commaunde them to find Surety of the Peace." Such persons were required to answer and post bond, and they faced commitment to gaol if they refused. Further, the justice was protected from retaliation in a way that other local officials were not. One of the most annoying weaknesses of parish and manor officials had been their vulnerability to vexatious litigation—usually actions of trespass—brought by those against whom they had exercised authority. By contrast, writes Lambarde, "no Action would lye against that Justice for so doing."[40]

Justices of the peace commonly supervised local officials in petty sessions. At these meetings, two or more justices (one a member of the quorum)[41] brought their power to bear on inefficient, corrupt, or reluctant local government. This system had been emerging for some time, and in 1605 the Privy Council gave it more formal shape by ordering that "convenient and apt divisions be made through every county and riding, and that fit Justices of the Peace be assigned to have the special charge and care of every such division, and these to be answerable for such defects as through their default shall happen therein." To a hardworking and hard-pressed local official, the presence of the justices was a welcome

---

Constitution, pp. 460–62. In practice, the justices had jurisdiction over all crimes but treason. D. H. Allen, ed., *Essex Quarter Sessions Order Book, 1652–1661*, p. xii.

39. Lambarde, *Eirenarcha*, p. 83. The forms and provisions of these bonds are set forth in ibid., pp. 84–132.

40. Ibid., pp. 86–87.

41. The quorum was a specially designated group among the justices, originally distinguished by their superior learning in the law and later by their greater experience, who were to be present at each petty session. Most Elizabethan social and economic legislation required the presence of a quorum member. Allen, *Essex Quarter Sessions*, p. xii.

source of support. On the other hand, their presence was less welcome to someone like High Constable John Crosbie, who was sent to quarter sessions and then removed from office in 1609 for his "evil government."[42]

The supervisory responsibilities of the justices were broad but explicit. Overseers of the poor, for instance, as well as surveyors of highways were accountable for the performance of assigned tasks and were required to report to the justices. The parish had to demonstrate that its whipping post, pillory, and other instruments of punishment were serviceable. Even in the administration of the poor laws—a major force behind the "rise of the parish"—the justices were indispensable, for they appointed overseers, examined financial records, and levied rates on wealthier parishes to assist less able ones in bearing the charges of the poor laws. With the power to punish specific officials for nonperformance, the justice of the peace and the petty sessions brought the power of the crown and gentry into local affairs and made resistance inadvisable, whether by recalcitrant parishioners or lazy officials. Even the vestry itself was subject to presentment at quarter sessions for neglecting its duty.[43]

Although the justices had statutory tasks of their own with regard to some local matters,[44] their primary contribution was not direct administration but rather their work above and through subordinate local officeholders. Disagreements over where responsibility lay for performance of a specific task frequently arose in a manor or parish, and it was the justices who assigned the unwanted job. Similarly, they might have to arbitrate the innumerable disagreements over rates, enclosure, or rights-of-way. Prodding reluctant officials, punishing corrupt ones, or assisting others, the justices saw to it that local government worked.[45]

Statute granted the justices of the peace only "inconsiderable" civil authority (generally confined to matters between masters and servants),[46] but justices occasionally construed their peacekeeping obligation broadly

42. Lambarde, *William Lambarde and Local Government*, p. 98. J. H. E. Bennet and J. C. Dewhurst, eds., *Quarter Session Records with Other Records of the Justices of the Peace for the County Palatine of Chester, 1559–1760*, p. 70. Holdsworth, *English Law*, 4:147.

43. Holdsworth, *English Law*, 4:141. Webb and Webb, *English Local Government*, 1:31. A recent study of Norfolk in this period concludes that parish officials "would have achieved little without oversight by the magistrates" in poor law administration (Smith, *County and Court*, pp. 105–6).

44. Holdsworth, *English Law*, 4:138–42. Lambarde, *Eirenarcha*, includes an appended "Table, conteining (verie neare) all the imprinted Statutes, both generall and particular, wherewith Justices of the Peace have in any sorte to deale."

45. Trotter, *Country Parish*, pp. 214–15.

46. Holdsworth, *English Law*, 4:139–41, fails to go beyond these explicit grants and ignores the wider capacity available in practice.

enough to cover many civil affairs.[47] While any local official or institution—such as the parish—might try to do the same and employ informal pressures to expand its formal jurisdiction, the justice of the peace was better equipped by his power to take bonds. If, for example, someone believed that a dispute would become violent and endanger the peace, he could ask a justice to intervene and require a bond of the person threatening him. Even when the parties admitted that there had been no "threatening words or blows," as several people of Chester did in 1635, they might approach a justice and receive his "lawful favour and assistance for the speedy ending of the differences, the poor men being freed of any further charge." The justice could arbitrate on his own, or he could refer the matter to other justices or eminent men of the locality and could then take bonds for adherence to the decision.[48]

It is not surprising, therefore, that many proposals for reform during this period placed much of the burden for bringing order and efficiency to the legal system upon the justices of the peace. To be sure, the variety of suggestions matched the political variety of the times, and there was also much support for reviving the older communal institutions. Yet the importance of the justice of the peace was almost universally recognized in the reform literature, and even the Levellers supported the continuation of the office, though they wanted it filled by popular election.[49] In a comprehensive treatise on law reform written in the Civil War period, William Sheppard integrated the stronger features of many systems to suggest a much greater supervisory role over local institutions for the justice of the peace. Like Lambarde before him, Sheppard cited the "tediousness, charge, and difficulty" of prosecution, the "neglect of Officers in execution of their Offices," and the fact that "men will not complain one against another, but do conceal the faults of each other." Sheppard's remedy drew upon his observation of the justice's role in local government, and he proposed "that there be more Justices of the Peace, one at least in every Hundred; and that they sit once a Month in every Hundred." Their authority should include all crimes except treason and felony, while conviction should be made an easy, prompt matter upon the testimony of one or two witnesses.[50]

47. Wrightson finds this function a primary one for the Lancashire quarter sessions in the years before the Interregnum ("Puritan Reformation," p. 138).

48. Bennett and Dewhurst, *Records of Chester*, p. 89. See also D. E. Howell James, ed., *Norfolk Quarter Sessions Order Book, 1650–1657*, p. 17; and Trotter, *Country Parish*, p. 210n.

49. For example, see Veall, *Popular Movement*, p. 75.

50. Sheppard, *England's Balme*, pp. 25–28, 30–31, 35–36. Veall refers to this book as "the most comprehensive set of law reform proposals put forward during the whole of the period covered by the Civil War and Interregnum" (*Popular Movement*, p. 84).

Sheppard also called for extending the justices' jurisdiction to civil issues, for in that area they had been notably restricted. He suggested that the county and hundred courts and the courts baron and leet would function more effectively if supervised by the justices and conducted by "able Judges setled and kept in them." He also proposed that there be "set up a Court of Judicature in every County, to be kept by some of the Justices of the Peace, with a Lawyer, for some special matters" as probate, tithes, and "poor mens Causes, matters of Equity."[51] John Winthrop, himself a justice, proposed that "any two Justices of Peace (one being of Quorum)" be given authority to make summary judgments in "all suites and demandes touchinge debt trespass batterye defamation or other cause not concerninge matter of tenure or title of or to any maners landes ten[emen]tes or hereditaments nor exceeding the value of x *li*, wherein any artificer husbandman labourer servant or spinster" was involved.[52]

Many Puritans supported these reforms. Although the justices were nominally the agents of a monarch who attacked nonconformity, Puritans did not fear the magistrates themselves. They recognized that justices could be useful allies in resisting the church and the crown. Many justices, for instance, refused to enforce unpopular statutes, while others protected Puritans presented at quarter sessions.[53] In a hierarchical society power was linked to status, and the role of the justice offered Puritans respectability as well as a measure of power to oppose the will of the crown. "They alone," wrote Calvin of the lesser French magistrates, "might defend true religion against heretical kings."[54] In addition, Puritan doctrine required that the community be free of moral sinfulness, and the justice was seen as protecting a society in that important sense. While Puritans emphasized the communal watchfulness of the covenanted, they knew that their communities included the unregenerate who would require discipline from "grave and religious magistrates." Even the radically presbyterian classis of Dedham, which tried to eschew all civil authorities in its affairs, sometimes had to enlist their aid. As it

51. Sheppard, *England's Balme*, pp. 62–63.

52. *Winthrop Papers*, 1:310.

53. Smith, *County and Court*, p. 112. That author cites M. G. Davies that justices enforced a new apprenticeship law "only when it met an urgent need of the local community or was in harmony with strong public sentiment" (*The Enforcement of English Apprenticeship*, p. 162). See also Allen, *Essex Quarter Sessions*, p. xiii.

54. Walzer, *Revolution of the Saints*, pp. 59–60. It appears that these "godly justices" were not removed from office because of such efforts or their religion. According to Gleason, there were recurring rumors that this would occur, but "the absence of all pertinent evidence argues that the Puritans as such were not systematically excluded from the county benches" (*Justices of the Peace*, pp. 73–74). The only instance of such a purge was the action taken against officials who resisted the Forced Loan in 1627.

discovered in 1586, it had become necessary "to compleine to the magistrates" about "some careles persons that had no regard of the word or Sacraments."[55]

Puritans in England and America recognized the interdependence of godliness and civil order. Hugh Peter, who came to Massachusetts in the Great Migration of the 1630s, believed that the two were inseparable and went so far as to say that justice was "more necessarie to the immediate subsistence of a Commonwealth" than either "religion or mercie." The reason, he explained in the preface to the tract on law reform that he wrote on his return to England, was that "manie Common-wealths subsist without true Religion, and much Mercie; but without Justice, no Common-wealth can long subsist; and it is this, of the three, the most immediate and proper work of the Magistrate's office, to see true Justice executed."[56] Peter urged that disputes be handled by the community before recourse to the justices of the peace. But to assure his goals, it was essential that "there bee in everie Citie, town, and hundred, appointed five, or seven able fit men, to determine all Controversies for Debts, and strifes."[57] Peter's view of the orderly and godly society was a typically Puritan attempt to fuse older communal values and institutions with contemporary institutions of social order, and it would be of central importance in the Puritan colony on Massachusetts Bay.

The creation of legal institutions at the Bay Colony closely paralleled the suggestions and ideas put forth by the English reformers. Responding to the concerns and goals of a shared experience, Massachusetts Puritans tried to revive old communal methods of achieving social harmony, but they also placed a strong reliance upon the coercive instruments of magistracy. They agreed with their contemporary Michael Dalton that the situation "most commonly" occurred that peace "is rather a restraining of hands, then an uniting of minds, And for the maintenance of this Peace chiefly, were the Justices of Peace first made."[58] Dalton's thumbnail analysis of English legal history would have applied to the earliest years at the Bay, for the colony's leaders—who were familiar with Dalton's *Countrey Justice* and later ordered copies of it for their use—knew that they were organizing a community composed of Anglicans and factious sectarians as well as adventure seekers and social outcasts. Understand-

55. Patrick Collinson, *The Elizabethan Puritan Movement*, pp. 54–55, 174, 204, 354–55. Hill, *Society and Puritanism*, pp. 224–25. R. G. Usher, ed., *The Presbyterian Movement in the Reign of Queen Elizabeth as Illustrated by the Minute Book of the Dedham Classis*, p. 55.

56. Hugh Peters [*sic*], *Good Work for a Good Magistrate*, pp. 27–28.

57. Ibid., p. 39.

58. Dalton, *Countrey Justice*, p. 7.

ably, the founders took full advantage of their charter privilege to make laws "for setling of the formes and ceremonies of government and magistracy," which included the right to make "impositions of lawfull fynes, mulcts, imprisonment, or other lawfull correction, according to the course of other corporations in this our realme of England."[59]

This right to act as a corporation was significant, for it meant that the Massachusetts Bay Company was not, like the old Dorchester Company, merely a type of business partnership with few powers of self-government. Rather, it possessed an authority granted only to corporate bodies and denied to lesser units of government: in the words of the Webbs, this was the right to give "one or more members . . . the well-known powers and authorities elsewhere conferred by the Commission of the Peace" and thus to hold its own equivalent of the county quarter sessions.[60]

The members of the company had had considerable direct experience with the commission of the peace as it was exercised in English counties and boroughs.[61] Richard Bellingham had been a justice of the peace of the quorum in Lincolnshire, and John Winthrop had held the like position in Suffolk, in addition to having been recorder (judge) of the Norwich borough court. Sir Richard Saltonstall, another justice of the peace, was also a nephew of an Elizabethan lord mayor of London. Moreover, there were close connections between these men and others who became the first magistrates of the colony, such as the obvious one between the John Winthrops, Senior and Junior, or the Richard Saltonstalls, Senior and Junior. Isaac Johnson and John Humfrey were both sons-in-law of the earl of Lincoln, whose steward was Thomas Dudley, the father-in-law of Simon Bradstreet. The Winthrops, Emmanuel Downing (the governor's brother-in-law), Bellingham, Humfrey, Dudley, and Nathaniel Ward all had had some legal training in England, which stood them in good stead as preparation for wielding the extensive legal powers they had received from the charter.[62]

While English county oligarchies did not migrate en bloc to America, Massachusetts did not lack an incipient oligarchy of its own. On the contrary, the governor, deputy governor, and the assistants (that is, the entire group of company members migrating to America) quickly constituted themselves as a tightly knit and powerful magistracy. With their

59. *Mass. Rec.* 1:16, 17.
60. Webb and Webb, *English Local Government*, 2:279.
61. This paragraph draws in large part from Robert E. Wall, *Massachusetts Bay*, pp. 31–32.
62. Thomas G. Barnes, "Law and Liberty (and Order) in Early Massachusetts," pp. 78–79. Thomas Lechford, *Note-book Kept by Thomas Lechford, Esq., Lawyer, in Boston, Massachusetts Bay, from June 27, 1638 to July 29, 1641*, pp. xv, 45.

English experience in law and government and with their particular social, religious, and political goals to advance they voted on 23 August 1630 that they were "in all things to have like power that justices of peace hath in England for reformation of abuses and punishing of offenders." These magistrates spent much of their time in the first years of the colony's existence in exercising powers that were as broad as those wielded by the justices of any borough corporation in England. They took their status and powers seriously and guarded them jealously: when Israel Stoughton had the temerity in 1635 to challenge them by "affirmeing the Assistants were noe magistrates," he was barred from office for a year. Their meetings were important affairs, and they were not reluctant to fine any of their own number who were late for morning assembly.[63]

Even before the Massachusetts Bay Company had received its charter in 1629, the officials who led a vanguard group to Naumkeag (Salem) for the short-lived New England Company in September 1628 exerted close control over the separate settlements hugging the coast to the south. These vestiges of the Gorges enterprise shared few of the Puritans' goals, and John Endecott, at the head of the Salem settlement, was suspicious of their heterodoxy. Samuel Maverick at Winnisimet (Chelsea) disliked Puritanism, while William Blaxton at Shawmut (Boston) and Thomas Walford at Mishawum (Charlestown) leaned toward episcopacy. Most seriously upsetting, of course, were Merrymount and Passonagessit (Braintree), where the revellers Thomas Morton and Captain Wollaston compounded their sins by selling guns to the Indians. Endecott had no authority to act as a "governor" because the New England Company was not a chartered corporation, but he nonetheless managed to command their obedience—with force when necessary.[64]

Endecott's personal control of affairs at the Bay was brief—it was reduced when the New England Company was reestablished and incorporated as the Massachusetts Bay Company in March 1629—but the role he had played anticipated the centralized direction of local affairs that his successors would continue. For the first six years of the colony's existence, the only instrument of authority (besides church discipline) was the General Court, consisting of the Court of Assistants and those freemen admitted to sit as delegates after 1632. Although the General Court experienced a great deal of internal turmoil as the governor, assis-

63. *Mass. Rec.* 1:74, 136, 181, 182. For a comparison with the powers of an English borough corporation, see Webb and Webb, *English Local Government*, 2:280.

64. Charles McLean Andrews, *The Colonial Period of American History*, 1:340, 361–62. A. C. Goodell, "The Origin of Towns in Massachusetts," p. 328. Endecott also drafted a set of laws. "Captain Indicotts Lawes" have been lost, however, and there is no evidence as to their content or effect. James Duncan Phillips, *Salem in the Seventeenth Century*, p. 81.

tants, and deputies struggled over the division of power, centralized control over local communities was not reduced.[65] Wary of placing too much responsibility on weak communal institutions, the assistants—sometimes meeting together as a court and at others acting singly or in pairs—virtually ran the small settlements that were taking shape outside Boston. These enterprises, initially referred to interchangeably as "severall plantations" or "towns," had no legal status and possessed no machinery of government. As such, they stood under the control of the Court of Assistants or those assistants/justices of the peace who resided among them. These men assumed the major responsibility of keeping the peace, resolving disputes, and carrying out the policies of the colonial government in Boston. They were, to use Edward Johnson's description, "able Pilots to steer the Helme in a godly peaceable Civill Government."[66]

Their work became progressively heavier as the Great Migration brought thousands of newcomers—and the attendant social problems—to Massachusetts Bay. Under the impact of this increased business, the legislature had to concede the need for decentralization and the delegation of some duties or powers to subordinate units of administration. Yet the founders of the colony were not about to create autonomous bodies that would rival their authority or become bailiwicks (literally, as well as metaphorically) of nonconformity. When the General Court dealt with this matter on 3 March 1636, therefore, it constituted town governments closely to resemble the limited structure of English parochial or manorial administration. The famous Town Act of that date is worth quoting in its entirety in order to demonstrate the strictly and traditionally circumscribed nature of town powers:

Whereas particular townes have many things, which concerne only themselves, and the ordering of their owne affairs, and disposeing of businesses in their owne towne, it is therefore ordered, that the Freemen of every towne, or the major parte of them, shall onely have power to dispose of their owne lands, and woods, with all the previlidges and appurtenances of said townes, to graunt lotts, and make such orders as may concerne the well ordering of their owne townes, not repugnant to the lawes and orders here established by the Generall Court; as also

65. This control was held fast even during the more serious political debates of the next decade. Wall interprets the debates over the Standing Council and the negative voice as efforts to confer greater powers on the lower house *and* the town boards of selectmen (*Massachusetts Bay*, pp. 21–22). Actually, nothing in those debates would have enhanced the authority of the towns. Whatever powers the deputies wrested from the assistants, they retained them for the lower house of the legislature and granted none of them to the towns. Judicial powers, moreover, were held securely by the assistants themselves. The lower house collectively shared some judicial power with the assistants, but its individual members had no magisterial authority.

66. Edward Johnson, *Wonder-Working Providence*, pp. 30–31. Darrett B. Rutman, *Winthrop's Boston*, pp. 43–44.

to lay mulks and penaltyes for breach of theis orders, and to levy and distreine the same, not exceeding the some of xx s[hillings]; also to chuse their owne particular officers, as constables, surveyors for highwayes, and the like; and because much busines is like to ensue to the constables of severall townes, by reason they are like to make distresses, and gather Fynes, therefore that every towne shall have two constables, and where there is neede, that soe their office may not be a burthen unto them, and they may attend more carefully upon the discharge of their office, for which they shalbe lyeable to give their accompts to this Court when they shalbe called thereunto.[67]

At a time when land distribution and management were of primary concern to the colony's population, these duties were, of course, a considerable responsibility. But the act was nevertheless drafted with the intent that the towns would be as strictly delimited in the powers conferred upon them as were manors or parishes. The General Court used language that clearly implied manorial and parochial precedent when it limited the towns to disposing of lands and woods, choosing parochial officers, making bylaws, and employing the restricted powers of amercement. In no sense was the legislature constituting anything to resemble the English system of powerful borough corporations as a pattern for these new towns. To have attempted that would not only have been politically unwise; it would also have been flagrantly illegal, because the Massachusetts Bay Company, as a corporation, had no authority to create other corporations. This principle was well known in the common law; as enunciated by Sir Robert Brooke in his standard abridgment, "cominaltie ou corporation ne poet faire aut corporation, ou cominaltie, p. usage ne prescription, nec aliter nisi p. chart le roy." Adherence to this restriction was rigid in England among corporations themselves, for they were reluctant to create independent sources of power that would challenge their own authority and they were quick to protest such efforts at subincorporation.[68]

The colony's corporate status has been one of the most commonly misunderstood aspects of its early development. Yet it is essential to understand because English corporate practices dictated the general course to be followed as the colony set up its system of government and law in the 1630s. When the Massachusetts Bay Company was chartered in 1629 it was incorporated as a joint-stock company; but because its true impulse was the establishment of a Puritan society beyond the reach of

---

67. *Mass. Rec.* 1:172.

68. Corporate powers are explained in Sir Robert Brooke, *La Graunde Abridgement, Collect and Escrit per le Iudge tresreuerend Syr Robert Brooke*, 1:188–92. See also William Sheppard's treatise, *Of Corporations, Fraternities, and Guilds*. On English corporation protest against efforts at subincorporation, see Derek Hirst, *The Representative of the People?*, p. 49.

royal or episcopal control, historians have interpreted the events of the first decade as the acts of a sovereign state. It is an article of faith in the existing scholarship, therefore, that immediately upon their arrival at the Bay the founders embarked on a policy of shedding their corporate status and assuming that of a "commonwealth."[69]

In fact, however, the colonists did not even arrive at the Bay as a true joint-stock enterprise. The company had undergone a complete financial reorganization in 1629 when a group of "undertakers" assumed control of the original capital stock. This change effectually divided the trading and governmental aspects of the venture, and at that point it "ceased to exist as a joint-stock body." The "undertakers" were trustees of the stock with no role in managing the colony, while the colonists took with them a charter divested of its business character and whose sole purpose now was the governing of a plantation in the New World.[70]

But once at the Bay, the colonists did not use their remoteness or the collapse of the old financial arrangements to erect a "commonwealth," if by that is meant an independent state. Rather, they interpreted their surviving charter as that of any English borough corporation, and they set up a system of colonial government consistent with it. Although still known as "governor" and "assistants" (terms associated with trading companies), they functioned as a mayor and his aldermen or burgesses— or, more specifically in some situations, as an incorporated borough's justices acting in their quarter sessional capacity. Freemanship followed borough practice in manner as well as name: just as some boroughs predicated membership upon prior admission to a particular guild or fraternity, the colony required admission to a Puritan congregation before anyone could be sworn to freemanship at its General Court. Even taxation of all residents, which has been cited as the primary example of "commonwealth" right and charter violation, was actually only a duplication of the traditional assessment made by boroughs on all householders through a variety of methods available to a corporation, such as the levy of a tax equivalent to the "county rate."[71] When the assistants assessed sixty pounds for defense in 1632, therefore, Watertown leaders might protest that the government "as a mayor and aldermen . . . have not power to make laws or raise taxations without the people," but their legal argument was weak against a background of corporate or county

69. See, for example, Wall, *Massachusetts Bay*, p. 6, or Andrews, *Colonial Period*, 1:430–61, "From Charter to Commonwealth in Massachusetts."

70. William R. Scott, *The Constitution and Finance of English, Scottish, and Irish Joint-Stock Companies to 1720*, 2:314–15.

71. Webb and Webb, *English Local Government*, 2:703n. Martin Weinbaum, ed., *British Borough Charters, 1307–1660*, passim.

practice in England where such taxes were commonly levied in that manner.[72]

Winthrop denied corporate limitations when he answered the Watertown protest, and historians have accepted his statement as representative of the colony's leadership. But Winthrop was isolated on this point, as he was on many other issues, and a reaction against his rule in 1634 removed him from the governorship. His successors Dudley, John Haynes, and Sir Henry Vane made no such claim, for external events were combining with internal factors to force the colony to conform to corporation practice. In the same year that Winthrop was defeated, the colony learned that the powerful Laud Commission for Regulating Plantations was investigating it. A year later Sir Ferdinando Gorges, who had rival land claims to the area, filed suit against the patentees and made numerous accusations about charter violations, while the Laud Commission added its complaints about heterodoxy and intolerance. With the outcome pending in litigation, the colony had to demonstrate that it was not the refractory, independent commonwealth that its opponents said it was. On the contrary, it had to solidify its position by showing that it was doing no more than what many other English corporations were entitled to do. Just as the colony's leaders publicly admonished John Endecott for cutting the cross of Saint George from the English flag in 1634 and two years later ordered the King's coat of arms erected in each quarterly court, they were careful to usurp no privilege generally denied to corporations. True, they did not stay within the *specific* limitations of the 1629 charter, but they did nothing that they could not later defend, if necessary, as being generally accepted corporate practice in England. And on close examination it does appear that the contours of the colony's governmental system remained consistent with county or general corporate precedent in England during the 1630s. For example, the creation of the "Standing Council" in 1636 has been viewed by historians as one more "commonwealth" prerogative, since its members were to serve for life. Such an action was not warranted by the charter, but neither was it an uncommon feature of English corporations, many of whom had groups of "principal burgesses" with life tenure.[73] Of course, those cor-

72. John Winthrop, *The History of New England, from 1630 to 1649*, 1:84.

73. *Mass. Rec.*, 1:175. See, for example, the charter of Dorchester, in Martin Weinbaum, ed., *British Borough Charters, 1307–1660*, pp. 29–30. Julius G. Goebel, in his classic article "King's Law and Local Custom in Seventeenth-Century New England," shifted the focus in Early American legal history from Westminster to the great variety of practices found in the localities. However, he unaccountably overlooked the justice of the peace—especially in his quarter sessional capacity within an incorporated borough—as an institution of some uniformity throughout local government that could serve as a model for New England.

porations had express warrant in their charters permitting them to create such positions, and the colony's efforts were no less ultra vires than those of English corporations that tried to do the same thing without express provision. But the colony's strategy was to interpret the colonial charter to be as broad as any English corporate charter (save the admittedly unique example of London) and in that way to be able to defend their acts as not "repugnant" to the laws of England.

This strategy was, to a degree, successful, because when the court of King's Bench finally did revoke the charter in 1637 the action was not taken because of charter violations; that is, the court did not rule that the actions of the colonial government constituted anything ultra vires. Rather, the court acted only on the grounds that the charter had been "surreptitiously obtained," and it even permitted the colony to continue with its existing government until Gorges could be sent over as "General Governor" with a new charter.[74] Fortunately for Massachusetts, its enemies were soon distracted by the Civil War, and Gorges never did arrive at the Bay. But until that became clear, the colony was left in a position of precarious survival, and its leaders hoped soon to move for a reversal of the judgment by a writ of error.[75] To aid their cause, they had to pursue a strategy of giving no further provocation by acting like a rebellious commonwealth and exercising royal prerogative.

The creation of corporations was one privilege reserved to the crown and not generally possessed by English corporations; among them only London, by a unique prescription ("lusage de Lond," according to Brooke), had that right.[76] For that reason, the General Court was as careful not to create guilds, trading companies, or educational corporations as it had been not to create borough corporations. Although the court did vote funds for Harvard College in 1636, for example, it did not specify any type of government for the institution until 1642 and did not confer "corporation" status until 1650—by which time Charles I was dead and his sons were in flight.[77]

Legal considerations as well as internal political ones, therefore, prevented the General Court from making the town a corporate entity,

74. *CSP*, 1:204–5; 5:129–30. *Acts of the Privy Council, Colonial Series*, 1:217. Andrews, *Colonial Period*, 1:423.

75. This strategy is described in a letter from Emmanuel Downing to Hugh Peter, *Winthrop Letters*, 6:58.

76. London, by this unique prescription, had created lesser corporations such as guilds. On London's exceptional character in this regard, see Brooke, *Graunde Abridgement*, 1:149, Title, "Prescription."

77. Harvard College was referred to as "The Society" in its early years. Andrew M. Davis, "Corporations in the Days of the Colony," pp. 184n, 190. *Mass. Rec.* 2:30; 4 (pt. i):12–14.

although some historians believe that town land policy suggests corporate practice.[78] However, the actual handling of the land suggests unincorporated tenancy in common and hints strongly at manorial procedures. Another privilege reserved to corporations would have been a town's ability to sue as a collective entity, but they did not actually do so in the 1630s. Instead, towns apparently followed the parochial method of designating a particular individual to appear privately for them.[79]

As a way of maintaining control over the towns and of being assured that they would not use their legal powers to gain too much autonomy, the General Court passed the famous Town Act (Order No. 285) only *after* it had created a supervisory level of magistratical government above the towns earlier that same day.[80] Thus, before the legislature delegated even manorial or parochial powers, it adapted rules and institutions from English legal practice that would be sufficient to oversee that authority. As a first step, the General Court repeated a rule made by the assistants acting alone in 1630 that the "sitting downe of men in any newe plantation" first be approved by a majority of the magistrates. Order No. 280 expanded on that rule, requiring that any new gathering of churches also receive that permission, in addition to that of the "elders of the greater parte of the churches in this jurisdiction."[81]

Order No. 281, however, was the most important limitation on the newly constituted towns, because it created a system of quarterly courts exercising civil, criminal, and administrative jurisdiction in the major population centers of Boston, Cambridge, Salem, and Ipswich. These courts could hear and determine civil cases of up to ten pounds in value and try all crimes except those punishable by banishment or by loss of life or limb.[82] The colony possessed no authority to create additional courts, but the quarterly courts were not, strictly speaking, an entirely new judicial system. In reality, they were a type of circuit court composed of those magistrates living in or near the four locations of the court.

78. Viola F. Barnes, *The Dominion of New England*, p. 184, expresses this view.

79. In 1639 Thomas Oliver sued George Harris for trespass, "according to ord. of Towne, Jos. Woodbury, tres" (SaMbk. 1636–41, p. 25). Conversely, a year later "Augustin Calem, Goatkeeper," sued "Mr Conant and Divers others" over a matter the "towne ordered" (ibid., p. 39). For an English comparison, see E. H. Bates Harbin, ed., *Quarter Sessions Records for the County of Somerset*, 1:xlviii, 156.

80. At this meeting the legislature also created the Standing Council and formalized the negative voice. *Mass. Rec.* 1:167, 170. Although the Town Act is generally considered by historians to be a single enactment, it was merely part of a larger comprehensive plan for effective local government in the colony. Perhaps one reason for historians' isolating the Town Act is an oversight committed by the clerk of the General Court when it was passed: he failed to enter the act with that day's business and later had to insert it where space allowed—with the business of 5 April 1636. Ibid., 1:172.

81. Ibid., 1:167, 168.

82. Ibid., 1:169.

These magistrates were assisted by "assotiates" who were appointed by the General Court on nomination by the freemen of the towns, but who were explicitly subordinate to the magistrates and had no independent authority of their own. Individual associates had none of the magistrate's powers, nor could they collectively hold a quarterly court without a magistrate present.[83]

Almost as soon as the magistrates began serving as judges of the quarterly courts, they had to assist the new towns. The institutions of the Massachusetts town were responsible for enforcing their own rules of land management, but they had little more success than English manors had had. It is clear from the region north of Boston—which would become Essex County in 1643—that the courts were filling a need created by the inherent weaknesses of the communal ideal and by the inability to duplicate the ancient routines of traditional agrarian life. This need was apparent in Salem, the oldest and most populous of these settlements and the one with the most highly developed institutions of its own. As such, Salem affords a good comparison between the town meeting (or its board of selectmen) and the quarterly court as instruments of governance. The town itself did not lack men of prestige or strong personality—Roger Conant and William Hathorne were among its selectmen—but the court had to intervene repeatedly in town disputes and problems. While Salem selectmen were able to refer to arbitrators issues related to town land, other problems went directly to the quarterly court. Between 1636 and 1640 it punished 29 Salem townsmen for various offenses, including pound breach, use of false weights, illegal sale of liquor, and abuse of constables. Since it is likely that no more than 419 adult males became even temporary residents during these years, the quarterly court thus was called upon to discipline 1 out of every 14 of them.[84] It also punished 15 women and 14 male servants, but no accurate estimate can be made for the total population of these groups. The court's civil jurisdiction is still more striking, for during this period it heard 192 cases; of these, 107 (56 percent) were intratown disputes from Salem. Moreover, another 20 cases (10 percent) were intratown disputes from Lynn, and it is possible that some of the 35 cases among persons of unknown residence were of a similar nature.[85]

Evidence of this sort suggests the weakness of the town's communal

83. Ibid.

84. This estimate of 419 adult males through 1640 is drawn from all names listed in the records of the town, congregation, quarterly court, and Court of Assistants.

85. The figures for the Ipswich court, whose records begin in 1641, are not as dramatic, but still suggestive: 47 percent of the cases that year were between Ipswich residents. This figure may be low because 35 percent of the litigants were of unknown residence and thus possibly of Ipswich.

institutions of peacekeeping and conflict resolution, as town records contain correspondingly few examples of such functions. But this conclusion is not a fallacious inference drawn from negative evidence. The Salem church records, for instance, also contain little evidence of conflict resolution, because successful cases were not recorded and the purpose of congregational mediation, like town mediation, was to keep a disagreement from reaching formal institutions. However, the success of the Salem church can be measured in a way that corroborates the lack of success of Salem town institutions: only three disputes between church members had to be taken to the quarterly court between 1636 and 1640, in suggestive contrast to the large number of intratown disputes among nonmembers in Salem that did require legal resolution. Of these three, moreover, only two came to final adjudication by the court, for one was sent to two fellow church members for arbitration.[86] Rather than indicating successful utopian communalism, town record books with little or no serious conflict may suggest, as do those of English manors, merely a restricted range of problems that the town was competent to handle. Such was the case among many English manors that entered *omnia bene* in their records while they sent their disputes to be settled elsewhere.[87] In point of fact, the Salem town records show explicit evidence supporting such a conclusion. In 1637 John Pickering enclosed a part of the town common "without Consent from the Towne." Elias Stileman, one of the town's seven selectmen, refused to concur in a decision by the other six to levy a twenty-shilling fine, however. On its own, the town was unable to punish Pickering, for it was following the traditional manorial practice of the court leet, which required unanimity to present and amerce for violation of local bylaws.[88] Unanimity, increasingly difficult to achieve in England, was to be ever more elusive in Massachusetts.

Even with unanimity, the towns—just as English manors and hun-

---

86. These three cases are "Ralph Fogg pl. (in behalf of himself and the caus[?]) against Ensigne Read def.," [1639], SaMbk. 1636–41, Dec. term #17; Humphrey v. Holgrave [1640], ibid., Sept. term #8; Verrin v. Pope [1638], ibid., June term #38, which was sent to arbitration. In addition, to the Salem records, see Ipswich, Massachusetts, Town Records, 1634 [–1660]; W. P. Upham, comp., *Wenham Town Records, 1642–1706*; Salisbury Records; Marblehead Records, *EIHC*; Benjamin P. Mighill and George B. Blodgette, eds., *The Early Records of the Town of Rowley, Massachusetts, 1639–1672*; and *Town Records of Manchester, From the Earliest Grants of Land, 1636 . . . until 1736*.

87. Town records devoid of serious dispute often have been presented as evidence of a successfully utopian communalism that obviated conflict in early seventeenth-century Massachusetts. But historians of Tudor-Stuart England have offered more plausible explanations for similar evidence found in contemporary English records. See, for instance, Dawson, *Lay Judges*, p. 254. Derek Hirst points out that localities may have concealed their disputes in order to create "the illusion of unanimity" where none existed (*Representative of the People?* p. 15).

88. *Salem Town Records, 1634–59*, p. 46.

dreds—lacked the sanctions necessary to make their decisions meaningful. They might send malefactors to the quarterly court or to Boston, but
their own sanction of a twenty-shilling fine was weak; indeed, it was only
half the sum allowed in manorial courts. Salem, the largest town in the
colony except for Boston, fined only two men as much as twenty shillings
in the 1630s, both for fencing town common: Gervas Garford by the
selectmen in 1637 and Edmund Giles in 1640 "by the generall towne
meeting." When the selectmen fined John Gatchell ten shillings for the
same offense, they agreed to refund half that sum "in case he shall cutt of
his lonng har of his Head in to a sevill frame." It seems that Salem was
still less stern in disciplining the negligence of its officeholders. In 1637 it
assessed insignificant sixpence fines against Thomas Scruggs and Daniel
Ray "for disorderlie standing and neglecting to spek to T[own] busines."
When an "agitation of matters which concerne the neatherd" also occurred that year, the town only voted its "sensure" should he fail to
do his job. Otherwise, Salem had to enlist the aid of a magistrate, as it
did in 1640 when constables were not collecting rates and it voted to
obtain "helpe from the Magistrate to [di]straine for such summes as are
behinde."[89]

For problems of this sort, Essex towns recognized the need to have a
resident magistrate. If necessary, they might extend lavish grants of land
as inducements to magistrates to settle among them, as Ipswich did when
it gave two hundred acres to Daniel Denison "for his better encour-
agement to settle amongst us." When the town feared that John Winthrop, Jr., was about to leave, it granted him the three-hundred-acre
"Castle Hill" and wrote to the governor that his departure would "de-
prieve our Church and town of one whose presence is so gratefull and
usefull to us. It was for his sake that many of us came to this place and
without him we should not have come." Keeping Winthrop at Ipswich
was all the more necessary, it said, because already "Mr Dudley's leaving
us hath made us much more desolate and weake than we were, and if we
should lose another magistrate it would be too great a grief to us and
breach upon us."[90]

Reliance on the magistrates increased as the defects of communal
discipline became painfully apparent to local leaders. Some of them nevertheless clung stubbornly to the hope of strengthening it, and they made
numerous futile suggestions to preserve the dominant communal ideal.
These suggestions, impractical as they were, only attested to the need for
magistrates. As early as 1635 Nathaniel Ward confessed in a letter to

89. Ibid., pp. 34, 38, 41–42, 45, 55, 101, 106.
90. "Petition from Ipswich" [21 June 1637], *Proceedings of the Massachusetts Historical Society*, 2d ser. 3 (1886–87):198–99.

John Winthrop, Jr., that Ipswich town leaders had been "awakened . . . by the confluence of many ill and doubtfull persons," and that henceforth they would have to be "carefull on whome they bestowe lotts." Only in that way could the town become "strong and of a homogeneous spirit and people, as free from dangerous persons as we may." Ipswich had been awakened "somewhat too late," but other towns could heed his warning to be more "carefull."[91] So, too, could the General Court. One reason for the failure of communal ideals to be effective had been their implicit repudiation by emigrants who moved into the far outlying regions of town grants, beyond community watchfulness and discipline. As a remedy, the General Court ordered in 1635 that no dwelling be built more than half a mile from a meetinghouse. The significance of this enactment was that it revealed the lingering force of the communal paradigm: the leaders of the Massachusetts Bay Colony continued to interpret their problems in its terms, and they therefore tried to impose by statutory order the conditions that would nourish a communal ideal withering in its New World environment. The effort, of course, was futile. Mobility could not be halted, and in 1640 the act was repealed.[92]

With the half-mile limit recognized as inadequate, Ward took the next logical step in 1640 and suggested to the younger Winthrop that the size of town grants be sharply limited. After all, communalism had flourished in England in small villages and manors. In such settings, proximity had promoted familiarity and had permitted neighbors to observe and, if necessary, influence the behavior of others. Seen against this background, Massachusetts towns such as Ipswich were outlandishly large. The contrast was obvious to Ward, who in that same year commented on the extraordinarily spacious "bounds of Ipswich" and added that the neighboring town of "Rowley is larger than Ipswich, 9 or 10 miles longe." By making smaller grants of towns on the scale of English manors, it was hoped that population could be more densely concentrated in order to permit effective community watchfulness someday to function properly.[93]

The need to depend ultimately on the coercive powers of the magistracy in community affairs was apparent even in matters of parish and church government. To begin with, the courts were given such traditionally parochial functions as appointing constables, enforcing church attendance, and punishing moral delinquency, while individual magistrates were given the cleric's responsibility to perform marriages and to record births and deaths. In England "clerical justices"—ministers com-

91. Ipswich, 24 Dec. 1635, *Winthrop Letters*, 7:24–25.
92. *Mass. Rec.* 1:157, 291.
93. Ward to John Winthrop, 1640, *Winthrop Letters*, 7:28.

missioned as justices of the peace—had fused the magistratical and clerical functions. Massachusetts leaders distrusted secular power in clerical hands, and their impulse toward county magistracy joined with this belief to confer these combined powers upon lay justices alone.[94]

Where possible, the handling of unacceptable behavior was to follow the rule set out in the Bible: "If your brother sins against you, go and tell him his fault, between you and him alone. If he listens to you, you have gained your brother. But if he does not listen, take one or two others along with you that every word may be confirmed by two or three witnesses" (Matthew 18:15–17). The assumption was that congregational resolution would follow: "If he refuses to listen to them, tell it to the church." In civil disputes where both parties were willing to submit, we have seen that this system apparently worked well. But it was not always possible to induce everyone—especially persons not belonging to the congregation—to accept the informal entreaty of the saints, and the soliciting of witnesses was becoming a preliminary of formal complaint to the court. This preference for legal punishment had been a problem in England, too, and bishops had ordered ministers to confront an offender and "to reclaim him if they can."[95] But the forces operating to diminish the power of congregational discipline in England were also at work in Massachusetts, where, in 1639, the General Court had to take action. So many persons were coming to the courts with complaints about their neighbors' excesses of dress that the courts were experiencing "trouble." As a result, the legislature took the extreme step of passing a stay law halting "all proceedings upon the said presentment" and ordering the churches to discipline their own members. The courts, it declared, were to act only after offenders "obstinately persist[ed]" and thus became "contemners of authority."[96]

Magistratical involvement in congregational discipline was necessary in a society where everyone, to a degree, was a newcomer and patterns of permanent residency had not yet emerged. In fact, church membership proved distressingly fluid to those whose concept of a congregation was a static (hence, stable) community: of the 256 persons admitted to membership in the Salem congregation by 1640, 48 (almost 1 out of 5) left to join another congregation. Although it was necessary, according to strict principle, for such persons to obtain formal letters of "dismission" to recommend their admission to the new congregation, in practice

94. Webb and Webb, *English Local Government*, 1:250–60. George Lee Haskins, *Law and Authority in Early Massachusetts*, p. 63; and George Lee Haskins, "Ecclesiastical Antecedents of Criminal Punishment in Early Massachusetts," pp. 21–35.
95. Haskins, "Ecclesiastical Antecedents," pp. 29–30.
96. *Mass. Rec.* 1:274.

it proved difficult to distinguish the actually "dismissed" (or "recommended") communicants from the excommunicants who presented themselves to other congregations as members. Disturbed by this problem in 1639, the Salem church wrote to that of Dorchester for assistance and asked it to read publicly the names of those whom Salem had excommunicated. "We can do no less," it complained, "than have such noted as disobey the truth."[97]

Until the previous year, as a matter of fact, the churches had been able to do no more. Excommunication in Massachusetts, unlike the penalty in England, did not bar the offender from receiving a legacy or suing at law. It did disfranchise the excommunicant (if the person was a male and thus had a vote to lose), but for many this was a small price to pay. The General Court described the problem in 1638: "[I]t is found, by sad experience, that diverse persons, who have bene justly cast out of some of the churches, do prophanely contemne the same sacred and dreadfull ordinance, by presenting themselves overboldly in other assemblies, and speaking lightly of their censures, to the great offence and greefe of Gods people, and incuragement of evill minded persons to contemne the said ordinance." As a solution, the legislature once again intervened to shore up failing communal authority: it applied the power of the state and ordered that anyone who did not mend his ways, repent, and seek readmission within six months of excommunication was to be fined, jailed, banished, "or further."[98]

As a small group of magistrates bringing justice and administrative efficiency to the general area of their residences, the quarterly court was reminiscent of petty sessions. Because the quarterly court had no grand juries of its own, it often acted on referral from the Assistants Court, in much the same manner that petty sessions received cases from quarter sessions. But the colonial quarterly court did have petit juries of its own, and like quarter sessions, its terms were held at similar times of the year: the English courts met at Easter (between 22 March and 25 April), the Translation of Saint Thomas (or "Midsummer"), Michaelmas (29 September), and after Epiphany (6 January), while those in Massachusetts met in March, June, September, and December.[99] In addition, the selection of locations had precedent from the English practice of holding quarter sessions at different sites in a county to assure accessibility. The Privy Council Order of 1605 had specified that courts be no further from

97. Thomas Hutchinson, *History of the Colony and Province of Massachusetts Bay*, 1:353–56.

98. *Mass. Rec.* 1:242.

99. Quarter sessions met according to 2 Hen. IV, c. 4. See SaMbk. 1636–41, pp. 2–48, passim.

anyone seeking justice than seven or eight miles—approximately the distance from any settled area in the colony in the 1630s to either Boston, Cambridge, Salem, or Ipswich.[100]

As the quarterly courts operated in Massachusetts, they embodied elements of quarter sessional practice and reform proposals for greater magistratical involvement in civil matters. For instance, the quarterly courts and the Court of Assistants appear to have divided criminal jurisdiction roughly in the way that quarter sessions and the assizes did in England. There was much overlapping of jurisdiction in both legal systems, and many of the same type of petty cases might be prosecuted at either level in Massachusetts or England. Nevertheless, similar rules of practice seem to have governed both systems: just as capital crimes in England were usually reserved to the assizes,[101] the Assistants Court heard the more serious offenses in Massachusetts. By statute, this court alone could order punishments affecting life or limb, and therefore those crimes that might involve such punishments were generally sent to the assistants. Clear-cut cases of adultery, a capital crime in Massachusetts, were thus heard by the Assistants Court and not by the quarterly courts —at least not by those of Salem and Ipswich in the 1630s and 1640s.[102] The civil jurisdiction of the quarterly courts was a novelty for justices of the peace (who soon came to be known simply as "magistrates" in Massachusetts), but it also had English impulses behind it. In the first place, the quarterly courts of Salem and Ipswich referred many civil matters to arbitration, following the practice of English justices: between 1636 and 1643, the magistrates of Salem and Ipswich dispatched twenty cases in this manner.[103] Second, the involvement of magistrates in local civil disputes was actually the embodiment of the reformist desire in England to confer such authority on the justices.

Although generally acknowledged as essential to community stability, the colony's legal institutions were not established without challenge. In addition to English pressures, the antinomian challenge of Anne Hutchinson and John Wheelwright threatened all ecclesiastical institutions at Massachusetts Bay and produced "great disorders" as well as "contempts" against legal authority. It was the most serious internal threat to the legal institutions of the colony in its first decade, and the

---

100. Holdsworth, *English Law*, 4:147.

101. Allen comments on the "marked similarity" between the business of the assizes and quarter sessions, though he points out that only the former handled capital cases (*Essex Quarter Sessions*, p. xxii).

102. *Assts. Rec.* 2:66, 70.

103. SaMbk. 1936–41, pp. 2–48, passim. Records of the Ipswich terms of the quarterly court before 1641 are lost. The earliest records of that court can be found included with the Ipswich Town Records.

degree to which the colony's officials felt endangered was demonstrated when they took the unusual step of disarming many supporters of the movement and banishing its leaders. To help prevent the recurrence of a movement that had called into question the legitimacy of the colony's entire structure of secular authority, the General Court enacted that persons defaming "any court of justice, or the sentences or proceedings of the same, or any of the magistrates or other judges of any such court, in respect of any act or sentence therein passed" could be punished by fine, imprisonment, disfranchisement, or banishment.[104] The legal system weathered the antinomian storm, however, because its strength lay in the broad popular awareness of its importance: its availability and effectiveness in assuring social stability and resolving community conflicts were highly valued by Puritans in England, and were no less appreciated in a wilderness. As soon as English interference was temporarily removed in the 1640s, moreover, the legal structure would adjust more flexibly to the many new and unanticipated problems of settling that wilderness.

104. Mark DeWolfe Howe, *Readings in American Legal History*, pp. 144–81. *Mass. Rec.* 1:212–13.

2 Real Property Litigation

The Social and Economic Backgrounds of Legal Change

The turmoil that characterized English politics after 1640 freed Massachusetts Bay of its fear of imminent charter revocation and therefore of its need to remain within the general confines of borough corporation government. When Charles I and Archbishop Laud were forced to turn their full attention to the challenges of the Long Parliament and the New Model Army, Massachusetts could create the institutional forms needed to continue its legal development along the path begun in 1629 but until now constrained by royal supervision. No longer was it necessary to heed Winthrop's warning that a written code of laws designed for a uniquely colonial and Puritan society would be "repugnant to the laws of England," and in 1641 the General Court ratified the *Body of Liberties*, written largely by Nathaniel Ward of Ipswich.

The historical attention given to Ward's code has obscured the importance of several other enactments that had a greater direct influence on the governance of the towns north of Boston. Also in 1641 the General Court granted the Ipswich and Salem quarterly courts grand juries of their own and a jurisdiction virtually equal to that of the Assistants Court. By this act, the quarterly courts received "the same power, both in civill and criminall causes, the Court of Assistants hath at Boston, except tryall for life, limbs or banishment, which are wholly reserved to Boston Court." Two years later the legislature established shires, or counties, into which all existing towns were grouped. Those between Boston and the Merrimack River became Essex County, and their quarterly courts became the Essex county court. Joined to the Essex court, too, were the towns of Haverhill, Salisbury, and Hampton. Though these were in Norfolk County, the General Court perhaps recognized that as new frontier settlements they lacked a resident gentry with sufficient prestige to constitute a bench able to command the necessary deference; alternatively it may have been concerned with keeping that remote and exposed region securely under reliable control. In either case, the court assigned Essex magistrates to serve a southern district of Norfolk, with courts meeting at Hampton and Salisbury once a year[1] (see map 1). Finally, in 1647, the legislature created the town office of "commissioners to end small causes," three of whom were to be chosen by each town that had no resident magistrate to handle civil causes under forty shillings. At that point, the structure of the colony's legal system was essentially complete, with four levels ranging from town commissioners to the General Court in Boston. Ultimately, the crown would revoke the charter and end this system in 1684, but until then the arrangement remained essentially unchanged.[2]

Although the legal system featured a multiplicity of levels, the county court—at least in Essex—became the most important court of first instance. More significantly, it became the critical institution for dealing with important matters of local community concern. The reforms of the 1640s gave no new authority to the towns, for their "commissioners" had a very limited jurisdiction, confined to the most petty of matters. Town institutions would reveal major weaknesses in handling difficult problems, and Essex residents came to rely increasingly on the county judiciary. Even the resident magistrates who were available for justice in the towns drew their strength not from the town, but from their commissions as justices of the peace. The commission of the peace in Massachusetts gave them a summary civil jurisdiction equal to that of the town commissioners, but it also included minor criminal matters such as breach of the peace. Perhaps more significant, the magistrates could bind offenders for trial at the county court. Together with the high social status associated with their commissions, the magistrates' legal powers made them a more important source of justice than any town institution in Essex. The magistrates, moreover, came to regard themselves as part of the county judiciary rather than as officials responsible to the towns, and they often—though not systematically—recorded their decisions and orders with the county court.[3]

The rules of substantive and procedural law applied by the new county legal institutions also departed, although perhaps more slowly,

---

1. *Mass. Rec.* 1:325–26; 2:38. The Hampton and Salisbury jurisdiction ended in 1679 when Hampton became part of the new royal province of New Hampshire; but Salisbury, Haverhill, and Amesbury (formerly part of Norfolk, too) became Essex towns.

2. Ibid., 2:208.

3. Timothy H. Breen, *The Character of the Good Ruler*, p. 83. After creating the office of commissioner, the legislature in 1649 spelled out the precise division of jurisdiction among the various judicial levels. Except on appeal, no cause cognizable by the commissioners (i.e., below 40 shillings) was to go to the county courts, and none cognizable by the county courts was to go to the Court of Assistants. *Mass Rec.*, 3:167. With few exceptions, this division was followed in practice. The General Court itself, of course, might also offer original jurisdiction, but by a statute of 1642, this was "onely to help in such cases where the party can have no releife in any other Court" (ibid., 2:16). This "releife" referred to equitable relief, which by the charter was confined to the General Court. Though the

MAP 1. Essex County, including the Southern District
of Norfolk County, 1643

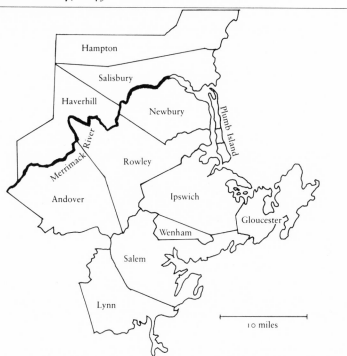

from the confines of the charter. It is an accepted fact that the substantive
law of the New England colonies did not follow only those patterns set
by the common law of England.[4] As at Plymouth, some practices of
English "local custom" found their way into the Massachusetts system.
According to the classic work on the subject, Massachusetts magistrates
felt free to "adapt legal rules which to their minds would best effectuate
the purposes for which the colony was founded," and as a result "the law
was not static, but . . . experimentation, expediency, and social and economic pressures continually influenced its growth."[5] What is less well

General Court used its adjudicatory powers flexibly, its equitable determinations were the
most distinctive function of its original jurisdiction. On this subject, see Barbara A. Black,
"The Judicial Power and the General Court in Early Massachusetts (1634–1686)." It
should be added that in Essex the county courts nevertheless applied equitable remedies,
too. See pp. 58–60, 79 of this volume.

4. Julius G. Goebel, "King's Law and Local Custom in Seventeenth-Century New
England," pp. 416–20.

5. George Lee Haskins, *Law and Authority in Early Massachusetts*, esp. chap. 8, "The
Path of the Law."

understood, however, is the specific nature of those changes, as well as their quantity and relative importance in the entire legal system. The changes can best be approached, analyzed, and measured by examining the way in which social and economic development and legal transformation were interrelated. It was a process that affected every aspect of life in seventeenth-century Essex, but the area that demands primary attention is that of real property, for in that aspect of the law changes first became necessary.

Conditions did not always require immediate change, however. Although the colonists arriving at Massachusetts Bay encountered an abundance of land unimaginable in the England they had left, it did not create legal problems for them at first: from 1636 to 1646, Essex residents brought only five land title causes to their local courts. In only one of these cases was the court's remedy suggestive of the changes that would become more common in a later period. When Richard Inkersell (Ingersoll) sued the town of Salem for a commonage share in 1639, the Salem court commanded Salem to make specific performance as demanded by the plaintiff, and ordered it to lay out the land in severalty for him.[6] In doing this, the Salem judges rendered a judgment for which no common law analogy existed. Although the common law knew of writs of partition for setting out land held by tenants in common, the social reality that existed in Massachusetts—land granted to towns and divided by them—was unknown in England, and hence the common law had not developed remedies to deal with such situations.[7]

Litigation over land remained at a low level during the 1640s and 1650s. Essexmen brought only three more land title cases in the next three years after 1646; lawsuits increased in the ensuing decade, but county residents still brought an average of only four cases each year before 1660. From that date onward, by comparison, the figures rose steadily until by the 1670s the county's courts were hearing approximately twenty cases annually. By that time they would rely frequently upon practices used rarely, if at all, by English common law courts in deciding disputes over freehold land.

That the Essex courts did not apply such novel forms to any great degree before 1660 was due to the great availability of land, a situation

6. Inkersell vs. Barney [1639], SaMbk. 1636–41, p. 26. EMbk. 1638–48, p. 42.

7. Charles Viner, *A General Abridgment of Law and Equity, Alphabetically Digested under Proper Titles*, Title, "Partition." For more on this point, see pp. 51–53, 60 of this volume. In England at this time the writ of *mandamus* was evolving, but this was a prerogative writ; i.e., issuing in the king's name and affecting the sovereignty of the state. In the period with which we are concerned, it was commonly used against negligent officials and was not used in civil suits at common law. On these early uses of *mandamus*, see W. S. Holdsworth, *A History of English Law*, 10:246–47.

that made serious competition for it unnecessary. In the earliest years of settlement, permanent farming or residential patterns were not yet established, and many people abandoned land in order to take up more fertile acreage readily to be had in other towns. The town of Lynn, it was soon discovered, contained hundreds of acres of marsh and rocky hills that were useless as either arable or pasture land. A large group left for Sandwich, in Plymouth Colony, in 1637, and forty more families went to Long Island in 1640. When the end of the Great Migration halted the flow of repopulation eager to obtain land, Lynn was dotted with abandoned tracts; by 1645 it was unable to collect its assessed colony rate, for there were between two and three hundred acres of unused, formerly cultivated land now "overrun with Sorrel."[8]

The outbreak of the Civil War in England further contributed to the land surplus. Not only did it stop emigration to New England, but it also lured many erstwhile colonists back to old England to fight against king and archbishop. Although such a decision in many cases meant giving up large parcels of land, the attraction of finally striking the long-awaited blow against popish vestiges was a powerful one. Hugh Peter is probably the best known of the many Essexmen who crossed the Atlantic and left their estates behind, but his 350-acre tract was small compared to John Humfrey's total holdings. The largest of these, although known modestly only as "Humfrey's Farm," comprised much of the present-day towns of Swampscott and Lynnfield.[9]

Still more land became available when its owners were forced to leave it because of religious disagreements with the colony's leadership. After the antinomian challenge was quelled by the authorities in 1637 and its leaders sent to Rhode Island and Long Island, heterodoxy was no more welcome in Essex County than in Boston. The fractious octogenarian minister Stephen Batchelor found Lynn, Newbury, and Ipswich all inhospitable despite receiving land in each; he abandoned it all—as well as a newly married third wife—to go back to England and enjoy a bigamous fourth marriage. When John Humfrey left Lynn to join Cromwell's Ironsides, Lady Deborah Moody was wealthy enough to buy the bulk of Humfrey's Farm. But along with her title and financial resources—she paid eleven hundred pounds for the property—Lady Deborah brought a strong and vocal opposition to infant baptism. Within two years she was on her way to Long Island to join others whose religious beliefs were incompatible with Bay Colony Puritanism.[10] Theo-

8. Alonzo Lewis, *The History of Lynn*, pp. 62, 72, 86–87.
9. Sidney Perley, *The History of Salem, Massachusetts*, 2:198. Peter preached at Salem before returning to England. His daughter later believed his Salem land to be hers.
10. Lewis, *Lynn*, pp. 49, 52, 54–56, 74–78.

logical disagreements or ecclesiastical rivalries, moreover, led several strong-willed Puritan divines to take groups of supporters to establish new settlements on their own. The most famous, perhaps, is Thomas Hooker, who left Cambridge in Middlesex, but from Essex a group followed Thomas Parker out of Ipswich. Of the 397 adult males who lived in Ipswich before 1660, in fact, it has been estimated that 146 left the town, many of them in a single body with Parker.[11]

Finding cheap or free land elsewhere, people like Lady Deborah Moody did not bother to sell their land, and it is unlikely that all of them could have found buyers if they had tried, in a market where land was so plentiful. Humfrey's Farm was quickly taken over by squatters whose only claim to it was their occupancy. Others who left did manage to sell their land, but few of them took the trouble to record the transaction. It was easy not to do so, for common English practice was not to record conveyances. A legal convenience, known as the "lease and release," had been developed to evade the Statute of Enrolments in England, and many people in Massachusetts knew how to use this device—in fact, they continued to employ it when transferring land they still owned in England. For their Massachusetts property, on the other hand, these same people dispensed with the technique entirely; although they went to the trouble of employing the lease and release for their property back in England, they conveyed their real property in Massachusetts by a simple document that they called an "indenture," and neglected to have it recorded.[12]

Of course, the absence of recorded land transfers had caused problems in England, and it did so in Massachusetts as well. Buyers had to be assured that the persons selling them land had legal title, and in 1634 the General Court ordered that all town land grants to freemen be recorded when made and that a transcript be sent to the court after surveying by a constable and four other freemen. The next year this requirement—in fact, a privilege, for it assured titles in writing—was extended to all town grants made to those taking the oath of allegiance. What appears to be an orderly and regular system befitting the supposed Puritan concern for orthodoxy in all aspects of life, however, was in reality rather less than that.[13] By 1637 the widespread failure of local officials to follow the

11. Edward S. Perzel, "Landholding in Ipswich," pp. 303–28.
12. Thomas Lechford, *Note-book Kept by Thomas Lechford, Esq., Lawyer, in Boston, Massachusetts, from June 27, 1638 to July 1641*, pp. 19–20.
13. Order and regularity were not usual in the land arrangements of the early seventeenth century. One of the first discussions of the land system there was Charles McLean Andrews, *River Towns of Connecticut*, p. 4. He included a map of lots in Wethersfield but cautioned against assuming any regularity there: "allotments cannot in every case be absolutely ascertained, as the records are often vague and faulty." Nevertheless, later historians

orders of 1634 and 1635 forced the General Court to act once again and demand "that some course bee taken to cause men to record their lands, or to fine them that neglect."[14] Although many landowners responded to the threat of fines, evasion of both the spirit and the letter of the law continued. Many men were still "apt to rest upon a verball bargaine, or sale," and abuses of the system occurred. In Marblehead, for instance, Thomas Davis sold a half share of commonage to Richard Norman, while Henry Pease sold the same half share to Richard Downing. George Corwin outdid either when he sold five shares of that town's common, even though he owned only three.[15]

The seeds of future conflict were being sown, but the first settlers of Essex had been preoccupied with the prompt cultivation of land and production of food to avoid the "starving times" that had decimated earlier attempts at colonization, and they soon grew accustomed to tolerating inexactness in allotment and record-keeping. In Ipswich, settlers had been particularly hasty in appropriating land in order to lay claim to that area before the French could occupy the northern fringe of the colony. As a result, few people there were troubled by the casual treatment of land arrangements during the first two decades. When a lot was surveyed for school revenue, for example, none of the lot-layers was willing to wade through a swamp to mark a boundary tree on the other side. One man was finally designated for the task, but he never recorded his effort and it was soon forgotten by everyone in Ipswich.[16]

While some residents did not bother to record their lots at all,[17] others recorded only vague and relative descriptions of their property.

were not as rigorous as Andrews and ignored his warning. See, in this regard, the assumptions made by A. C. Ford, *Colonial Precedents of Our National Land System as It Existed in 1800*, passim. Ford used Andrews's map—but not his text—to demonstrate seventeenth-century precedents for the orderly patterns of the Northwest Territory. Percy Bidwell and John I. Falconer then drew on Ford's error to assert that early land arrangements possessed "remarkable regularity" (*History of Agriculture in the Northern United States*, p. 52). Despite the central importance of land affairs in the life of early Massachusetts towns, historians have failed to go beyond these formalistic analyses to probe the actual workings of the "system."

14. *Mass. Rec.* 1:116, 137, 201. In part, this situation may be attributed to the absence of any precedent in England, where no common or general deed registration system operated. Even New Netherlands, however, which did have a precedent upon which to draw, did not act for many years and experienced similar confusion. Massachusetts was also one of the last colonies to create the office of surveyor general, in 1682. Richard B. Morris, *Studies in the History of American Law*, pp. 69–71. Clarence W. Rife, "Land Tenure in New Netherlands," pp. 50–51. *Col. Laws* 1672–86, p. 296.

15. Marblehead Records, *EIHC*, 69:247–50.

16. Epps v. Bennett [1678], EP 28:8. For similar treatment of a lot between Rowley and Andover, see Selectmen of Andover v. Fuller [1677], EP 26:147. In each of these cases, witnesses in court in the 1670s were describing the events of earlier decades.

17. Manchester, Massachusetts, *Town Records of Manchester*, p. 33.

Town meetings were no more careful; in some instances they specified the length of the lot, but more typical was Salisbury's record of its grant to Thomas Barrett: "two acres more or less of meadow lying between the meadow lots of John Hoyt and John Clough, butting upon the great creek and the great neck."[18] The major concern in these land arrangements was the prevention of fraudulent land sales; it was not the establishment or enforcement of precise boundaries. So lax was concern for precision that no protest was raised when a man in Lynn needed lumber and obtained it by felling a "bound tree."[19]

The famous land recording act of 1640 testified to the lack of concern for border certainty. According to its preamble, this law was "[f]or avoyding all fraudulent conveyances, and that every man may know what estate or interest other men may have in any houses, lands, or other hereditaments they are to deale in." To assure its purpose, all land transfers were to be recorded, but no great detail was required. One clause explained that "it is not intended that the whole bargain, sale, etc., shalbee entered, but only the names of the graunter and grauntee, the thing and the estate graunted, and the date."[20] Further limitations were added at the revision of the law in 1652, but more precisely described boundaries were still not required.[21]

Real property transactions, therefore, were characterized by a casual treatment of boundaries. In addition to factors unique to the New World, the English background of the colonists contributed to the relaxed attitudes. In an agrarian society where customary rights were well known to the members of a community, great concern need not be paid to defining explicit boundaries. In Massachusetts, on the other hand, such implicit and generally shared understandings did not always exist. In one Salem neighborhood, different people believed different men to be the owner of a specific lot. There was no house erected on it, nor was it fenced. Daniel Southwick frequently cut wood there and called it "Davisons, or Captain Corwins plaine"; Corwin, for his part, regarded the land as commons. Eleazer Taylor referred to it as "Bartholmew's playne," while John Putnam said that it was "reputed and commonly called Captain Trasks plain." However, at Trask's death the estate appraiser heard

18. Salisbury Records, p. 15. For a like entry by the town of Salem, see Salem Records, EIHC, 9:14.

19. Mansfield v. Newhall [1682], EP 37:33–35. The man left a pile of rocks, but that was less reliable.

20. Mass. Rec. 1:306–7. The best discussion of this act is Mark DeWolfe Howe, "The Recording of Deeds in the Colony of Massachusetts Bay." Also helpful is George Lee Haskins, "The Beginnings of the Recording System in Massachusetts."

21. Max Farrand, ed., The Laws and Liberties of Massachusetts, pp. 13–14. Mass. Rec. 3:280; 4 (pt. i):101.

no mention that it had belonged to Trask, and no written proof could be found to determine ownership.[22]

John Cotton was exceptional when he addressed himself to the general unconcern in 1642. Cotton, with a Puritan minister's ability to conflate theological and social issues, observed that in the colony there were "good meddowes and accomodations [and] these are great things." But he added that the ability to enjoy such open land had prevented any effort toward regulation. He asked, "[I]f we could have large elbowe-room enough, and meddow enough, though we have no ordinances, [and] we can then goe and live like lambs in a large place, what shall I say then?"[23]

Most landowners were content to "goe and live like lambs" because many of the disputes that did occur could be settled with little trouble within the mechanism of town government. In some cases, farmers who discovered that hasty distribution of lots had left them with "little or no marsh or medow ground" were able to request and receive additional land, or tracts "in lieu of" worthless ones. Compensatory grants were common in the 1630s; even the town surveyor of Salem had to petition for such land in 1638 after he realized that he had taken "50 Acres of rocks . . . which are not of any use."[24] When the town had to lay out a highway in 1657, it produced a "difference" between neighbors William King and Roger Hasscoll that was also settled in this way. King and his neighbors needed access to bring their grain to a mill, but the proposed path went through Hasscoll's land. Jacob Barney and Jeffrey Massey were appointed to settle the matter, and they were able to give Hasscoll another parcel of land.[25]

Litigation to recover land, therefore, was less frequently necessary when abundance minimized competition. Reliance on unapportioned land to settle disagreements was a seductively easy policy, and in the early decades the General Court abetted that by extending town borders into the vacant wilderness if necessary. As early as 1638 the residents of Lynn

---

22. Woolcott v. Trask [1686], EP 46:16–24.

23. John Cotton, *The Churches Resurrection*, pp. 25–26.

24. Salem Records, *EIHC*, 9:45, 76, 78, 67. For similar complaints in Salisbury, see Salisbury Records, pp. 5–6, 28, 68, 109. Obviously, different towns underwent different processes, but this pattern was very common in the county as a whole. Only Marblehead managed to escape such difficulties because in its first years it was almost exclusively a fishing community. As part of Salem in 1637 it was decided to grant only the standard small fisherman's lot to each resident there, and no meadow or upland figured in its first division. Instead, allotments consisted of house and garden lots of two acres, with rights to common woods and pasturage for goats and cattle. Samuel Roads, Jr., *History and Traditions of Marblehead*, p. 12.

25. Salem Records, *EIHC*, 9:205. On two other occasions in the winter of 1656, Massey and Conant had been chosen for this purpose. Ibid., p. 189.

MAP 2. Settlement of Available Arable Land in Lynn, to 1660

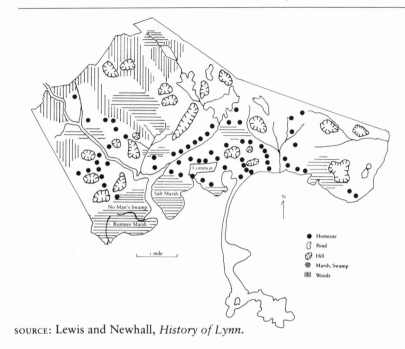

SOURCE: Lewis and Newhall, *History of Lynn*.

complained of a land shortage, although only 8,680 of the town's 18,000 acres had been distributed. The land scarcity had occurred because the remaining acreage was of little value, consisting largely of hills and wooded waste, rather than the meadow and upland that the residents preferred. Two large swampy marshes straddled the Saugus River in the center of town, and no settlement was even attempted there (see map 2). The General Court eased the shortage by granting Lynn 6,400 adjacent acres, which became known as "Lynn End."[26]

A temporary lag in immigration during the 1640s reduced pressures on Essex land, but in the 1660s renewed pressures found many towns in the county unable to solve disagreements as easily as before. By that time, the towns had discovered that an open frontier was no longer available and that all future land grants would have to be made within existing limits. Never again would Lynn be able to expand "six miles into the

26. Lewis, *Lynn*, pp. 64–68. John Humphrey Sears, *The Physical Geography, Geology, Mineralogy, and Paleontology of Essex County, Massachusetts*, p. 21, app. A. The wooded areas of Lynn were kept as undivided common until 1708. Commonwealth of Massachusetts, *Historical Data Relating to Counties, Cities, and Towns in Massachusetts*, p. 41.

countrey." Salem, beset by the same problem, made a final addition in 1660, but it had to reach offshore to obtain "Miseries and Bakers Island." Even a newer town like Wenham saw its sources of additional land disappear, and in 1678 it had to turn to Salem—from which it had been set off in 1643—with a request for more land. Salem replied with a complaint of its own: "[W]ee find that the Towne of Salem had already granted away so much land that they canot Spare any more without much Streightening themselves."[27]

Although many towns in the colony had large areas of land suitable for cultivation to ease the sense of scarcity, others—at least in the perception of their residents—did not. The end of the Great Migration helped matters temporarily, but as early as 1641 a Cambridge man observed of the colony that "theis Townes [are] so thicke planted" that people would have to "improve the trade of fishing, and other trades" in order to survive. The same awareness was present in several Essex towns after 1660. A town like Andover was able to provide its second generation with sufficient land for planting or pasture, but only because it was relatively large, and a higher proportion of its approximately thirty-eight thousand acres was meadow and upland. By contrast, towns such as Lynn, Salem, Ipswich, Newbury, and Salisbury had large treeless tracts of swamp and began to feel a scarcity of timber. Studies of historical geography have shown that a family required fifteen cords of wood (three-fifths acre of standing timber) per winter. To assure an adequate supply, these smaller coastal towns had to limit the cutting of trees from their common lands as early as the 1640s.[28]

The absence of freely available land also made it necessary for Essex towns to make serious efforts to increase their diminished reserves. One method was to expand their borders at the expense of neighboring towns. Salem, for instance, had border disputes with Topsfield in 1653, Ipswich in 1660 and 1661, and Beverly in 1672. Seeking more land and trying to discover what was rightfully their own, its residents began to change the lax land arrangements that had existed for decades. In 1673 they voted for the first time to perambulate the town limits, although required to do so by colonial law since 1647. There followed land discussions with other towns and efforts to establish exact boundaries: Salem officials met with representatives from Reading in 1673, Lynn and Marblehead in 1679, and Wenham again that year.[29]

Another result of this emerging land shortage was a new and scru-

27. Salem Records, *EIHC*, 48:348.
28. *Assts. Rec.* 2:109–11. Perzel, "Landholding in Ipswich," p. 309.
29. *Massachusetts Data*, p. 66. Salem Records, *EIHC*, 9:174; 40:286, 108; 42:262; 43:45, 46; 49:76, 148, 155. *Mass. Rec.* 2:210.

pulous attitude toward encroachments on town land. The Salem town meeting in 1673 directed its selectmen to search for town land being used illegally, and they discovered numerous violations. Significantly, they reported a practice that indicated more than mere casual inattention: "We found . . . a bound tree newly Cut downe and hewed on the Sids," they observed. "It was marked to deface the markes."[30] Trespasses on town land were not limited to isolated mowing or planting lots on the outskirts, moreover. "Jonathan Southwicks fenc neare his house [was ordered] to be personally pulled down" by town officials in 1661. In a more serious case, Thomas Bell was directed to tear down his home in 1683 because it was on town land; if he refused, the selectmen were authorized to sue him "for his Trespasse and presumption." Suits such as these, with towns suing their own residents for encroachments on undivided land, became common in the decades after 1660.[31]

The appearance of the county courts in intramural town disputes attested to the scope and perplexity of a problem emerging from years of indifference. The distribution of open land to satisfy demands had been an expedient as dangerous as it was seductively easy, for it had prevented towns from formulating a general policy to be used when the supply was exhausted. Belatedly, Andover tried to locate "clear and certaine" grants of land, and to declare them "as valid and authentick, as if they had been entered and recorded at the time when they were graunted." But such a declaration meant little when disputes arose over holdings that were less than "clear and certaine" or if no easy compensation existed for men who lost a town decision.[32]

As the acquiescent town founders passed away, their land holdings were inherited by sons who were eager to place relationships on a more formal and economically assured basis. Some, of course, were also interested in increasing their holdings in the process, and they could not be expected to rely on the tacit understandings that their fathers had held. The earliest settlers had been able and content to tolerate uncertainty or to settle problems informally—in Cotton's words, to "live like lambs in a

30. Salem Records, *EIHC*, 42:261; 43:43–45; 49:76; 44:65; 49:79; 83:273, 275–76. For efforts in Marblehead, see Marblehead Records, *EIHC*, pp. 252–53.

31. Salem Records, *EIHC*, 9:216; 40:114; 44:80, 207. For other such suits against residents, see Selectmen of Rowley v. Nelson [1672], IpMbk. 1666–82, Sept. term #15; Selectmen of Lynn v. Edmonds [1673], EP 20:25–28; Sambourne, on behalf of Town of Hampton, v. Tilton [1673], NorMbk. 1672–81, p. 26, and NorWbk., p. 93.

32. Poor v. Wright [1681], EP 35:40–42. In Haverhill, Johnson v. Herriman [1684], EP 42:101–6. In Newbury, Gerrish v. Dummer [1675], EP 23:77–81. In Wenham, Poland v. Patch [1679], EP 31:68; 53:29–32. In addition, purchasers began recording deeds in full at the county registry, although not required by law to do so. The first such recording appeared in 1658. Essex County Land Records, 1:95–97.

large place," or in those of a man from Salem, to make agreements that were "only verball." Less acquiescent successors, by comparison, went to court.[33]

Essex landowners might have sought guidance from their town meetings. These bodies could not take cognizance of actions involving title to land, but they could settle factual questions regarding the town's actions in the past. However, disputants perceived important advantages in having the decision rendered by the county court. Significant decisions affecting someone's possession of land—indeed, his livelihood—could polarize an entire town and do serious damage to local harmony if brought before the town meeting. When such a dispute was discussed at the Salem town meeting in 1678, it produced only an unpleasant stalemate, as the leader of one group taunted the other, "I know I stick in sum of your eies. I had rather stick in your throats."[34] Scenes of this sort occurred because at a town meeting every voter had to take sides publicly when the issue came to a full vote. Blame and recrimination were inevitable by-products of mandatory taking of sides in emotional cases, but settlement in court helped reduce these dangers. In the first place, only those persons who were involved in the dispute or who wanted to take sides came to court. Supporting testimony might be solicited by the litigants, but it appears that persons were not summoned to court by subpoena and required to testify. In addition, the final decision was made by a relatively impartial third-party institution, removed from the jealousies and rivalries of town politics. The five judges presiding at each quarterly term included those assistants from the General Court residing in Essex, as well as "associates" chosen at large in the county. Also hearing civil causes were petit jurors summoned by the sheriff from various towns; jurors were rarely challenged for partiality—indeed, only once after 1672.[35] A final, and perhaps most important, advantage was the force behind the court's

33. One of Hugh Peter's old lots in Salem illustrates this process in Norman v. Orne [1685], EP 43:110–20. For another example, in which two brothers made an exchange of land that was "only verball" and led to later dispute, see Balch v. Price [1680], EP 33:52–59. On other litigious sons of acquiescent fathers, see Bennett v. Pengry [1674], IpMbk. 1666–82, Mar. term #20; and Savage v. Hathorne [1681], EP 36:86–101. An extreme case of a grandson's attempt to overturn an earlier generation's arrangements was Fowler v. Needham [1681], EP 36:18–21. The most explicit confrontation occurred in Lynn, with Witter v. Richards [1680], EP 34:2–3. In fact, Hugh Peter commented on this phenomenon as early as 1650 when he was sued by Robert Saltonstall over £100 and complained that it was "monstrous thus to thinke to cheat his fathers friends" (*Saltonstall Papers*, p. 45).

34. Bridges v. Batter [1678], EP 28:129–31.

35. *Col. Laws 1672–86*, p. 36. The obligation to take sides in a dispute before the town meeting—and, hence, the danger of being drawn into conflict—was paralleled in the church. John Humfrey discovered this fact in 1637 when "he was loath to offend the church" over a dispute. He had tried to abstain from a dispute, but the question was put to the church, "whether a brother may abstayne, when he is like else, to give offence to

judgment. Towns were empowered by statute to levy minor fines (up to twenty shillings), but as late as 1671 their reluctance to wield even so limited a power prompted them to request that the General Court reaffirm that responsibility.[36] By contrast, forty shillings was the *minimum* for the cases the county court could hear. It could, of course, award lesser damages—or none at all—but its sanctions were markedly more effective.

The residents of Lynn discovered the advantages of resolving local disputes outside the town meeting in 1683 when the entire eastern end of town was drawn into a major confrontation (see map 3). On a geographical basis, the men at the southwest corner of Humfrey's Farm opposed those of the northwest side across Humfrey's Brook. The difference arose when selectmen found it necessary to lay out a new highway across the Farm to its eastern extreme, where Ezekiel Needham had acquired a tract of land. The road was to be run between Benjamin Farr's land and Josiah Witter's. Neither man wanted the existing land arrangements upset by a road, and both were "much averse to having it laid out upon either of their lands." Farr prevailed upon the selectmen to cross Witter's land, but this was "much to the dissatisfaction" of Witter's tenant, who "went along and pulled up the stakes." One of the three selectmen was William Bassett, a friend and neighbor of Witter's; a second survey, not surprisingly, relocated the road on Farr's land.[37]

No one would yield the land necessary for the road, and the dispute threatened to paralyze the town. A majority of the selectmen were allied to the Witter-Needham faction, but they could gain no final victory as long as Farr and his supporters viewed themselves as "extremely damnified" by their actions and regarded the selectmen's decisions as partisan. One of Farr's group typified the opposition when he vowed to keep fighting the issue at the town meeting until his death. With positions so hardened, the only solution was to take the problem away from town institutions. Each side sued the other for trespass in 1684, and Farr's right was finally upheld.[38]

Disputes like the Farr-Witter problem began to appear as soon as a town's population had dispersed to the point that highways and cart-

---

another." To Humfrey's chagrin, the answer was a simple "No." This episode is recorded in John Fiske, Notebook [unpaged], at "10th of 11th month" [10 Jan.], probably 1638, as "Mr Humphre's case."

36. *Mass. Rec.* 4 (pt. ii):486.

37. Farr v. Needham [1684], EP 41:113–16. Witter v. Farr [1684], EP 42:90–97.

38. Witter v. Farr. Farr lost at the county court in this latter action, but only because of a disputed letter of attorney; at the Court of Assistants Witter was nonsuited, and Farr gained a reversal of the judgment. *Assts. Rec.* 1:269–70.

MAP 3. Approximate Locations of Property Holdings
at Humfrey's Farm, 1683

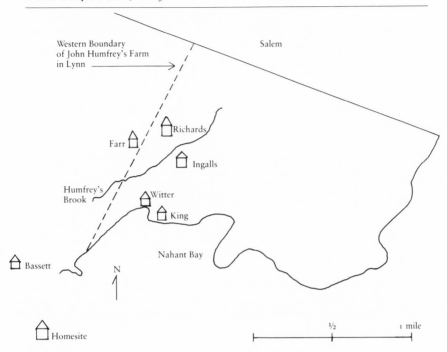

ways became necessary for outlying farms, or when secondary clusters of
population developed far from the center of town so that mills and other
service facilities for them had to be established. Town officials in the first
decades of settlement had provided for such needs and had either reserved certain corridors or obtained the necessary land by giving compensatory grants to persons who had yielded lots for that purpose. These
highways were not always built, however, and reserved land was sometimes reoccupied by the initial grantee or by a third party. In 1653, for
example, Hampton had set aside land for access to the area on the other
side of the town's millbrook; no one occupied the reserved land until
Abraham Drake fenced it as his own. By 1674 it became necessary for
people living in that area to use the pathway, and they had to sue him in
an action of case in order to have it opened for their use. The court ordered the way laid out and awarded the plaintiffs two pence damages.[39]

39. Colcord v. Drake [1674], NorMbk. 1672–81, p. 34. See also James v. Northy
[1672], EP 18:49; and King v. Town of Lynn [1673], EP 20:7–8.

Similarly, a town might require land to be used for a new mill to accommodate its increased population, as Salem attempted to do in 1663 when it granted several men a tract on the South River on which to erect a gristmill. The town's right to make the grant rested on its customary right to reserve all waterside land up to a certain point above high water. On the other hand, John Pickering believed that the land was part of his adjoining property. When construction began on the mill he pulled up the surveying stakes and threw the workmen's tools into the river, and he also entered trespass actions against the mill owners. In both cases the town custom prevailed. Specifically, Richard Davenport, who had lived in Salem from 1631 to 1648, testified that the town had reserved to its own use two poles' width of land between all waterside lots and the high-water mark of river or tide and that "it was a very usual thing" for residents to use that particular land as a highway. With that point established, the jury decided for the mill owners, and "South Mills" became an important enterprise in Salem. Two years later, moreover, John Leighton was able to plead the same two-pole custom to win a replevin case when Thomas Borman impounded Leighton's livestock for allegedly trespassing on his private property.[40]

Town land affairs were particularly prone to dispute after 1660, when the General Court strictly limited the creation of new commonage shares.[41] No longer was erecting a dwelling within a town sufficient to merit a share in the commonage; only on the vote of the town meeting could such shares henceforth be obtained. The result was that even in a town with land as relatively abundant as Andover, those who held no shares felt deprived. As several of that town petitioned the General Court in 1675, they were "much straitened in their p[er]sonall accommodations and most of their children grown up and many others of the petitioners wholly destitute of land for settlement and soe under a necessity to look for inlargment and places of habitation."[42]

With new rights harder to obtain, people began competing for old ones and seeking commonage shares about which their fathers had not cared. In Rowley, John Elithorp asked the town to lay out for him a share to which he was entitled, he said, by the descent of his late father's right. When two town officials refused his request on 4 and 5 March 1672, Elithorp (on his own behalf, and as attorney to his mother, brother, and two sisters) sued the officials (on the town's behalf), demanding that they lay out his share.[43]

40. Pickering v. Price [1664], EP 10:48. Leighton v. Borman [1666], IpMbk. 1646–66, Sept. term #8. Perley, *Salem*, 2:336–39.

41. *Col. Laws 1672–86*, p. 149.

42. Greven, *Four Generations*, p. 64.

43. Elithorp v. Pickard, in behalf of Town of Rowley [1672], EP 18:68.

The questions he raised and the remedy the court applied typified the general problems of imposing order on the seventeenth-century land system in Essex. The plaintiff declared that his father Thomas Elithorp had purchased the share from Thomas Sumner and in turn had agreed to sell it to Thomas Burckbee, who paid for it "partly with a cow." Before he completed payment, however, Burckbee decided that he did not want the land and requested return of the cow. Both Elithorp and his wife refused to return the animal, and Burckbee assumed that the land was his after Elithorp, he said, "told mee that he would make mee deeds of Land when I would." All of this had taken placed before the recording act of 1652 required that all conveyances be made in writing; but, as Burckbee deposed, even "after the Law was made of makeing deeds in writing I sould it to Joseph Jewett, deceased, and never askt any deeds of it nor gave any when I sould it, nor troubled myself further about it." John Pickard, one of the town officials being sued, defended and testified that he was present when Thomas Elithorp had made up his will shortly before his death in 1644. Elithorp, he said, had commented at the time that all he was able to bequeath to his wife was forty pounds, having sold all of his rights in Rowley. Ezekiel Northend, the other official named in the suit, added that he had been present when Elithorp, refusing to return the cow to Burckbee, had explained that he was selling all of his Rowley property in order to move to Haverhill or Andover. Nevertheless, his son John Elithorp sued for the right that the town said his father had given up, and the jury returned a verdict for him. The court thereupon ordered the town to lay out a full share's lot to the plaintiff within a month and to pay him seventy-five pounds should it fail to do so.[44]

The clamor to revive dormant rights became a subject of frequent litigation after 1660 because town founders had not provided their successors with any policy for transferring rights to future allotments. Unless an explicit statement were made in a deed, it was not clear among Essex commoners if the purchaser of a commonage share also obtained the right to future allotments, or if the seller—as a town founder—retained it. This problem would not be solved until the eighteenth century; only then, when legally recognized groups of town proprietors were incorporated and set apart from the town meeting, did allotments become economic commodities to be bought and sold freely.[45] Until that time,

44. Ibid. For this type of dispute in Salisbury, see Stevens v. Clement [1692], EP 52:47–54. Similar disputes arose over the early commonage grants made in Amesbury when part of Salisbury, as in Weed v. Barnard [1674], NorMbk. 1672–81, p. 37; and Fowler v. Weed [1679], ibid., p. 105. On 13 May 1661 the Salem town meeting, seeing the increasing number of revived dormant claims, ordered "thatt all men that have any former grants of Land from the Towne are to come to the selct men and make their Claime within one yeare after the date hereof or els Loose it forever" (Fletcher v. Town of Salem [1673], EP 19:128–30).

45. *Acts and Resolves*, 1:704. On the later pattern, which emerged after that statute

however, no general rule existed, and competing interpretations had to be settled in court.

Adding to the difficulty was the absence of any well-known rule from English practice, for the Massachusetts system of commonage differed from its English predecessor. Land in England was rarely subdivided and then distributed as individual holdings in severalty to members of a commonage. Instead, the land was shared collectively ("stinted"); and thus if a commoner wished to enclose a specific portion as his own property, he had to buy it from the commoners as a private individual. He had no claim to such a grant in severalty as a commoner, because it was not customary to set out land in that manner. Distribution of holdings in severalty from the Massachusetts town common, on the other hand, had developed into a familiar fact of town life. This difference made a share in the commonage potentially far more valuable, but it also made the situation a novelty to the rules of English agrarian life.[46]

It was left to the courts to assert the precise customary arrangements needed to determine a person's right to the newly valuable but frequently contested allotment shares. The manner in which they did so was demonstrated in Rowley. Traditionally in that town, a share in the ox pasture gave its owner only herbage; i.e., the right of placing a certain number of animals there to graze. In monetary terms, each of these shares (usually referred to as "gates") was worth ten shillings a year, and in 1664 John Johnson purchased one and a quarter gates from Thomas Remington for fifty shillings, a price that another potential buyer had refused to pay, believing it to be too high. But in 1674 Rowley decided to distribute its undivided common land on the basis, among others, of ownership of pasture rights; as a result, the value of a gate increased enormously. One resident commented that sixteen pounds was too low a price for a gate he owned, while another agreed that twenty pounds would still be less than the value of Johnson's gate. But shortly before the distribution was to be made, Remington asserted that the allotment would belong to him, and Johnson had to sue him in an action of case for not "making good" the right to the allotment share. Johnson won his suit, and three years later Daniel Wicom was able to sue the town for failing to grant him land that he deserved "according to the custom of the town"—that is, the customary right of purchasers to share in commonage divisions, as that right had been established by judicial precedent.[47]

---

separated the economic body of proprietors from the political body of the town meeting, see Roy H. Akagi, *The Town Proprietors of the New England Colonies*, pp. 44–77.

46. On the English background, see R. H. Tawney, *The Agrarian Problem in the Sixteenth Century*, pp. 95, 157–60, 245, 284–94. New intakes in England were not governed by past custom, moreover, but were treated as an entirely "new thing" (ibid.).

47. Johnson v. Remington [1674], EP 21:17; and IpMbk. 1666–82, Mar. term #8, #9. Wicom v. Pickard [1677], EP 27:85.

Because of their importance in governing future distributions of land (and, thus, of wealth) in Essex towns, customary arrangements were essential. Ironically, the outside institution of the judicial system often had to determine and assert what such "custom" was in a specific town. A multitude of local customs existed in England, and each emigrant to Massachusetts brought with him the memories of the customary arrangements of his specific locality. Each new town, therefore, had no single custom on which to rely, and towns often divided over which interpretation of its "custom" should prevail. Land distribution was a source of many disputes, and the general problem was worsened if it also involved questions of political rights when town meetings tried to put questions to a vote. Questions related to voting were a source of disagreement even in England at this time, and Massachusetts settlers brought these uncertainties with them.[48] Essex towns had relied on unanimous votes in their early years, but split votes and conflicts pitting town meetings against selectmen soon caused legal problems. If a vote was not unanimous and a minority entered a dissent to a land distribution, was the majority a legal grantor? In Newbury in 1654 a group of town inhabitants challenged the right of the previous group of selectmen to have granted land. The Rowley town meeting tried to limit this danger in 1648 by requiring the selectmen to obtain the consent of the town meeting to grant land, but it appears that the meeting could be equally capricious; in 1672 the county court had to uphold an earlier Rowley grant against the challenge of a subsequent town meeting. Unless land titles were to become subject to the turnabouts of town politics, rules for distributing town land had to be established and enforced by the court.[49]

Especially after 1650, the bench possessed the continuity of membership needed to bring consistency to the procedural and substantive law applied in court. Because the judges of the county court were those assistants residing in Essex, plus several "associates" chosen at large in the county, they benefited from colonial electoral practices that effectively returned incumbent magistrates to office. Each November the freemen of the colony submitted the names of those men whom they wished to nominate as candidates for election as assistants; from all the names submitted, the twenty who were named most often were actually nominated to stand for election the following May. At that time, lists of the twenty candidates were read at town meetings, and the ten men receiving the greatest number of votes became the colony's magistrates. In practice, however, incumbents were always renominated and placed at the top of the lists, with the new candidates following in descending order accord-

48. Derek Hirst, *The Representative of the People?* p. 15.
49. Emery et al. v. Merrill [1654], IpMbk. 1646–66, March term. Selectmen of Rowley v. Nelson [1672], IpMbk. 1666–82, Sept. term #15.

ing to the number of nominations they had received. "Consequently," writes the scholar who has studied this system most carefully, "when the names of the nominees were read off in the town meetings it would be necessary for a voter to withhold his ballot from an incumbent before he could give it to a new candidate." In addition to this practical advantage, Massachusetts magistrates benefited from the popular belief at the time that magistrates were to hold office indefinitely unless specific cause for removal existed.[50]

The manner of electing associates is less clear from the papers surviving in the county court files, but its effect was the same, for the membership of the county bench was essentially stable from 1650 until the end of the Old Charter period in 1684. Twenty-four men served on the county bench during that period, and four of them (Samuel Symonds, Robert Bridges, William Hathorne, and Daniel Denison) served until they died, averaging more than twenty-nine years of service. Simon Bradstreet, a venerable survivor of the founding generation, also sat for twenty-nine years. When most of the others with shorter terms left office, it was for reasons unconnected with removal by the electorate. John Endecott, for example, left upon moving to Boston in 1655 after serving eighteen years; although he had been governor of the colony for many years, he had resisted the move to Boston, preferring to remain at Salem. The establishment of the royal colony of New Hampshire, in addition, meant the removal of three men (with an average tenure of five years) living in towns that became part of the new colony. Seven other magistrates were in office at the revocation of the charter; several of these had been added in 1680, when the size of the colony magistracy was increased to eighteen, but their average tenure was still just under seven years. The eight other judges or associates averaged only one and a half years, but the men of longer tenure obviously dominated the court. It was from their ranks, for instance, that the presiding judge at each term was chosen. Moreover, four judges (Bradstreet, Symonds, Denison, and Hathorne) constituted a majority of the bench at every Salem and Ipswich term for a quarter century, from April 1653 until Symonds's death in 1678; from 1663 to 1672, in fact, these four were the only men on the bench.

This continuity was important as land competition provoked conflict in the older coastal towns of the county. Greater age and population placed greater pressure on their land supplies, and farmers there began quarreling over land of less and less quality. A lot that had been sold for only a blanket or two in 1640, for example, was being sought eagerly in

50. This description of electoral practice is based on the analysis made by Stephen Foster, *Their Solitary Way*, app. B, pp. 180–81.

1685, and marshland was becoming the object of lawsuits to a degree never seen before. In Salisbury, Robert Pike sued Samuel Weed in trespass upon the case over some freshwater marsh in a part of the town where the land was so poor that the slaughterhouse was located there, away from the inhabited neighborhoods. Selectmen had not even laid out the area at first "[b]ecause it was low and [with] many small Creeks and ponds, and we thought it would be a damage to those whose Lots should fall there." For Essexmen to sue over marshes was a sign of the increasing scarcity of land. Boggy Essex marshland was of less value than meadow because it was often flooded by fresh or salt water, and the natural grass that grew there was, unlike English grasses, useless as a winter fodder.[51]

At a time of tightening land supply, Essex farmers were impelled by agricultural realities to make the best possible use of what land they possessed. Natural considerations of efficient farming led many of the second generation to consolidate small, scattered holdings into single units that could be more productively plowed, seeded, and harvested. Echoing the opinion of others, John Bartoll of Marblehead observed that a certain subdivided area would be a "brave farm" if the separate parcels could be assembled into a single unit; as they were arranged then, however, they were worth little. Unable to buy any adjacent lots, he gladly sold his own section.[52]

This trend was more evident in Essex towns that had been settled according to the open-field system known in England. In Massachusetts, this practice took the form of grouping residential lots around a central common ("compact" settlement) or along a stream ("linear") and then distributing portions of larger lots set aside for planting, pasture, and mowing in different outlying parts of the town. As each of the older Essex towns made additional allotments a farmer might possess lots in different areas of the town. By the 1660s many of these men were actively amalgamating their scattered lots and moving their residences to a suitably large tract. Even where there were no serious land shortages, problems might result. Andover, in spite of its relative abundance of land, experienced much litigation as its residents sought to create large homestead farms in place of their several dispersed smaller lots.[53]

Not everyone was willing to sell, of course, but it was possible to employ the courts to assert a better claim to a coveted lot in order to oust its present occupant. Few men attempted it, but Nathaniel Putnam of Salem was the most notorious practitioner of this tactic; in 1674 Putnam

51. Bidwell and Falconer, *Agriculture*, pp. 19–20.
52. Brown v. Smith [1673], EP 19:149.
53. Greven describes this process in Andover and Haverhill (*Four Generations*, pp. 56–61).

hatched what a neighbor called a "grand designe" to wrest title to a valuable piece of land from him. The land in question was part of the late Governor John Endecott's farm along the Crane River. Perhaps because of the governor's status, his neighbors always had accepted his interpretation of their borders and little need was felt to formalize something that was already confirmed by the word of the eminent Endecott. Sometime around 1660, for instance, Richard Ingerson (Ingersoll) had rented a parcel of land next to the governor's. One day, related Ingerson's son, "the said Governor Endecott came to my father when we wear at plow and said to my father he had fenced in some of the said Governor Endecotts land. My father Replied that he would remove his fence. Noe, said Governor Endecott, lett it stand and when you sett up a new fence we will settle in the bounds." Endecott had no fear that his understanding of the borders would be challenged, for his neighbors always had deferred to it.[54]

After the governor's death in 1665, however, his son and grandsons were less able to command such deference, and Putnam found the uncertainty of the boundaries to be an opportunity for expansion and consolidation of his own nearby holdings. His "grand designe" rested on a strict reading of the town book's record of the original grant made to John Endecott. According to that grant, a certain hemlock tree was specified as a "corner" of Endecott's farm. Strictly applied to the landscape, this reading would rearrange the placement of several rectangular grants in the area by rotating them ninety degrees. This change of boundaries would, in turn, place a corner of the lot owned by another man, Francis Nurse, well into the Endecott's farm, dividing it into two separated parts. It was Putnam's hope that the Endecotts would then be forced to sell one of these parts.[55] As Zerobabel Endecott told the court when he sued Nurse for trespass in 1678, Putnam was challenging the generally accepted understanding of community boundaries and was seeking "to Catch what he can . . . [and] to devide or cut in two that part of his [Endecott's] farme and to make it like unto a kites tayle, the like president not being knowne in the Cuntry." The Endecotts realized that Putnam had discovered "some Improper and doubtfull expressions in the Recordinge," which threatened their title to the governor's property. To demonstrate how absurd an interpretation Putnam had made of the original grant, they likened the would-be shape to that of a "kites tayle" and included a drawing. Fortunately, the jury accepted the traditional neigh-

54. Endecott v. Preston [1690], EP 49:3–21.
55. The two main cases in this dispute, with the important documents, are ibid., and Endecott v. Nurse [1678], EP 28:79–95, with a map at p. 94.

borhood understanding of the grants made there, and its verdict was in Endecott's favor.[56]

Putnam's effrontery had capitalized upon the precarious state of many titles and boundaries in the county, a situation that had a socially and economically disruptive impact on communities. Title uncertainty reduced the value of any property and seemed to be a particular problem in Salem. When William Sergent wanted to buy a parcel from John Holgrave, Holgrave could give no assurance that he had a good title from William Piney, from whom he had bought the land. Sergent thereupon refused to complete the bargain for fear that the title would "be troubled" in the future. As Thomas Gardner of Salem remarked about another house and land there, he "would not give as much as he would have done" before a third party questioned the title.[57]

The county court, therefore, found it necessary to perform a function that the more informal, nonjudicial local institutions were proving less able to do on their own. This new role of the court was occasionally demonstrated when men petitioned the court to appoint a committee to settle a problem so "that each man might know his own." More often, however, people brought an action at law. It was essential, they recognized, that a community have a mechanism of conflict resolution capable of reaching a decision and enforcing it when economic pressure was so intense that neighbors were incapable of agreement and powerless to "run the line between them that they might live like Christians."[58] A county court decision need not have been the final resolution of the problem, for a losing litigant could appeal to the Court of Assistants. But in actual practice such a solution afforded a large measure of finality. Only thirty land disputes were appealed between 1672 and 1684, and seven of these were not prosecuted. The Court of Assistants, moreover, reversed only eight of the Essex court's judgments; it confirmed twelve and sent three back for local arbitration. A losing litigant had another option, for many of them had challenged the title in question by committing a trespass. When sued, he would admit the general issue (the act of entering the land and mowing hay, for instance) but plead specially that the land was his and the plaintiff had disseised him. The question then became one of who had the better right. But since trespass was a personal action, it concerned only the act of committing the trespass and other trespasses could be made if a loser so wished.[59]

56. Endecott v. Nurse.
57. Holgrave v. Sargent [1654], EP 2. See also Marshall v. Fellowes [1684], EP 40: 124–30.
58. Nealand v. Kimball [1682], EP 38:114–18. Maverick v. Griggs [1685], EP 44:57.
59. Holdsworth, *English Law*, 5:323. It has been remarked that in trespass "One

To create its system of adjudication, the Essex county court departed in some degree from the procedures used in English common law courts of the time. "Real actions" to recover land in England were highly technical and time-consuming and so very specific that many litigants entered the wrong one. By the seventeenth century, the action of ejectment had become a relatively convenient way of avoiding many of the real actions, and according to Coke it was the most widely employed action to try title to land. This action, too, however, had procedural requirements that led people in Essex not to use it. Because it had been developed to grant recovery of a term by a lessee, a fictitious lease (usually to a "John Doe") and ouster (by a "Richard Roe") had to be alleged in order to bring ejectment. These steps were hardly difficult, but they were nevertheless necessary for an action of ejectment to try title, and a frontier legal system demanded even greater simplicity. Despite its routine employment in England, ejectment was not used in Essex throughout the Old Charter period and appeared only when the Dominion of New England government required strict common law procedures.[60]

In its place the Essex county court applied procedures that English common law courts did not. In the so-called Epistle to the *Laws and Liberties* of 1648, it was stated that the Massachusetts legal system drew upon that of the ancient Israelites, in whose laws "there was also somewhat of equitie." The reference to equity used the term in two different senses. The first—to cite the Epistle again—was the conduct of human affairs "according to the light and law of nature." This sense of elevating substance over form had been described by Christopher St. German's *Doctor and Student* as "a right witness that considereth all the particular circumstances of the deed, the which also is tempered with the sweetness of mercy."[61]

Equity was also the system of law applied by the chancellor in England, and by the seventeenth century it had become less a vague body

---

litigant had no fewer than five bites at the cherry" (A. W. B. Simpson, *An Introduction to the History of the Land Law*, p. 139). The personal nature of trespass was a problem in spite of the efforts of the court to prevent repetitious actions. See the observation that "Thomas Russle frequently threateneth that whosoever shall have Thomas Cauley's Land Thay shall never Injoy it peaceable and he will Cutt downe the fence from tyme to tyme soe it shall not be Beneficall to anyone, which hindreth the sale of the Land, because of his threatening Language" (Complaint against Thomas Russell [1682], EP 37:10–12). The principle of res judicata would not apply to repeated trespasses against the same property, between the same parties.

60. Roe v. Doe, of the demise of Henry Rhodes [1686], EP 46:101–11, was the first instance of its use. For more on the Dominion judiciary, see pp. 59, 160–64 of this volume.

61. Farrand, *Laws and Liberties*, p. 42. Christopher St. German, *Doctor and Student*, p. 44. Edwin H. Woodruff adds that the legal system of Massachusetts Bay was based on the authority of God, "an authority in which the conscience of equity must have been supposed to inhere" ("Chancery in Massachusetts," p. 371).

of principles drawn from "natural justice" or the conscience of the chancellor and more a system of definite rules and remedies. This movement had begun earlier, but it was particularly apparent during the Restoration period under the direction of Lord Nottingham. Borough courts, it should be added, exercised powers analogous to these, and the Mayor's Court of New York often operated much like a chancery court when, for example, it supervised trusts or chancered bonds. Since the courts of Massachusetts assumed many characteristics of the borough model, they too sometimes employed equitable rules and remedies such as the chancering of bonds when the situation appeared to merit them. As the colonial laws read, "[I]f there be matter of apparent equity, as the forfeiture of an Obligation, breach of Covenant without damage, or the like, the Bench shall determine such matter of equity."[62] And, as has been shown with the Suffolk records, the bench there occasionally granted injunctions to abate nuisances and ordered sequestrations, neither of which were common law remedies.[63]

The Essex court was little different in this regard. It too ordered the sequestration of estates, and litigants there might request an equitable determination if, for example, they felt that there had been a defect in the recording of a grant. Residents of Ipswich pleaded such a "poynt of Chancery or equity" in 1647 when they said that a grant recorded to John Winthrop, Jr., was "generally knowne to be upon a grosse mistake."[64] In this case the court decided against them, but when the Endecott family made the same plea in 1678 against Nathaniel Putnam's "kites tayle" claim, both the jury and the bench decided for them and rejected Putnam's claim. Significantly, Putnam persuaded Nurse to bring suit again under the common law rules of the Andros regime when local courts had no equity authority, and Nurse won the case.[65]

---

62. *Col. Laws 1672–86*, p. 86.

63. Zechariah Chafee, Jr., ed., "Records of the Suffolk County Court, 1671–1680," pp. 103, 629. In addition, in 1642 the General Court provided what was probably a chancery procedure for new trials. It enacted that if a party who had lost an action at the county court presented new evidence for a trial de novo, he was to obtain it at the "same Court, upon a bill of reveiwe." This was a procedure unknown to common law courts, in which a writ of error was used and the new trial was at a higher court. George Lee Haskins suggests that the Massachusetts procedure may have had chancery antecedents (*Law and Authority in Early Massachusetts*, p. 183), while Barnes contends that it undoubtedly came "from the practice of English-bill procedure as followed in chancery, Requests, and Wards" ["Law and Liberty (and Order) in Early Massachusetts," p. 73]. On the activities of the New York Mayor's Court, see Richard B. Morris, ed., *Select Cases of the Mayor's Court of New York City, 1674–1784*.

64. *Winthrop Letters*, 7:125. See also "Bill in Equity," Robbins v. Pinson [1689], EP 44:76, entered after the Dominion's overthrow and during the so-called Interregnum before the arrival of the second charter.

65. Nurse v. Endecott [1686], EP 46:31–36.

Court orders to deliver land or pay a specific sum are also suggestive of equitable remedies. In discussing this type of order as applied by the Suffolk court in this period, Zechariah Chafee, Jr., observed that the court might only have been following Coke's "theory that a promisor has the option of performing or paying damages." He added that this would be the case if the specified sum equaled the value of the land. On the other hand, as Chafee pointed out, such an order to pay money would be very much like a chancery "penalty for disobedience of the order to convey" if the amount ordered was greater than the value of the land and if it was clear that the amount did not simply constitute damages.[66] The latter situation seems to have occurred in Essex in *Elithorp* v. *Pickard*, where the court ordered that seventy-five pounds be paid if land was not laid out within a month. While there were parcels worth that much in Rowley, they were only the largest, choicest, and already cleared tracts. Elithorp, whose right derived from a one-and-a-half acre lot, was entitled by the town meeting vote of 1658 to only fifty acres, and county probate records indicate that "wilderness" land such as Elithorp was to receive was of relatively low value (forty acres were worth twelve pounds in 1670). Of course, he was also gaining a right to potential future divisions, but commonage shares were worth only twenty pounds and even a house with an acre of land and a commonage share was inventoried at twenty-four pounds. The sum of seventy-five pounds, therefore, was considerably in excess of the value of the rights and real property awarded, and it is clear from the wording of the court's order that the amount was not to be seen as accrued damages.[67]

But it was not usually necessary to employ equity procedures, and Essex litigants more often used a remedy that—although not equitable— was also not generally employed in English common law courts. This expedient procedure was the use of the action of "case" to obtain title to land. The widespread use of case has been remarked upon in several studies of Early American law, and different explanations have been offered. Julius Goebel identifies English county court practice as the reason for such usages by the Plymouth county courts,[68] while Zechariah Chafee, Jr., has examined the Suffolk county court records very closely to suggest that the practice was a product of the way that a summons was worded. Chafee explains that in Massachusetts the "same form of sum-

66. Chafee, "Suffolk County Court," pp. liv–lv. He adds, "There was no absolute rule in England that imprisonment was the only penalty for disregard of the orders of Chancery."

67. Elithorp v. Pickard, in behalf of Town of Rowley [1672], EP 18:68. Mighill and Blodgette, *Early Records of the Town of Rowley*, p. 101. For representative land and commonage values in Rowley at this time, see George F. Dow, ed., *The Probate Records of Essex County, Massachusetts*, 2:147–51, 224–25, 387–89.

68. Goebel, "King's Law and Local Custom," pp. 437–48.

mons was used in all civil suits (except replevin), regardless of the nature of the claim. There were no technical key words to indicate the form of the action automatically, and the writ merely set out the basic facts which must have been in many instances rather informally stated." According to Chafee, therefore, clerks simply "would describe the action as 'case' and let it go at that."[69]

These are quite plausible explanations, but another one—more related to the problems of possessing land in a wilderness—also seems possible. Although the action of trespass was a convenient form for contesting land, it had an important drawback. The disadvantage was the requirement of the plaintiff's actual possession of the land at some point in time so that he could declare that someone had, in actual fact, committed a wrong by entering illegally—to mow hay, for instance—or otherwise to disseise him. Simply detaining land that one entered legally when vacant was not actionable as trespass.[70] But it often occurred in Massachusetts that someone with the right of property never had occupied the land and later discovered another person in possession when he finally tried to occupy it. If he wished, he could commit a trespass in the hope that the occupant would sue; but even if he successfully defended the act of the alleged trespass, as a winning defendant all he could recover were costs of court and he could not obtain an order putting him in possession. In some specific cases, he could obtain such an order by suing in ejectment—if, for example, he had gained the right to the land as heir to someone who had died seised of it. In that situation, the heir had what was known as a "right of entry" because his ouster had been by "abatement." On the other hand, it more usually occurred that the person being kept out had bought the land or had been granted it by a town, in which case his ouster was by "deforcement," and he had no right of entry.[71] Unable to sue in trespass or ejectment, he would have to use one of the highly technical "real actions."

It is unlikely that legal officials in Massachusetts were unfamiliar with ejectment, the most commonly used form of title trial in England, and with the limitations that governed its usage. People in the colony clearly knew how to use the "lease and release" to convey land but preferred a simpler "indenture." So, too, it is likely that they avoided using ejectment and instead drew upon the residual action of case to develop a simple and effective means of trying title when technical complications might have required the use of the complex real actions. The product was a form they called "case, for trespass" or "case upon title to

69. Chafee, "Suffolk County Court," pp. xxxviii–xli.
70. Viner, *Abridgment*, Title, "Trespass."
71. William Blackstone, *Commentaries on the Laws of England. Book the Third,* chap. 10.

land." This was a sophisticated adaptation of the common law, offering the simple procedure of a trespass action as well as the feature of ejectment that put the plaintiff in possession of the land rather than merely awarding damages; in one case, the combination of the two forms was very apparent: the court awarded both possession and damages.[72]

Innovations of this sort were part of a transformation of the legal system that made the Essex county court an important and effective instrument of local governance. While town meetings possessed only a questionable ability to handle these issues, the county court successfully adapted and applied traditional English legal rules and institutions to deal with them. Litigation enabled individuals and communities to clarify rights and establish customs, and it demonstrated the advantages of a legalistically grounded social order. The court offered a body of rules, forms, and remedies that could be relied upon to impose order in Essex society.

These transformations in the New World, however, took place in the context of political turmoil in London. While that climate had allowed the changes to take place, the later efforts of the Stuarts to limit local autonomy and borough privileges would endanger them. English observers long had been critical of Massachusetts legal departures, and as early as 1642 Thomas Lechford (who styled himself "a student or practiser at law" as well as "solicitor") expressed his shock at the practices of the colonial legal system. During the Restoration period, criticisms of Massachusetts justice continued to reach London, and a letter to the Council for Foreign Plantations in 1660 complained of laws in Massachusetts "not mentioned" in the colony's written code but existing only "in the Magistrates breasts to be understood."[73] Whatever the accuracy or ani-

72. For trespass upon the case "for fencing" land that plaintiff bought but had never occupied, see Hussey v. Green [1663], NorMbk. 1648–78, p. 63; court awarded possession and damages. For possession and damages, see Colcord v. Drake [1674], NorMbk. 1672–81, p. 34. For possession and no damages, see Lever v. Scails [1682], EP 37:59–63. For "case upon title to land," see Johnson v. Herriman [1684], EP 42:101–6. For "case, for trespass," see Ingersoll v. Barney [1669], EP 14:28–34, 83–89. See also Mansfield v. Browne [1682], EP 38:100–14; Sanford v. Putnam [1674], SaMbk. 1667–79, June term #8, and EP 21:65–70.

73. Thomas Lechford, *Plain Dealing*, p. 66. Lechford, *Note-book*, pp. ix–x. Captain Thomas Breedon to Council for Foreign Plantations, 11 Mar. 1660, E. B. O'Callaghan, ed., *Documents Relative to the Colonial History of the State of New-York*, 3:39–40. It should be added that English perceptions of Massachusetts legal practice were not always accurate, and they sometimes misunderstood colonial law. Michael G. Hall points out how Randolph "misinterpreted" the colonial statute on the possession of land and reported his misperception back to London (*Edward Randolph and the American Colonies, 1676–1703*, pp. 26–27). For the text of Randolph's report, see *Edward Randolph, His Letters and Official Papers from New England, Middle, and Southern Colonies*, 2:312–15, 231–33.

mus of these attacks, Essex magistrates shared the perception that their system of justice had deviated from strict English legal standards. Applying their legal knowledge to a broad and bewildering range of problems, they had fashioned a reliable institution to cope with growth and change in the New World. It was a system that had become as necessary to preserve as it was vulnerable.

3   Outsiders and Subgroups

The Coordinative Function of the Court

The concept of membership in a particular community required redefinition in seventeenth-century Essex, for neither ownership of land nor residence by itself meant that someone shared a community's ways of thinking and acting. Many men owned property in a town but did not live there, and for that reason stood apart from the other landowners in the town. Others, though resident in the town, were set apart for other reasons. Although all people residing within specific geographic limits attended the same town meeting and referred to each other as "townsmen," beyond that classification existed a variety of economic interests, occupations, and cultural attitudes that differed from those of the general community. The appearance of these groups could not be prevented or ignored, for towns could not forbid land sales to outsiders forever nor could they continue to warn out every invalid or pauper who turned up among them. By the 1680s the process of warning out had evolved into a means of freeing towns of the obligation to maintain these groups without actually forcing them to leave town. The county courts, whose authority was required to remove someone who ignored the town's warning, typically reacted by recording a "caution" and noting that such people "may not by resyding become chargable to the Towne."[1] Even the banishment of criminal deviants or objectionable sectarians proved impractical except in the most extreme cases. After the colony banished several Quakers and executed four of them for returning between 1659 and 1661, the Court of Assistants banished only thirteen other persons under the Old Charter.[2]

1. Petition of Ipswich Selectmen [1681], IpMbk. 1666–82, Sept. term #45. Petition of Beverly Selectmen [1686], IpMbk. 1682–92, Mar. term.

2. Besides three antipedobaptists, persons banished included "a gemester at dice," a rapist, a French "Dancing master," two "Incorrigible Theeves," two black arsonists, a man who had plotted with Indians against the colony in wartime, a witch, and one man convicted of "revileing the Courts of Justice and the magistrates in base and unworthy terms" (*Assts. Rec.* 3:177, 201, 217, 255; 2:102, 158, 189, 197, 198). The county court could not, by law, banish, but in 1684 John Hathorne arranged to have two horse thieves "shipt to Barbadoes" as servants. As Hathorne commented on one of them, "And soe Selling himself was shipt of[f] for Barbados and I hope the Country well Rid of a horse thiefe." Another factor in their case was the "Extreame Cold" that winter, leading to fears that they would freeze to death in the ramshackle Salem gaol (EP 45:49).

Instead, some type of modus vivendi had to be established. Litigation did not create perfect harmony any more successfully than communalism, nor did it create the single-minded consensualism that had remained an unrealized ideal since 1630. Indeed, such an ideal was proving increasingly unrealistic as time passed. Especially as towns grew larger and commerce expanded, Essex was becoming less of a face-to-face society capable of sustaining any sort of communalism. Through litigation, however, a new sort of equilibrium emerged, one that was capable of coordinating or integrating the various outsiders, subgroups, and identifications present within the general community.[3]

The anomalous status of the absentee landowner caused problems in many Essex communities. The land distribution system of the colony did not provide for the absentee owner but was designed to apportion land only to those people who would put it to permanent use. Townships were granted to groups of persons with definitely avowed intentions of settling the land or to those who already had taken up residence on ungranted sites in the hinterland. If house and planting lots were given by towns to individuals who had not expressed such intentions, the land was offered as an inducement to settle on it. But these offers of ownership—usually made to a craftsman whose skills were needed by the town—were contingent upon residence there, and they were withdrawn if he did not come. Because the General Court and town meetings could not effectively control the disposition of land after they had granted it, however, their plans were frustrated. The law might specify that a town could overrule the sale of land to someone to whom it objected, but even if that law were enforced there was no law barring an outsider's acquisition of land by marriage or inheritance. Much of the available land in the county thus fell into the hands of nonresidents or was purchased by them speculatively. These holdings, which were often unoccupied, increased in value throughout the century, as prices in the Essex Land Book amply demonstrate. Those who owned—or claimed to own—land recognized that this strong demand made the sale of property a source of ready capital for further investment in many other enterprises, and a brisk trade developed in land.[4]

Absentee owners were thus more willing to sell property to the many

3. The notable exceptions were the nineteen "witches" executed in 1692. For an explanation of that failure, see chap. 7 of this volume. The functional integration of various social groups as a persistent theme in American history is well discussed by Rowland T. Berthoff in "The American Social Order."

4. The Essex County Land Records contain ample evidence of steady price increases. See, for example, the rising value of a tract in Lynn, 1:53–57. The value of improved land as "by far the most important constituent of capital" in the colonies is described by Stuart Bruchey, *The Roots of American Economic Growth, 1607–1861*, p. 23.

people in Essex who were seeking to increase or consolidate their holdings. Unfortunately, absentees were particularly susceptible to the general
problems of boundary and title uncertainty.[5] Purchasers, as a result,
often discovered that they had been dealing with men who were not
entirely scrupulous about assuring the validity of those boundaries and
titles. For reasons that will be discussed later, the selling of false claims
by local people to unsuspecting outsiders had not yet assumed the pro-
portions of the American tradition it later became—only one such complaint was made to the county court between 1672 and 1692.[6] More
typical was Samuel Bennit of Boston, a land speculator whose lack of
attention or scruples produced a considerable amount of litigation before
the Essex county court. The main source of confusion was a large tract of
land at Rumney Marsh on the border between Lynn and Boston. This
land had been of little value during the first decades of the town, but
Bennit later found a ready market among Lynn residents who saw the
spread of settlement moving southward from the older districts of Lynn.
Bennit, however, took a distressingly lax position regarding the reliability
of his sales. When told that he was selling land that was "surely beyond
the bounds" of an adjacent farm as well as the Lynn commons, he
answered that he could always offer "enough of boston Land to make it
up." The people of Lynn "were much displeased" with this attitude, for
they knew that Lynn commonage made up of "boston Land" was a
logical and legal absurdity. No one occupied the land until Thomas
Browne, a Lynn potter, fenced it in 1680; two years later the Lynn
commoners forced him, as a grantee of Bennit's, to defend his rights by
suing them in an action of "case, for cutting and carrying away wood."[7]

Bennit's attitude was not unique among Bostonians with land in
other counties. In several cases merchants from Boston sold land in Essex
and caused such problems. John Paine sold salt marsh on Plumb Island
to two local men who were more inclined to use it than he had been.
When others on the island later mowed that marsh, the vagueness of the
true ownership became obvious and resulted in a trespass action.[8] Bostonians were not the only nonresident owners of land in Essex County,
and people from far beyond the boundaries of the colony were in possession of land there. They included residents' sons who had gone to sea and

5. For example, Fellowes v. Marshall [1691], EP 52:61–63; Patch v. Hobbes [1692],
EP 52:3–5; Wade v. Wade [1683], EP 41:49–61; Putnam v. Gould [1674], IpMbk. 1666–
82, Sept. term #11; Town of Lynn v. Ottoway [1674], EP 22:34–38; Knight v. Leach
[1679], EP 31:25–29.

6. Tilton v. Palmer [1678], NorMbk. 1672–81, p. 80.

7. Browne v. Laighton [1681], EP 35:123–26, and 39:49, in review.

8. Dole v. Pengry [1692], EP 52:9–21. See also Rootes v. Kenney [1683], IpMbk.
1682–92, Sept. term #4. Taylor v. Rhodes [1691], EP 50:115.

relocated in another colony, such as the mariner William Chichester of "Lower Norfolk County, Virginia, only son and heir of William Chichester, late of Salem." Others, like Isaac Hull of "Topham, Dorset," were husbands of women who had received legacies of Essex land.[9]

Absentee landowners were particularly susceptible to many of the same problems that plagued resident owners, especially that of imprecise boundaries. Captain John Wade petitioned the Essex court in 1683 that an estate appraisal was "illegal and very oppressive to my selfe" because his brother had "presumed to put persons in another County" as appraisers although they had no idea of the true extent of the property belonging to his deceased father's estate. A Newbury man, owner of land in Salisbury, was unable to put his land to use because he had no firm notion of its exact boundaries. When told to mow his hay in order to pay rates due to the town, he confessed that he could take no hay there because "I know not how to have it done."[10] Landowners and town meetings thus had to establish in court the precise limits of landholdings. As Richard Russell of Gloucester wrote to the Manchester town meeting concerning his land in the latter town, efforts to determine his boundaries had resulted in "soe barren an accompt" that he proposed to "seeke the favour of the Court to supply yow with some other waye If your need require it." Russell was upset at the contrariness of the Manchester town meeting toward settling the matter, but he insisted that he was only trying to obtain his "just right." "I should have bin farr enough from makeing the least clayme with Tendency to your rong," he wrote to the town, "whose welfare is more joyous to mee then your Impoverishing." A final resolution of the dispute through town institutions—of Gloucester as well as Manchester—was beyond reach; a survey was attempted, but the surveyor, told by observers that his line was wrong, at last concluded that "if twenty men ran it, they would differ." Russell finally sold the land to Robert Knight of Marblehead, who sued a town resident over the line. Although Knight lost his case, he at least obtained an accurate boundary.[11]

More than casual uncertainty was caused by the absentees, however, because land was more than simply an economic commodity to many members of premodern communities. Nonresident ownership of land depersonalized it and destroyed the ancient equation of land tenure with membership in the community. At a time when social, economic, agricul-

9. Chichester v. Dutch [1690], EP 49:54. Hull v. Fairfield [1680], EP 34:34–38. Edwards v. Maverick [1681], EP 35:53–61.

10. Petition of John Wade [1683], EP 41:49–61. Fellowes v. Marshall [1692], EP 52:61–63.

11. Knight v. Leach [1679], EP 31:25–29. Knight v. Leach [1680], EP 33:125–40.

tural, and demographic changes required closer and more precise management of land, absentee owners were unable to participate in collective efforts of regulation. Physically removed from the town, they were unfamiliar with the community's unwritten customs and relationships. Occasionally, therefore, they were less reluctant to pursue material gain at the expense of local harmony. If not so cynical, they were more likely to blunder into socially disruptive actions whose consequences they had not anticipated.[12]

Overturning town custom was generally considered bad neighborliness. It was "unneighborly," complained the commoners of Ipswich, for an absentee to insist that the town strictly enforce commonage bylaws that traditionally had been ignored for "the Owners Convenience." An absentee might have clear legal rights, but townsmen became irritated, as one litigant from Lynn told the court when sued for trespass by an outsider in 1680, because the absentee "canot be contented to run loose in his own pasture but he must break over fences."[13]

It was this breaking of a community's social and property "fences" that led many people in Essex towns to resent absentee landowners. These nonresidents, having little or no acquaintance with town standards, were thus often embroiled in boundary disputes and conflicts over the maintenance of obligations toward property.[14] Joseph Browne of Lynn had to sue his landlord, John Keazer of Haverhill, for "not making the living at Lin tenantable with barns and fences."[15] Fences, which were essential to neighborliness, meant less to the nonresident Keazer, but they were of great importance to Browne in his daily relations with others in the community.

As on English manors, the requirements of an orderly agrarian existence demanded that local customs and standards of neighborliness be observed. In uniting against outsiders who upset these conventions, Essex towns were demonstrating the persistence of local control over farming practices, but at the same time they were revealing the inadequacy of town institutions to enforce them. Absentee landlords were beyond informal community pressures such as ostracism, hostility, or noncooperation. They were also protected, in many cases, from the formal sanctions of the town: if one simply owned and rented out land but did not pasture

12. Rogers v. Graves [1690], EP 51:46–49. See also Ayres v. Pengilla [1678], EP 29:65–67.
13. Rogers v. Graves, pp. 48–49. Witter v. Richards [1680], EP 34:2–3. See also Holyoke v. Farrar [1672], EP 19:34.
14. Taylor v. Rhodes [1691], EP 51:40–46.
15. Browne v. Keazer [1684], EP 42:73. Rhodes v. Appleton [1686], EP 44:49–59. Nelson v. Woolcott [1676], IpMbk. 1666–82, Mar. term #16. Nelson v. Savery [1676], ibid., #15.

his own livestock there, the town would have difficulty distraining his chattel property in satisfaction of its amercements. Towns were limited to distraining chattel property, but a writ of *capias* from the county court could attach his real property—or his own body—to compel his appearance at court to confront those whose customary rights he was violating. Thomas Fuller of Rowley, for example, defied Andover town officers when they refused to give him permission to cut cedars on Andover common land. Fuller cut them anyhow, and the town had no recourse but to sue him for trespass.[16]

Bringing together residents and nonresidents, groups whose interests often set them apart, the county court contributed to a new ideal of local harmony that could not be obtained through local pressures or weak town institutions. The court's decisions were thus coordinative in the sense that they helped establish and enforce a "totality of norms" to regulate the relationships of private individuals.[17] This function was seen in Lynn, where Henry Rhodes, a local farmer, disagreed with his absentee neighbor James Taylor about a boundary. Rhodes could gain no settlement of the problem because Taylor was never present to negotiate; his farm was being managed by another man. Rhodes, preferring to deal directly with the owner, therefore arranged a trespass in order to force Taylor to meet with him. Rhodes and his son simply removed their section of the fence and led eight or nine horses onto Taylor's farm. Another neighbor watched this and asked the son what was going on. Young Rhodes explained that "he had taken up the gate by his fathers order and said itt should Lie open all the next Sumer Except [i.e., unless] Mr Taylor would Come and agree with him." This method of conflict resolution was not inexpensive—the court awarded Taylor five pounds in damages, plus costs—but it had been effective when other attempts had been useless.[18]

Not all "outsiders" were nonresidents, however. Problems with absentee landowners were the problems of a society that still retained many characteristics of its traditional English agrarian origins, but other adjustments had to be made to accommodate town residents whose backgrounds were neither English nor agrarian. Such were the economic attractions of New England that migrants came to Essex County from many parts of the British Isles and even from the tiny Channel Isle of Jersey.

The integration of groups from different regions of England was not

16. Selectmen of Andover v. Fuller [1677], EP 26:147.
17. Max Weber, *Economy and Society*, 2:642.
18. Taylor v. Rhodes [1691], EP 51:40–46.

accomplished without difficulty in the first decades of the county's settlement. Frictions between East Anglians and Westcountrymen at Salem,
for example, had led to the splitting off of Beverly. Besides their differing
ideas about land usage (either open- or closed-field agriculture) an early
clash had occurred between these groups when East Anglians misinterpreted a bit of Westcountry doggerel as an insult directed at them. The
Scots and the Irish occasionally clashed with the English population, but
they migrated there in such small numbers that their adjustment was
relatively easy. The Scots were English-speaking Lowlanders, but the
Irish, who were Roman Catholic and for the most part had come to
Essex as captives of Cromwell sent over as indentured servants, spoke
Gaelic. The county court, therefore, had to order in 1643 that Teague
O'Mahoney be taught English.[19]

Relations with emigrants from the Channel Isle of Jersey, however,
became a persistent problem in Salem.[20] Jerseymen, while nominally
subjects of the English crown, were separated from Englishmen by great
cultural differences. Geographically much closer to France than to England, they were also culturally closer. Indeed, by language, laws, and
customs, the island was a medieval French anachronism in the seventeenth century.[21] Philip English was probably among the first Jerseymen
to take up residence in Essex County when he arrived around 1670.[22] He
quickly contributed to the increase of the French-speaking community by
bringing over large numbers of Jerseymen as servants. Young women
were indentured to serve for seven years in Essex households, while
young men were usually engaged to work four years at sea. The Salem
Jerseymen—approximately two dozen families by 1685—were numerous enough to maintain a community of their own. Unlike the few Scots,

19. Presentment of William Snelling [1652], EP 2:17. Order with regard to Teague
O'Mahoney [1643], EMbk. 1638–48, p. 146.

20. The Jerseymen have escaped historical notice and have been confused with the
larger number of Huguenots who came to Massachusetts after the revocation of the Edict
of Nantes. Partly, this error has been due to contemporary references to the Jerseymen as
"French," after their language. For a fuller discussion of that island's history and the role of
its emigrants in Massachusetts, see David T. Konig, "A New Look at the Essex 'French.'"

21. See, generally, A. C. Saunders, *Jersey before and after the Norman Conquest of
England*, passim.

22. The identification of Essex residents as Jerseymen is a difficult investigative task,
for many quickly anglicized their names: Zachiah LeBlanc arrived in Salem in 1678 and
became Zachariah White, for instance. Sidney Perley, *The History of Salem, Massachusetts*,
3:135–36. Others emigrated by way of England, and their arrival aboard a ship from an
English port led genealogists to the conclusion that they were English. See, for example,
James Savage, *A Genealogical Dictionary of the First Settlers of New England*, 2:545, in
which Nicholas Jennings is identified as "probably a Suffolk man," when in fact he was a
Jerseyman. Philip English came to Salem as Philippe L'Anglois. Bernard Bailyn, *The New
England Merchants in the Seventeenth Century*, p. 144.

Irish, or Dutch in the county, the Jerseymen did not assimilate into the larger community around them for at least a generation, and despite their relatively small numbers they were a distinct group that did not escape the notice of the English population.[23] Although they generally arrived as servants and thus were unable to live together as they pleased, in Salem they were able to obtain homes or land near each other after leaving servitude. Philip English, who owned large tracts of land on the south side of Salem Neck, became the center of a community that included the Searles, Mazurys (formerly LeMessurier), Feveryears, Beadles, and Brownes (formerly LeBrun).[24]

Because they remained a thriving and separate community, Jerseymen were still not completely integrated at the end of the seventeenth century. Although the islanders had been forced to give up their Anglicanism by the Huguenots and a Puritan conquest, they did not accept the New England Way entirely.[25] Philip English took the trouble of rowing to Marblehead to attend Church of England services and toward the end of his life even refused to pay rates for the support of the Salem Congregational church. In Ipswich the Jerseyman Thomas Baker slept through William Hubbard's efforts at "exsortation"; when threatened with censure, Baker's reply was a laugh and he had to be admonished by the secular authority of the county court.[26]

The authority of the legal system was thus brought to bear upon the Jerseymen to impose conformity, and the English were not reluctant to resort to official action against these outsiders when disagreements arose. John Waldron, the constable of Marblehead, once tried—and failed—to make the Jerseyman John Brock stand more than his obligatory share of the town watch. Some time after that attempt, the constable found Brock at a public house with "three strange men" and ordered them all to leave. According to witnesses (including two watchmen) this order was "more than they could or should doe," and Brock justifiably ignored it. Heated words followed, and Waldron used his authority as constable to bring Brock to court. The judges, however, saw the ethnic motivation for the arrest; the court wisely admonished both sides—and the innkeeper—for allowing the disagreement to get out of control.[27]

23. Perley, *Salem*, 3:97. Ralph Bartram Harris, "Philip English." An arrest warrant in 1675 was drawn up simply as a "spechal warrant . . . to haprend two french men," with no names affixed (EP 24:89).

24. James Duncan Phillips, *Salem in the Seventeenth Century*, endpiece map.

25. A. C. Saunders, *Jersey in the Fifteenth and Sixteenth Centuries*, p. 141. Philip Falle, *An Account of the Isle of Jersey*, pp. 36–40.

26. Henry W. Belknap, "Philip English, Commerce Builder," p. 23. Presentment of Thomas Baker [1678], EP 28:52.

27. Complaint against John Brock et al. [1672], EP 19:26–30.

The levying of rates on Jerseymen was a particularly difficult and contentious issue. Many considered themselves to be only transient residents of Essex towns, spending much of their time at sea fishing or trading with their compatriots on Jersey. In Salem, this problem led to violence and lawsuits. Edward February (or Feveryear) and Nathaniel Beadle were both brought to court for "abuse of authority" when they objected to the manner and amount of the constables' tax demands.[28] Philip English was a defendant in a major lawsuit by the town of Salem in 1684 when as constable he refused to be held responsible for rates assessed on men—probably Jerseymen—who were not living there any more.[29]

With a litigious tradition from the mercantile life of the Channel Isle, the Jerseymen found the courtroom a familiar forum for defending their interests against the general Essex community.[30] These encounters were not uncommon, because there existed a stereotype in the county that the French-speaking Essexmen plotted with one another to deal dishonestly with the rest of the population. For example, one objection that Andrew Tucker made against arbitration and a reckoning of accounts with Abraham Ketville was that the latter would pick a fellow "Jarsey man." Constable John Waldron suspected that John Brock was cheating in his job of weighing fish that local Jersey fishermen were selling in Marblehead, and in a drunken rage he assailed Brock as a "knave, cheater, and French dog."[31]

It was in matters of suspected theft that the English image of Jerseymen as surreptitious and threatening found its fullest expression. This image was given impetus in 1673 when Peter Leycros (or LeCras) was arrested for theft in Ipswich. Two English colonists were also arrested and convicted, but it was obvious that Leycros was the most active, and his position as a servant in the household of his victim, the eminent

28. Complaint against Edward Feveryear [1674], EP 22:23, and SaMbk. 1667–79, July term #92. Complaint against Nathaniel Beadle [1679], EP 32:35. Evidence in these cases suggests that the constables may have recognized the difficulty of collecting rates from other Jerseymen and that they used excessive force in demanding payment from the two defendants.

29. No proof survives that the men in English's case were Jerseymen, but inasmuch as Philip was constable for a precinct that included many of these people, it is quite likely that a few of them were. Selectmen of Salem v. English [1684], EP 43:8–23. The two nonresidents named specifically as being absent for two years were William Ingland and Philip Muddle (or Mudell), for whom no genealogical information exists, but whose names may very well be of French or Jersey derivation.

30. Philip English sued so often and with so little provocation that he developed a reputation for rapacity. On the peculiar way that he and other Jerseymen used the courts in Jersey and Essex, as well as a discussion of the peculiarities of Norman-French legal tradition on the island, see Konig, "Essex 'French,' " pp. 173–74.

31. Ketville v. Tucker [1681], EP 36:84–85. Complaint against Brock, p. 92.

William Hubbard, made the Jerseyman seem all the more spectacular a reprobate and his crime all the more insidious.[32]

At least after Leycros's discovery, the identification of Jerseymen and larceny was an easy one for the English residents of certain towns in the county. When Zacheous Perkins was arrested for thefts in Salem and Topsfield, he confessed to the crimes and his only defense was that he had been persuaded and instructed by "a Frenchman named Nicholas Jennings."[33] In 1683 John Best spread a rumor around Salem that the Jerseyman Nathaniel Beadle had received fifty pounds that "Black Dick, Mr Browns negro, had stolen from his master." As it turned out, Beadle was entirely innocent, and Best was actually the man who had encouraged the slave to steal from Browne. Attempting to hide his actions, Best had found it a convenient and credible excuse to direct suspicion toward a Jerseyman.[34]

The conspicuous wealth of Jerseymen like Philip English also served to create distrust. In fact, his great wealth led to rumors—indicative of the prevailing popular attitudes—that he was a cynical and conniving suitor who had married the daughter of trader William Hollingworth and had become a merchant prince, through inheritance, at Hollingworth's death in 1677. It is true that his wife inherited a fortune, but it was not simply a windfall that enabled a disinherited miscreant to become a wealthy merchant overnight.[35] Rather, English's rapid accumulation of wealth was part of a phenomenon that second-generation colonial Americans were beginning to resent deeply in the years after 1660. As a Restoration emigrant to the colonies, English was one of a group of men who brought with them money as well as broad mercantile contacts in the Atlantic trading community.[36] What distinguished English from all those other newcomers and added to the resentment against him was the fact that his contacts were with the Isle of Jersey, which possessed a charter dating from Richard II exempting it "from all manner of Taxes, Imposts, and Customs, in all Cities, Market-Towns, and Ports of England." Another charter (from Edward IV) extended that right "to all Places within the King's Dominions beyond the Seas."[37] These special

32. Complaints against Peter Leycros [1673], IpMbk. 1666–82, Mar. term #56–#60, #63.

33. Presentment of Zacheous Perkins [1680], EP 32:144–50.

34. Beadle v. Best [1683], EP 40:49. See also the comment by Richard Young in Ketville v. Tucker, concerning Ketville's character, or the suspicions directed at George Major in Complaint against George Major [1677], EP 26:54–55.

35. The myths about Philip English's background are effectively refuted by Belknap, "Philip English," pp. 19–20.

36. For a deeper discussion of this process, see Bailyn, Merchants, pp. 112–42; and that same author's "Politics and Social Structure in Virginia," pp. 90–115.

37. Falle, Account of Jersey, p. 206.

privileges, plus English's undoubted skills, enabled him to become one of the richest men in the colony. Possessing vast property, privileges denied to others, and a certain "arrogance of manner," he was the preeminent symbol of the Jersey community that his English neighbors regarded suspiciously and enviously.[38]

In spite of these feelings, the Jerseymen were integrated into the larger Salem community. Within a generation, in fact, they were able to assimilate to the point that their ancestry has been difficult to discover. Among their first generation, however—when language, religious practice, and custom set them apart—the court made an essential contribution to the assimilation process. Its authority prevented Salem town officials from abusing their powers at the expense of the Jerseymen, just as it prevented baseless accusations of larceny from defaming them. Taken together, these judicial acts restrained the force of prejudice, protected a minority, and served an important coordinative function in a Puritan society notoriously distrustful of outsiders.

The economic development of New England that had raised land prices and drawn people from all parts of the British Isles also produced in Essex County a vigorous mercantile community that had to develop its own standards and rules, especially in its dealings with the general agrarian community around it. An ambivalence toward business and competitive capitalism lay at the root of Puritanism, and the need to establish standards of behavior was a logical result of the uncertain position of the merchant in a Puritan society. This need had existed from the earliest days of the colony—as someone like Robert Keayne could attest—but it coincided with the needs of the merchants themselves, especially in the last third of the century.[39] As Essex merchants extended their operations throughout the Atlantic world, they found themselves engaged in an elaborate trading "mechanism" that required an increasing degree of order, rationality, and certainty—qualities absent or rare in the haphazard efforts of the first generation of New England merchants. The fishing trade, no longer the "desultory" and "uncertain" business of 1635, employed two thousand fishermen in New England in 1670 and dealt with markets from Jamaica to Calais. To supply this vast demand

38. English's trade with Jersey is amply demonstrated in his business account books at the Essex Institute in Salem. Ralph Bartram Harris, "Philip English," p. 278. Belknap, "Philip English," p. 21. Another such merchant was Philip Nowell (or Noel), who was lost at sea en route to France in 1675. George F. Dow, ed., *The Probate Records of Essex County, Massachusetts*, 3:39–41.

39. On the Puritan ambivalence toward business, see Michael Walzer, "Puritanism as a Revolutionary Ideology"; and Bailyn, *Merchants*, chaps. 1–2. See also Robert Keayne, *The Apologia of Robert Keayne*.

and to reap the highest profits from it required organization. Fishing was no longer only an offshore operation. After 1670 efforts were shifted to long-range northern voyages lasting many months; for enterprises of this scale sufficient labor and capital had to be organized.[40]

Neither was readily obtained, but rationalizing the labor supply remained a particularly annoying problem among Essex enterprises. A fishing voyage needed at least four men before a boat could leave port—a master, two fishermen, and a shoreman to dry and pack the catch. These jobs demanded a certain amount of skill and a willingness to risk one's life at sea, and if any of these men failed to appear when the boat was ready to sail, costly delays occurred while the owner of the vessel tried to locate a replacement before the season had passed. So prevalent was the difficulty of finding replacements promptly that in 1679 the General Court ordered that fishermen "shall not presume to break off their Voyage" without consent and directed that violators be liable to damages recoverable by litigation.[41] Job Tookey, as an example, violated this law when he agreed to ship with Richard Knott on a venture to the Maine coast but later withdrew. Knott was enraged, and he hurled a stream of oaths at Tookey, calling him "Rogue and Severall other Names" before ordering his body attached by a *capias* to satisfy nine pounds in damages.[42]

Reliability became a primary concern of those in the fishing trade. Fish had to be properly dried, packed, and readied for shipment to Salem, Ipswich, or Marblehead, where it was transshipped to faraway customers.[43] Conditions in a fishing camp were disorderly, however. As hard as they tried, employers found it difficult to get their fishermen to work regularly. The arrival of a trading ship (known as a "walking tavern" for what it brought) could instigate a drunken revel, and all work would stop for days—"nay, sometimes a whole week," remarked a contemporary witness. Observers explained this behavior by noting that these men

40. For a fuller description of this mercantile group, see Bailyn, *Merchants*, esp. pp. 76–91; and Raymond McFarland, *A History of the New England Fisheries*, pp. 57, 69–72. A trader could earn 50 percent on shipments to the West Indies and up to 100 percent if he stopped in England and brought merchandise back to the colony.

41. *Col. Laws 1672–86*, p. 266.

42. Knott v. Tookey [1682], EP 37:149–51. See also Hunniwell v. Cannon [1678], EP 30:66; Tucker v. Keene [1690], EP 49:139–42. Discipline might also be a problem on voyages far from the law for long periods of time. Unable to exert force while at sea, masters of these small vessels sometimes had to wait until returning to port in order to discipline a crewman before the county courts. Complaints against Richard Bale and Robert Bray [1683], EP 40:90. Bartlett v. James [1684], IpMbk. 1682–92, Sept. term #6.

43. These requirements are explicitly referred to in a letter from the Boston merchant Sampson Sheafe to his son-in-law and partner Jonathan Corwin of Salem, 20 June 1680, Curwen Papers, box 4.

"never had any government among them; most of them are such as have fled from other places to avoid justice."[44]

With a labor source of this sort, a merchant fisherman easily might have to wait several weeks for a load to be completed. Samuel Pearce, for example, hired Stephen Hasscott as a shoreman to load fish, but on his arrival Pearce found nothing ready. He received the fish two weeks later, but in the meantime he had incurred heavy demurrage costs for which he had to sue once back in Ipswich.[45] Usually a merchant had to sue for breach of covenant or in trespass upon the case because no delivery at all had been made. Such was the situation for Francis Johnson, who returned to Monhegan Island only to find his shoreman Richard Bedford so drunk that he had failed to dry and salt the fish left with him. Lying untreated in the sun, the fish had rotted, and Johnson had to sue Bedford for damages.[46] Lawsuits were a vital method of obtaining monetary compensation and enforcing, through threat, work schedules and supply responsibilities. It was a function supplied nowhere except in the courts.

Economic conditions and necessities in the timber trade resembled those in the fishing trade to a large extent, although control and rationalization of the logging industry were somewhat easier. Because the felling and sawing of timber were all done on land, larger and more stable communities arose around this industry than the makeshift camps that supported the fishing expeditions. It was possible, therefore, for a timber merchant to construct his own mills and retain a permanent resident manager to oversee all operations.

The Corwins (or Curwens) of Salem—Captain George and his son Jonathan—were major Essex timber dealers, and their sawmill at Wells, Maine, was a typical operation.[47] Like so many seventeenth-century New England business enterprises, this mill was managed by a relative, Eleazer Hathorne. It was Hathorne's duty to organize the numerous loggers of the area into a group whose purchases from a company store could be followed and balanced in a "Generall Account" with the value of the timber they supplied. He was responsible, too, for making sure that a full load of timber was always ready for the ships that the Corwins sent to Wells. To assure full loading, agreements had to be enforced between the owners and the loggers who contracted to furnish a steady stream of logs "so that the said mill shall not stand still." As Jonathan Corwin (who

44. John Josselyn, *An Account of Two Voyages to New England*, cited in Lorenzo Sabine, *Report on the Principal Fisheries of the American Seas*, pp. 107–8.

45. Pearce v. Hasscott [1679], EP 31:141–43.

46. Johnson v. Bedford [1672], EP 18:52. See also Wade v. Moore [1672], IpMbk. 1666–82, Mar. term #26, #27; Cromwell v. Rainsbury [1673], EP 20:2–3, 137; English v. Mazury [1677], EP 27:55–56.

47. The Corwins were also partners in a sawmill at York. Agreement between Charles Martin and Jonathan Corwin, 7 July 1679, Curwen Papers, box 4.

was in charge of the business) insisted from Salem, every ship must be fully loaded "that I may not have dead fraight to pay." Dead freight, however, was not his only worry: Corwin was also involved in the fishing trade and needed prompt delivery of barrel staves in order to pack and ship that valuable commodity.[48]

The Corwin enterprise at Wells was thus a model of the newer business methods being developed to rationalize a growing industry. Nevertheless, problems arose that required court action to protect its interests and commitments. Almost immediately—as an absentee landowner—Corwin was forced to sue at court to vindicate his rights to the franchise and land at Wells. Fortunately, the written records of the town supported him in his suit at the York county court, and he was able to certify the precise extent of his holdings against challenge by a resident of the town.[49]

Further difficulties were precipitated by the death of Eleazer Hathorne in 1680. Corwin promptly contacted a man in Wells, Joseph Storer, to take over. Because the enterprise had been such a closed family affair, however, Storer had not been able to gain any "insight into the way and manner" of the business. "Your things have been keept Dark from me," complained the new manager, who was beginning to run into problems. The Sayward family of Wells renewed its claim to possession of the mill and seized it. To make matters worse, the loggers were not fulfilling their obligations and Storer was at a loss to enforce them. Sending a ship back deadfreighted, he apologized to Corwin for what was "a great trouble to me" as well as "to your damage." He concluded his letter with the desperate request that Corwin come to Wells "as soon as you can."[50]

Appearing there quickly, Corwin demonstrated seventeenth-century business practices at their best. His presence helped to restore the logging operations to normal; just as important, he went to court at York for assistance in putting his affairs back in order. There, he and the widow Mary Sayward "mutually agreed" to settle the first phase of their dispute. Mary still refused to surrender a claim to the mill, but Corwin was able to regain its possession and to settle the matter finally at the York court three years later.[51] Corwin had been quick to employ the courts, but only

48. Articles of Agreement between Jonathan Corwin and Henry Browne, 16 July 1680, ibid. John Corwin to Joseph Storer, 3 Feb. 1679, ibid., box 3. Hathorne kept the Corwins' "Wells Ledger Book" for the town; this book, with accounts for the year 1679, can be found at ibid., box 2.

49. Grant by the Town of Wells to Henry Sayward and James Johnson [1669], ibid. Request of Eleazer Hathorne to Town of Wells [1679], ibid.

50. Jonathan Corwin to Joseph Storer, 3 Feb. 1680, ibid., box 3. Joseph Storer to Jonathan Corwin, 9 Feb. 1680, ibid.

51. Charles Thornton Libby, ed., *Province and Court Records of Maine*, 2:353, 518. Corwin v. Sayward [1682], ibid., 3:84, 105.

out of necessity. Like other suppliers of raw materials, he knew that litigation was a standard business procedure in a system of production and
distribution that was rapidly expanding but still fragile and uncertain.[52]

Essex merchants engaged in more general trading enterprises were
also aware of these difficulties. The trade of New England involved men
from all over the Atlantic trading world—many of them newcomers or
part-time venturers—who possessed varying ideas about mercantile obligations and relationships. Compounding their problems were the novel-
ties and unanticipated situations of seventeenth-century trade.[53] For
example, the developing Atlantic commercial system had few firmly established trade routes, and the vagaries of supply and demand frequently
dictated changes of course. Seaman James Cox signed on as a foremast-
man with Nathaniel Veren between Salem and Virginia, but in the course
of trade Veren found it necessary to alter his ship's itinerary. Cox felt
entitled to higher wages as a result; when his request was refused by
Veren, he had to sue for what he reasonably deserved.[54] Unforeseen
developments might also require a master or agent to conclude business
transactions that a merchant back in Essex County had not authorized,
creating differences of opinion over the bailment of property and the
implied contract between the master and the merchant. Until trade routes
and relations could become more stable, the uncertainties of Atlantic
trading made court resolution of conflicts necessary. If a merchant persistently refused to reimburse a master for unexpected expenses, the courts
stood as a handy ally that could, if necessary, jail the recalcitrant partner
until satisfaction was obtained. As master Stephen Cross of the *Adventure* asserted in 1681, he was taking Joseph Emerson to court to "sue
him and plague him" for not coming to terms.[55]

Reckoning mercantile accounts was a difficult affair in a society as
chronically short of currency as Massachusetts, and the county courts
performed the valuable service of untangling the confused obligations of
a barter economy. When fisherman Peter Murrell was unable to present
in cash the £3.17s.5d. he owed to Lieutenant John Higginson, the court
had to levy execution on a sufficient amount of fish to discharge the
obligation. The town constable was able to determine the quantity by
consulting the fishermen of the town, but it was not always that easy.[56]

52. Bailyn, *Merchants*, p. 87. Bernard Bailyn and Lotte Bailyn, *Massachusetts Shipping, 1697–1714*, pp. 16, 35, 57.
53. For a discussion of the uncertainties affecting Massachusetts trade on the Atlantic,
see Bailyn and Bailyn, *Massachusetts Shipping*, pp. 69–71.
54. Cox v. Veren [1684], EP 43:37–38.
55. Cross v. Emerson [1681], EP 36:36. See also Ashby v. Clarke [1679], EP 31:
114–15.
56. Higginson v. Murrell [1681, execution], EP 36:149.

For all the veal and mutton that Nicholas Bartlett had bought from John Cromwell between 1676 and 1681, how many porringers, "basons," kettles, trenchers, andirons, and chamber pots was Constable Richard Prythrich to attach?[57] Extensive and detailed accounts were brought before the county's judges for collection, and some determination had to be made when agreement between creditor and debtor was hard to reach.

Even when bonds of indebtedness were given, the court sometimes had to make difficult reckonings, because a bond (a sealed instrument setting forth a specific sum) could be sued on for only its face value—no more and no less. To account for potential damages and interest, therefore, creditors usually obtained a bond stating a sum considerably in excess of the original obligation—for £60, say, on an obligation for £33.8s. payable in cash and wheat, or for £2,000 on an obligation for £200 and one-fourth share in an iron mill. Once judgment was given against the debtor, it fell to the court to chancer, or use its equity power to reduce, the award to its actual amount.[58]

Satisfaction of obligations was sometimes difficult for merchants dealing in a retail capacity, too. The economic leverage of merchants in their own local communities, however, was such that only infrequently were they forced to use the court system to recover money owed them in the towns where they lived. On the contrary, the major retail merchants in Essex County—George and Jonathan Corwin of Salem, and John and Francis Wainwright of Ipswich—were able to exert their economic influence to obtain satisfaction from fellow townsmen without recourse to litigation. While communal pressure in general may have been weakening, the economic pressure they could exert was still formidable; they were major sources of credit in their towns and their displeasure was not provoked lightly.[59]

As a result, Essex merchants sued fellow townsmen proportionally much less often than persons living in other towns; fellow townsmen sued by the Corwins and the Wainwrights between 1672 and 1692 for the recovery of money due for goods sold and delivered or for monies lent, for instance, were only nineteen (25 percent) of the seventy-eight debtors whose residences can be verified (thirteen cannot be located). Francis Wainwright's litigation reveals this very clearly; he sued only six

57. Cromwell v. Bartlett [1681], EP 37:23. Plaintiff's writ was "debt . . . due by book."

58. Godfrey v. Corles [1672], EP 18:114 (£60 bond chancered to £45 on debt of £33.8s.). Walters v. Gifford [1680], EP 32:82–93 (£2,000 bond chancered to £500 on debt of £200 and one-fourth share of iron mill).

59. For a study of the informal powers wielded by one seventeenth-century Massachusetts merchant, John Pynchon of Springfield, see Stephen Innes, "Land Tenancy and Social Order in Springfield, Massachusetts, 1652–1702," esp. p. 36.

Ipswich residents during that period but twenty-four outsiders. Customers named as defendants in his lawsuits included men from Chebacco parish (part of Ipswich technically, but by this time a separate community), Bradford, Haverhill, Exeter, Marblehead, Amesbury, Newbury, Salisbury, Boston, Lynn, Great Isle, and the Isles of Shoals.[60] Jonathan Corwin's correspondence also indicates the efforts needed to obtain satisfaction from out-of-town customers. Reminding one of them that he was behind in his accounts, Corwin explained that he was sending a short "Memento" of what was owed, adding that "otherwise I must seek my redress in a Court of Law." Such redress was necessary, he realized, because distances caused men to forget or delay payment of their obligations. As he reminded one of them in 1677, "Out of Sight, out of mind."[61]

Persons like Corwin and Wainwright had another reason to use the court, however, for they found it necessary to deal with a traditional source of friction in the Puritan community—the popular suspicion directed at business practices. It was not unusual for charges of "oppression" in trade to be directed at the artisans and merchants of Essex who were thought to be exceeding a "just price" for their goods.[62] Similarly, in an economy that relied heavily on credit, Essex residents sometimes suspected that their local merchants were altering accounts or not recording payments made. One man in Ipswich, for example, believed that John Wainwright of that town had charged him three times for a single peck of salt and thus had "salted his conscience." Thomas Knowlton was accused of adding a fake five-shilling charge to the accounts of Abraham Fairfield, while Walter Fairfield or John Lee was said to have inserted the word *and* to increase the obligation due him from John Gifford.[63]

In situations such as these, the county court stood as the most effective authority to settle grievances or to enforce standards of workmanship in Essex, because merchants' associations and crafts guilds had not been transplanted there. In 1648 the General Court chartered, for three

60. See Wainwright v. Griffing [1673], EP 19:94; Wainwright v. Ayres [1673], IpMbk. 1666–82, Mar. term #18; Wainwright v. Lattamore [1676], SaMbk. 1667–79, Nov. term #13; Wainwright v. Gross [1677], IpMbk. 1666–82, Sept. term #12; Wainwright v. Knowlton [1677], ibid., #77; Wainwright v. Needham [1685], IpMbk. 1682–92, Mar. term #18; Wainwright v. Hendrick [1689], EP 48:26–27; Wainwright v. Allin [1690], EP 48:100.

61. Corwin to Thomas Sously, 30 Aug. 1677, Curwen Papers, box 3. Corwin to Robert Wooley, 30 Aug. 1677, ibid. See also Richard Waldron to Corwin, 12 Feb. 1682, ibid.; and George Jaffray to Corwin, 18 May 1683, ibid.

62. Complaint against Dennis [1675], IpMbk. 1666–82, Apr. term #73. Complaint against Scammon [1676], NorMbk. 1648–78, p. 57.

63. Hasseltine v. Knowlton [1672], EP 18:65. Fairfield v. Gifford [1678], EP 28:3–7. See also Ireland v. Dolbear [1691], EP 50:35; Banton v. Fowler [1690], EP 48:101–3; Wainwright v. Swan [1690], EP 48:136–42.

years, a guild for coopers in Boston and Charlestown and one for shoe-makers in Boston, but no counterparts ever existed in Essex.[64] With no institutions of self-regulation available, business practices as a result had to be dealt with by the external authority of the legal system to a greater degree than in England. Statutory standards had to be enforced—not only for the benefit of the general public, but for aggrieved customers in the business community, too. Accordingly, suppliers were sued for pack-ing underweight barrels of fish or for producing inferior bricks, unusable coke, and nonmerchantable lumber products.[65] The court's competence was a broad and effective one, for it was not limited to the assessment of fines. Once a merchant or artisan was convicted of doing business unethi-cally—"either through falsehood or extreme neglicenc"—he was liable for damages. The miller Freegrace Norton was fined forty shillings for giving short measure in 1674 and was further punished when the magis-trates left "persons injured to take there remedy by law."[66]

Not only was litigation a weapon to protect consumers from dis-honesty, but it also protected the merchants. In a Puritan community, charges of "oppression" or exceeding a "just price" were serious matters that could harm a merchant whether he was guilty or not.[67] So fearful were Essex merchants of rumors about their integrity that they were quick to sue for defamation in order to vindicate their reputations to all who might think of dealing with them. The Derby family of Salem told the court how another shopkeeper, Thomas Maule, had persuaded "many not well acquainted with us" not to trade with them and had damaged their business. Roger Derby, like other merchants in the county, recognized that Maule's "Riseing such scandols . . . might have proved [Derby's] Ruin." Numerous merchants came before the court with com-plaints that their businesses were being damaged by such tales. The ru-mors were sometimes spread quietly, such as Richard Rowland's "pernis-ciously suggesting misapprehensions to peoples minds in [James Smith's] dealings." On the other hand, they could result from a public outburst like the one directed at Erasmus James of Marblehead, who was openly denounced "in a railing manner" as a "base, cheating Rogue and one eyd dogg." The effect, at any rate, was the same: a merchant would have "suffered much in name and credit in other counties" as well as in his

---

64. *Mass. Rec.* 3:132–33.

65. *Col. Laws 1660–72*, pp. 129–30 [1641, 1647, 1651, 1652], 152 [1646]. Make-fashion v. Leonard [1673], EP 20:87. Cogswell v. Morgan [1673], IpMbk. 1666–82, Mar. term #4. Cross v. Needham [1673], EP 20:10–12. Bishop v. Lord [1683], EP 39:62. Presentment of Josiah Clark [1684], EP 41:65. Maule v. Stearnes [1687], EP 47:66–67.

66. Presentment of Freegrace Norton [1674], IpMbk. 1666–82, May term #2. Davis v. Tawley [1681], EP 35:116. Presentment of John Davis [1681], EP 36:13.

67. For an earlier instance of this situation, see Keayne, *Apologia.*

own town.[68] As the Derbys explained to the court at Salem, going to court was necessary "only to clear our selves to the World from all such things as the said Maul would make the people believe we are subject unto, whereby to keepe our Trading for our Livelihood."[69] Jonathan Corwin jailed (by *capias* to begin a defamation suit) persons who had made such statements about his business practices. Two men were thus forced to seek their release by promising to do nothing else in word or deed "to wrong or damnify you." One also promised to move to Virginia, while the other pledged "my bond to Depart from this Jurisdiction."[70]

The county court, therefore, served an important role in the functioning of the Essex economy. But to emphasize the employment of the court as an exclusively mercantile institution obscures the no less important role it played in relationships among persons not primarily engaged in trade. For them, too, court actions to recover money were important. Colonial New England was an agrarian society in which lending and borrowing were common facts of life. With currency scarce and vital farm implements sometimes unavailable, it was necessary to extend credit for money obligations as well as to share farm tools. Payment for rates (taxes), goods, and services was often made with quantities of grain, and reimbursement frequently had to wait for the autumn harvest.[71]

That "neighborly loans" operated in this way in late-seventeenth century Essex is amply demonstrated in the inventories of estates probated with county officials from 1675 to 1679. These inventories reveal the debits and credits held by a man at death. Significantly, these obligations never had been brought to court; in contrast to obligations that had to be settled in court, these had been allowed to remain unpaid until the debtor's death, implying at least some degree of familiarity or trust between lender and borrower. It is quite likely, moreover, that probate records actually underrecord the true extent of personal indebtedness, because it was a common practice for aged persons to "clear" their estates when death was imminent. Their creditors had trusted them until

68. Smith v. Rowland [1669], IpMbk. 1666–82, Mar. term #16, #17, #18, #42. Fairfield v. Gifford [1678], EP 28:3–7. James v. Chin [1684], IpMbk. 1682–92 Sept. term #5 (for the defendant's saying that plaintiff was "a drunking cheating Rogoue and that he would cheat any boddy and deserved hanging"). James v. Glasse [1684], ibid., #7. Derby v. Maule [1686], EP 46:38–41. See also Browne v. Smith [1672], EP 19:6; Palmer v. Colcord [1674], NorMbk. 1672–81, p. 37. Browne v. Farrington [1691], EP 48:100.

69. Derby v. Maule.

70. William Godso to Jonathan Corwin, 2 Oct. 1684, Curwen Papers, box 3. Nathan Pickman to Corwin, 2 Oct. 1684, ibid. See also Joseph Bennit to Corwin, 6 Dec. 1679, ibid.

71. William B. Weeden, *Economic and Social History of New England*, 1:119, 326. The author alludes to the practice of "neighborly loans" made in anticipation of a later harvest (ibid., pp. xv, 408).

that time, and many people felt obliged to settle accounts without being asked to do so. As John Godfrey lay dying in 1675, for example, his son Peter discussed this matter with him. Peter related how "I Askd the said Godfary when he would Com and order mattrs conserning his bills or bonds. hee told me vary speedily. said I to him, you may dy and leave youar things to you know not hoo. to which John Godfary Answered, as for Jams Jakman hee shall have his bond or bill upe of wheat and Indian corne."[72] If necessary, a dying man might direct his son to settle "any du debtes or demands what so ever that can justly demand of me."[73] Nevertheless, the pattern of obligations revealed by the probate records is a vast one. Essex probate records account for only one of every four deaths among householders there in the seventeenth century, but of the 202 inventories probated from 1675 to 1679, 167 (83 percent) listed obligations owing to or from them.[74] As a raw quantitative figure, this percentage is significant, for it reveals—if only roughly—the extent of interpersonal indebtedness in the society.

Unfortunately, most obligations were not specified by name. Though individuals were sometimes named, it was common simply to list, for instance, "debts from severall persons, 8 li."[75] But omissions can also be historically revealing. One important reason that so many estate inventories did not list specific debtors or creditors was that the executor, administrator, or widow—or sometimes even the testator himself, when alive—did not know who they were or the value of the obligation. When Anne Roundy brought in the account of her late husband's property, she was forced to list "Possibly some debts that may be owing to this estate but what the widdow cannot tell, neither doth she know how much the abovesaid estate of her deceased husband's may be indebted."[76] Thomas Oliver of Salem attempted to determine his own debts and credits during "his sickness" in 1679 but was unable to figure them out and upon his death left "several other debts owing not yet knowne" for his executors to try to locate.[77]

The lax treatment of so many debts suggests the presence of positive ties between members of the Essex community. People trusted others to

<hr>

72. Estate of John Godfrey [1675], Dow, *Probate Records of Essex County*, 3:20. See also Estate of Sarah Charles [1676], ibid., p. 144.

73. Estate of Edmund Needham [1677], ibid., p. 152.

74. The period was chosen for the convenience of available published inventories. Those consulted can be found at ibid., pp. 1–348. Debts incurred from funeral expenses are not included. For an estimate on the extent of probated inventories among decedents, see William I. Davisson, "Essex County Price Trends," p. 150.

75. Estate of James Bailey [1677], Dow, *Probate Records of Essex County*, 3:164.

76. Estate of Philip Roundy [1678], ibid., p. 236.

77. Estate of Thomas Oliver [1679], ibid., p. 319.

hold their property; although they generally remembered that certain persons were in debt to them, they did not always know the precise amount involved and were content to allow the obligation to remain unpaid as a gesture of faith in the relationship. When Jacob Preston was lost at sea in 1679, Thomas Preston was able to determine most of his outstanding obligations, but not those between Jacob and one William Bowditch. Both men were from Salem, but Thomas had to confess that it was still "Unresolved how the account stands between Mr Willim Bowditch and the abovesaid Jacob Preston, Thomas Preston haveing don his best endeavor to have a settlement but cannot as yet attaine it."[78]

As in other agrarian societies where such obligations have been studied, these "neighborly loans" were measures of trust as well as implicit social bonds between creditor and debtor.[79] Attesting to this is the fact that very many of the sums owed were intrafamily debts, usually between fathers and sons or between brothers by birth or marriage. John Breed of Lynn owed money to his sons Allen and Timothy, for example, and Benjamin Chadwell was a debtor to his son Moses. In both examples these family debts amounted to large sums by comparison with other outstanding obligations, but they required no enforcement in court.[80]

Obviously, such acquiescence did not characterize all monetary obligations: creditors demanded repayment, debtors refused (or were unable) to pay, and creditors sued to recover the money owed to them. If it may be assumed that undemanded debts were directly related to effectively acquiescent relationships, a comparison of such loans with legally demanded debts sheds much light on the Essex community. In what sort of relationships were debts more likely to be demanded in court? Among merchants and their customers, it has been shown, distance was a real factor: merchants more often had to sue those who did not live in their own communities.

A spatial (geographic) analysis of indebtedness in the town of Lynn indicates a roughly analogous situation among nonmerchants. Manageable size and particularly extensive surviving evidence make Lynn a good case study for a test comparison of undemanded and litigated indebtedness. One of the older towns in the county, Lynn was smaller than Salem and more typical of the noncommercial, agrarian towns of Essex. The locations of seventy residences can be determined quite reliably, moreover, from a map prepared for a nineteenth-century bicentennial history

78. Estate of Jacob Preston [1679], ibid., p. 342.

79. For an analysis of this phenomenon in a modern rural society, see Conrad Arensberg, *The Irish Countryman*, pp. 173–76.

80. Estate of John Breed [1678], Dow, *Probate Records of Essex County*, 3:254–55. Estate of Benjamin Chadwell [1679], ibid., pp. 307–9.

of the town as well as from testimony in the county court records.[81]

For the purpose of examining the nature of undemanded obligations, the inventoried estates of Benjamin Chadwell (1679) and John Breed (1678) may be used. They are unusually complete with regard to indebtedness, and most of the persons listed can be located as to place of residence within the town. Breed died in 1678 with debts outstanding to ten persons. One creditor was a Bostonian, and the towns of another four cannot be determined. But the other five can be located, and if they are typical they give some indication of the type of relationship in which an obligation was allowed to continue undemanded. Two creditors were Breed's sons Allen and Timothy. The remaining three (Samuel Johnson, Clement Coldam, and Samuel Hart) all lived in Lynn.[82] They were not Breed's next-door neighbors, but they did live in the same general neighborhood, in an area set off from the rest of the town and definably circumscribed by Lynn Harbor on the south, Strawberry Brook on the west, Flax Pond on the north, and Rock Pasture on the east. They were neighbors by any definition of the term, though not "near neighbors," as owners of contiguous house lots were designated at that time. Benjamin Chadwell's undemanded obligations reveal the same pattern. Of his eighteen creditors, twelve were fellow townsmen; three were Salem merchants (Francis Croad, Bartholomew Gedney, and Edmund Batter); the sixteenth was a Newbury man; the seventeenth was from Ipswich; and one cannot be located. Besides his son Moses, six of the dozen Lynn residents can be pinpointed. As with Breed's group, these persons lived in the same recognizable neighborhood as Chadwell, within a triangle formed by Strawberry Brook and Rock Pasture on the northwest, Stacy's Brook on the east, and the common on the south. They all lived within easy reach of Chadwell's residence by way of the town roads linking them.[83] Neither Chadwell nor Breed, it should be added, was engaged in lawsuits with anyone else in the town.

If these undemanded obligations suggest an optimum distance (under two miles) for the smooth functioning of economic relationships, the obligations that Lynn residents brought to court may reveal the limits beyond which such acquiescence did not operate and may shed light on economic relationships in the Essex community. One point to be noted is the relatively low number of intratown cases brought to court to recover money lent or due for goods sold and delivered. Of the seventy Lynn townsmen whose residences could be located as a test, only seven used the county court for that purpose against fellow townsmen during the

81. Alonzo Lewis, *The History of Lynn*.
82. Estate of John Breed.
83. Estate of Benjamin Chadwell.

years 1672 to 1692. In all likelihood some used the "commissioners to end small causes" if damages were less than forty shillings, while others probably resorted to the mediation of neighbors or the church. But the figure is still low if compared with the large number of appearances that these same people made as plaintiffs or defendants in trespass actions, or as witnesses or defendants in prosecutions for assault, defamation, drunkenness, and fornication. While these cases frequently involved neighbors, those to recover money more usually involved men living at a considerable distance from one another in different neighborhoods. Unlike the men who tolerated the existence of an unpaid debt, the litigants were not drawn together by the geography or communication routes of the town. Though "townsmen" in name, their contact with their opponents was probably limited and less frequent—except in two cases—than that among persons living in the same neighborhood.

John Gifford is a good example with whom to start, for he lived in the west end of town at the ironworks, while two of his opponents lived in the east and center of the town: Edward Richards, who sued Gifford and was later sued by him, lived more than four miles away across town at Humfrey's Farm, and Clement Coldam made his home three miles away next to Flax Pond (see Map 4). Besides the longer distances between them, they were separated by water, hills, marsh, and woods. In three other actions, the same distances and obstacles obtained: the lawsuits by Joseph Browne and John Stacy against Matthew Farrington, and by Henry Rhodes against John Ballard.[84] In the suit of John Armitage against Richard Hood, the distance was only one and a quarter miles, but they lived in distinct and different neighborhoods—the former along Strawberry Brook and the latter in a small community along Nahant Bay across the harbor.[85]

By contrast, the obligations that never came to court involved men living closer together. The only exceptions were the lawsuits between Gifford and Henry Dispaw in 1675 and between Walter Taylor and Obadiah Bridges in 1672. However, Bridges, who lived directly across the street from Taylor, simply acknowledged his obligation in court without joining issue.[86] In the other case, Henry Dispaw was an employee living at Gifford's residence, and their dispute exhibited a personal animus not seen in the other money suits, as the exaggerated tensions of living in the same household may have imparted a significant noneconomic feature to their disagreement. When the two disagreed over the

84. Browne v. Farrington [1691], EP 50:100. Stacy v. Farrington [1689], EP 48:49–51.

85. Armitage v. Hood [1674], SaMbk. 1667–79, June term #2.

86. Taylor v. Bridges [1672], IpMbk. 1666–82, Sept. term #21.

MAP 4. Locations of Lynn Residents Engaged in Intratown
Litigation to Recover Money Owed

wages due Dispaw and Gifford refused to pay, the former sued Gifford
for the amount; Gifford was unable to satisfy the judgment, and Dispaw
took execution against Gifford's body, causing him to be imprisoned for
twenty-one weeks while Dispaw took over Gifford's home and business.
This type of disagreement is, in all likelihood, an exception proving a
more general rule about the noneconomic tensions generated by proximity in the Essex community.[87]

    As in any society, those obligations requiring no court enforcement
far outnumbered those that did come to court. But the latter category is
nonetheless suggestive, especially if one can generalize about the rela-

87. Gifford v. Dispaw [1675], SaMbk. 1667–79, Nov. term, for twenty-one weeks'
false imprisonment. For more on this particular type of dispute, see chap. 4 of this volume.

tionships between creditors and debtors involved in litigation. In local noncommercial debts as well as in more far-flung mercantile ones, distance was probably the operative factor causing litigation to recover money for goods sold and delivered or for monies lent. The Essex town may, therefore, have contained within it smaller discrete neighborhoods in which face-to-face contacts contributed to some degree of order in economic relationships. These small neighborhoods very closely resembled English villages in size and hence embodied the social context necessary to nourish a communal village ideal. But as Essex society developed geographically and economically, the limits of that ideal became apparent to many of its people: outsiders owned land among them, the large size of their towns generated separate neighborhoods and reduced the effectiveness of the town meeting, and economic dealings brought people into contact with others less familiar to them. In these situations the county court served an important role by resolving conflict among the diverse elements of the larger community and affording them a common set of rules by which to live.

4 From Communalism to Litigation

The Elevation of Law and Legal Forms

In the establishment of a society at Massachusetts Bay in 1629, two concepts had had paradigmatic force: the gathered church with its congregationally ordained leader and the compact community of neighbors and families.[1] While the colonial leadership had recognized the realistic limitations of those ideals and had set up powerful legal institutions to support them, the ideals themselves had possessed a strong exhortatory and symbolic quality. Whatever their actual effectiveness, they stood for the founders as ultimate goals and as the very symbol of the colony's "errand into the wilderness."[2]

But that concept of "errand" underwent a profound change after 1660, as the work of Perry Miller has demonstrated with such subtlety and insight. In large part, the transformation was a by-product of disillusionment with the Puritan cause in England. Whether it was the ascendancy of Presbyterianism or of Cromwellian tolerationism, the initial impetus of the movement as the emigrants had known it seemed lost. The identity of the colony was called into question, and its ministers and secular leaders who reflected carefully upon their society were forced to acknowledge that their unique experiment was becoming a provincial culture; their litany of the prosaic sins present in Massachusetts was vocal testimony to that fact. Miller was perceptive enough to recognize that the breast-beating "jeremiad" sermons called for a redoubling of efforts to redefine the precise nature of the colony's "errand" and to discover a new identity. Nevertheless, subsequent scholars assessed the conflict and litigation of the late seventeenth century and concluded that no new ideology or generally accepted identity emerged before the eighteenth century; until then, one study concludes, there was "as yet no ideology

1. See chap. 1 of this volume.
2. This and the following two paragraphs owe much to Perry Miller's classic essay "Errand into the Wilderness" and to his *The New England Mind*, 2:130–31. Although it is apparent that Miller's model of "orthodoxy" and "declension" does not in all ways agree with the thesis of this book, Miller's understanding of the Puritan mind in the late seventeenth century offers many suggestive insights into the perception that the ways and goals of the Founders were no longer within reach and that new goals, with methods of attaining them, were called for.

which could persuade men to embrace it as a positive good."[3]

Actually, the Puritan colony at the Bay did not sink into confusion or discouragement, for the falling away of the old communal paradigm could not have occurred without the appearance of a new mode of reference to replace it. Upon the fading of the ideal of the gathered community of the elect, there emerged a fresh understanding of the colony's identity and uniqueness, as well as a reformulation of positive ideals. One of the more recognizable features of that new identity was the colonial charter, for it protected the colony from Anglicanism and Stuart divine right monarchy on the one side and from social disintegration and Quaker or anabaptist heresy on the other. On an individual level, the charter embodied the mass of prescriptive rights held by the residents of the colony. No other colonists, James Oxenbridge told the General Court in his 1671 election sermon, enjoyed the liberties that the residents of Massachusetts Bay possessed in their charter. Election sermons became a regular part of Massachusetts politics after 1660, and they repeatedly emphasized the importance of the civil government under the charter. Gradually they pointed toward a new way of viewing the social order. Charter and liberty—these were the two quantities that were increasingly recognized as positive foundations of the Bay Colony. Both, of course, needed defending: the charter was constantly threatened by the crown, and personal liberties had to be asserted and defended in courts of law. Acknowledging and finally accepting the increasingly legalistic character of their society, the ministers of the colony placed an ever greater emphasis on the responsibilities of the magistrates in protecting colonial liberties—not the least of which was "the great liberty of an English subject to be tryed by his peers, before whom he hath free and full libertie to plead law for his endempnitie and safety."[4]

The idea of "gathering" congregations in Massachusetts rested on the limitation of church membership to those who could relate a conversion experience and demonstrate a knowledge of the Bible, as well as the "outward signs of inward grace" (proof of living an upright life). The first requirement was an innovation in congregational practice, for it had not been required in England.[5] As a way of sharply restricting membership, it was to be a source of strength as well as weakness for the church

---

3. Kenneth A. Lockridge, *A New England Town, The First Hundred Years*, p. 117.

4. Miller, *New England Mind*, 2:131. On the transition between paradigms, see Thomas S. Kuhn, *The Structure of Scientific Revolutions*, p. 77. Kuhn cautions that a new paradigm is needed before an old one can be abandoned, and the "decision to reject one paradigm is always simultaneously the decision to accept another."

5. Edmund S. Morgan, *Visible Saints*, chap. 2.

in Massachusetts. On the one hand, requiring a conversion experience made certain that the congregation would be a collectivity of "visible saints" committed to the ideals of the "errand." On the other, however, a restricted membership had the very practical result of confining the church's effective disciplinary powers to only those who had signed the church covenant and thereby agreed to submit to the authority of congregational discipline.

Assuming that the saints would constitute a majority of the population, congregational authority would be a powerful means of bringing order to the community. But church membership, at least in Salem where the available figures permit an accurate comparison, did not keep pace with the population increase. In 1629, it will be recalled, only 30 persons of the 200 living at the colony signed the Salem church covenant. By 1640, the Salem church had admitted 256 people as the town's population rose to approximately 1,000, but 48 of those admitted either "removed" themselves from Salem or were "recommended" or "dismissed" to other congregations. In the next decade church admissions continued to rise proportionally to the general population, as 142 persons became members, while 35 left. After 1650, however, the trend reversed. The congregation experienced a period of sluggish growth in the 1650s, when it recorded only 24 admissions, with 3 departures. In the 1660s, 88 persons joined, but most of these were children of members, and 67 communicants removed themselves to form a congregation at Bass River (Beverly). Only in the 1670s and 1680s, in the aftermath of King Philip's War, was there an upturn: 84 joined in the 1670s, 64 of them in the four years after the disasters of 1675. Despite these new admissions, the decline in membership was apparent and in 1682 it was necessary for the church's pastor to impress upon its communicants their "duty of observing and Encouraging such as they knew to be Godly to joyn the Church." Nevertheless, when the town compiled its list of ratepayers the next year, only 17 percent of those listed were members of the congregation.[6]

Salem was not unusual in late-seventeenth-century Massachusetts, where declining church membership was a widespread source of concern.[7] At any rate, the fact that the percentage of Salem church member-

6. Richard D. Pierce, ed., *Records of the First Church in Salem, Massachusetts, 1629–1736*, passim, p. 154. Richard Gildrie counts 94 members and 542 ratepayers (*Salem, Massachusetts, 1626–1683, A Covenant Community*, p. 163); my own count of ratepayers is 563, but the percentage remains roughly the same.

7. Contemporary awareness of this fact first appears to have taken the form of explicit statements in the controversy over the "Half-Way Covenant" at the Synod of 1662, attended by ministers from Congregational churches of every part of New England. For a good description of the issues involved, see David D. Hall, *The Faithful Shepherd*, pp. 197–202.

ship was no longer any higher in 1683 than it had been in 1629 testified to the continuing importance of secular institutions—and the legal system in particular—as agents of social control. From the beginning of the colony's existence it had been assumed that the state would lend support, whenever necessary, to the church: church and state, according to the *Laws and Liberties*, would each "help and strengthen [the] other."[8] Ministers were expected to support the state through their personal influence and their sermons and to give guidance on thorny issues when consulted. Conversely, the state assured the financial support of the ministry by ordering in 1637 that all inhabitants (i.e., not just church members) were to "contribute to all charges, both in Church and Commonwealth." Recognizing that not all inhabitants had been willing to pay voluntarily, the General Court also provided that recalcitrants could be "compelled thereto by assessment and distres to bee levied by the cunstable, or other officer of the towne."[9]

Besides external financial support, the church required secular force to maintain its internal cohesion. As early as the 1630s, the fractious nature of the Salem congregation—and the centrifugal forces of Separatists and Antinomians within it—had called into question the ability of the congregation by itself to enforce its standards of belief and practice, and in 1636 Hugh Peter explicitly acknowledged the need for secular aid when he added to the Salem church covenant the provision that its adherents would "carry our selves in all lawful obedience, to those that are over us, in Church or Commonweal."[10] The purpose of this clause was to assure that future dissidents of the Hutchinsonian type would recognize the state's authority if it were later applied to reinforce a congregational decision. Its fundamental underlying assumptions, of course, were that church and state would not be in conflict and that the courts could be expected to uphold the will and actions of the congregation.

But in later decades the legal institutions of Essex County proved to be something other than the unwavering and consistent bulwark of the church that had been anticipated. Indeed, two major cases—one in 1657, the other in 1663—revealed a shift in emphasis within the county. Essex was hardly becoming a tolerationist society when it came to matters of doctrine (witness the Quaker persecutions), but it was beginning to move toward the position that certain personal liberties were to be protected as zealously as the church—in fact, that they might have to be protected *from* the church. The courts were the source of that protection, for it was

8. Max Farrand, ed., *The Laws and Liberties of Massachusetts*, p. A2.
9. *Mass. Rec.* 1:240–41.
10. Pierce, *First Church in Salem*, pp. xxiv, 4.

there that individuals could defend their personal liberties against a town meeting or congregation.

The background of the first case was a vote by the Ipswich town meeting in 1657 to "give £100 towards building a house for Mr Cobbet," the minister of its congregation. Ten years earlier the General Court had empowered towns to raise money to "grant, build, or purchase" a dwelling for their ministers, "provided always that such grant" was "to the use of the present preaching Elder and his next successor." When Ipswich voted to raise a hundred pounds, however, it also planned to grant the house to Cobbet as a freehold rather than only to his use. George Giddings objected to what he regarded a "gift," and when he refused to pay his assessment Constable Edward Browne distrained "his pewter dishes or platters" to satisfy the rate. Giddings therefore brought an action of trespass on the case—though trespass would have been the proper form of action in England—before Magistrate Samuel Symonds sitting out of sessions to end small causes. Symonds found for the plaintiff; although he assessed only a shilling in damages (and 5s.8d. costs), he recognized that "the case being of very weighty concernment in the countrey . . . I shall express the groundes of my judgment."[11]

Symonds's opinion remains a remarkable document, ranging as it did from the unjustness of Charles I's ship money and the folly of "Levellisme" to the limited powers of Parliament and drawing upon the authority of Dalton's *Countrey Justice*, Finch's *Law*,[12] the Ten Commandments, earlier Essex decisions, and the general principles of legal reasoning. Symonds began by asserting that "it is against a fundamentall law in nature to be compelled to pay that which others doe give," and that neither king nor Parliament could compel it. Comparing the gift of the parsonage to "knighthood-money, ship money, etc.," in England, he cited the authority of "histories, lawyers bookes of reports, records, etc.," to elevate "fundamental lawe" and state that "it cannot be made to appeare that in the most exorbitant times any man hath had his estate taken from him as by the guift of others, under colour of lawe, or countenance of authority." Symonds interpreted the grant of the parsonage as a gift and stated that a gift "doth not bind such as doe not consent" to it. Nevertheless, he was willing to consider the plea that it was "a bargain or contract." Even then—and "setting aside the consideration of the fundamentall lawe"—he found it illegal, for "such bargains as bind the nonconsenters must be equalle, rationall, and the termes or conditions also

11. Symonds's opinion can be found in Mark DeWolfe Howe, *Readings in American Legal History*, pp. 232–40.

12. Sir Henry Finch, *Law; or, a Discourse Thereof.*

expressed or certayne: If any of these fayle," he explained, "noe law will bind them." To Symonds, the contract was certainly not equal and was "a very blind bargain." Congregations, he also said, possessed only "a derived power in trust, being a society; for they have not such an unlimited domain over other mens estates or persons." Symonds conceded that the law providing for ministerial support "in its true sense is good," but that a wrong "construction" was being put on something that "may lawfully be done in the particular." Such a law therefore "must needs be voyd, if it should be necessarly construed against the right or liberty of the subject."[13]

The county court meeting at Salem in November 1657 reversed Symonds's judgment and was upheld by the General Court, for he was attacking financial support of the established church, a basic principle that was not overturned in Massachusetts until 1817. But he had stated several important points for the first time in Massachusetts. One was the primacy of fundamental law over "colour of law, or countenance of authority" even if that authority was the church's. "If repugnant to fundamentall lawe," he said, any act is "voyd." Second, Symonds had delimited the congregation's role and power over its members by comparing it to an ordinary "society," which was "limited by statute law." Finally—and perhaps most important, for it was his concluding argument—he asserted that laws compelling support of the church must be "grounded upon such principles as both here and in other nations will be owned as just and equall."[14]

It would be a serious mistake to wrench Symonds's opinion out of its seventeenth-century context and compare it to First Amendment principles and related nineteenth-century decisions about church and state. To do so would obscure its very close resemblance to parallel English legal reasoning and, possibly, even to Sir Edward Coke's argument in *Dr. Bonham's Case* (1610). Symonds did not refer directly to that case, but it is likely that he had it in mind. The part of Coke's *Reports* that contained the case was available to Symonds—having been purchased by the colony for its magistrates—and it is significant that in his opinion he warned, "Let us not (here in New-England) despise the rules of the learned in the lawes of England, who have both great helps and long experience." Specifically, he followed the same line of reasoning that Coke applied against broadening a statute. In a manner suggestive of the 1610 case, he explained what was unambiguous in the Massachusetts law ("to compell

13. Howe, *Readings in American Legal History*, pp. 232–40.
14. Ibid. On the problem of church and state in the nineteenth century, see Adams v. Howe [1817], in D. A. Tyng, *Reports of Cases Argued and Determined in the Supreme Judicial Court of the Commonwealth of Massachusetts*, 14:340–50.

men to pay necessary duties in church and common wealthe, as necessary maintenance"); this, he said, was "consonant" with the statute and with the intent of its framers. On the other hand, the town's interpretation of the law was a "wresting," a "corrupt interpretation" whose effect was to "overthrow" the proper construction. In the way that this interpretation took property for the church, it was "repugnant to fundamentall law" and thus "voyd." Only its narrower interpretation was to be followed.[15]

Symonds's decision reveals how the general English principles of statutory interpretation were operative at the most basic level of the Massachusetts Bay legal system. He had used them to assert a principle that limited the power of individual congregations and elevated the rule of law to protect certain fundamental liberties—in this case, not to have one's estate "unduly taken." In calling for adherence to the legal standards of "other nations," moreover, he was implying the end of the colony's unique errand to create a Bible commonwealth, although he was far from rejecting the Bible entirely. He was simply and clearly stating that piety and justice together must be acknowledged as the basis of Massachusetts society. Citing the Bible to support his opinion, he concluded, "I doe sometymes remember what is said of Levy. In poynt of right and truth, he tooke noe notice of father and mother. And that is the way to establish love and peace in this our Israel. And the holy scripture doth oblige the doctrine and practice of piety according to the first table, and of distributive justice in the second, both expressly, or by necessary consequence."[16]

State support of the church was too important a general principle to challenge, but Symonds's decision and argument either prompted or anticipated legal actions by others against the authority of individual congregations. The most significant of these grew out of a Lynn commonage dispute in 1661, and before the action was finally settled two years later it struck a real blow against the power of a congregation to discipline its members. The initial action was brought at the Ipswich court on 16 March 1661 by William Longley against the town of Lynn for withholding and refusing to lay out a forty-acre commonage allotment. His suit was successful, and the court ordered Henry Collins and John Ha-

---

15. Howe, *Readings in American Legal History*, pp. 236–37. For an excellent discussion of the Bonham case that dispelled the mistaken historical analyses given to it, see Samuel E. Thorne, "Dr. Bonham's Case." In 1647 the General Court purchased "two [copies] of Sir Edward Cook Reports" (*Mass. Rec.* 2:212). Dr. Bonham's Case is in the eighth part of Coke's *Reports*, eleven parts of which were available at the time. The report can be found most easily in *The English Reports*, 77:638–58. On the availability of Coke's *Reports* in Massachusetts, see Thomas G. Barnes, "Law and Liberty (and Order) in Early Massachusetts," n. 31.

16. Howe, *Readings in American Legal History*, p. 239.

thorne, who had been named defendants to appear in behalf of the town, to lay out the forty acres by 1 June or pay Longley forty pounds. When Collins and Hathorne refused to lay out the land, Longley obtained a writ of execution on 14 October, and Marshal Robert Lord seized a horse (worth fifteen pounds) belonging to Hathorne. He delivered it to the plaintiff and then proceeded to levy execution for the balance on the property of the codefendant Collins. But Collins refused to yield any property; it was not "his propper debt," he protested, and said to the marshal, "here is Towne Comon before my dore; take that for your satisfaction." Lord instead levied execution on Collins's body and arrested him.[17]

When the court met again at Ipswich in March 1662, both Hathorne and Collins sued Lord for illegally levying execution. Hathorne withdrew his action, and the jury returned its verdict for the defendant in the other after Longley and another witness, Andrew Mansfield, testified in Marshal Lord's support. Hathorne, they deposed, not only had refused to aid in levying execution at Collins's home, but he also had obstructed Lord by pushing him away from Collins. Hathorne, according to Longley, had said, "I owne the authority of the country, but you [Lord] I will not owne; I will see better cloths upon your back first." Lord had explained to Hathorne after arresting Collins that he would be a "fool" to levy execution a second time even if goods were offered. To that, Longley continued, Hathorne had snapped, "I hope to make a fool of you before I have done with you."[18] Though Hathorne failed to "make a fool" of the marshal, he was not finished, for later that summer he charged before the Lynn congregation that Mansfield and Longley had lied in their depositions. Specifically, he accused them of breaking the ninth commandment by bearing false witness against a neighbor, and the congregation, after spending much of the summer on the problem, voted to censure them.

Mansfield and Longley thereupon challenged the power of the ecclesiastical discipline by bringing defamation suits against Hathorne at the Ipswich court in March 1663. In each case the jury found for the plaintiff and ordered the defendant to make a public confession of his erroneous accusation within thirty days and to do so before the Lynn meeting.[19] The bench, however, was not quite willing to overthrow a

17. Longley v. Collins and Hathorne, on behalf of Town of Lynn [1661], EP 6:75–77.

18. Hathorne v. Lord [1662], IpMbk. 1646–66, Mar. term #7. Collins v. Lord [1662], EP 8:61–64.

19. Mansfield v. Hathorne [1663], EP 8:105. Longley v. Hathorne [1663], EP 8:118.

congregational censure without giving the Lynn church an opportunity to meet again and reverse the vote on its own. The judges therefore sent a letter, drafted by Robert Lord as clerk of the court on 4 April, explaining to the church that Hathorne had been duly convicted of defamation after "a full and impartiall heareing and due examinacon and by the verdict of the Jury." They commented that "it is much to be desired that contrary judgment in one and the same case may be prevented if possibly it may be attained and one power not to clash against the other. Wee thought it expedient before we give judgment in the case to comend the same to the serious consideration and further examinacon thereof." They then expressed their hope that the congregation would "change their mind and reverse [the] sensures," and they promised to defer judgment until the next court term.

But the congregation rejected the suggestion, and in May the judges wrote once again to the Lynn church. This time their tone was not as conciliatory. They began by denying any intention to encroach upon or destroy "the right or power of the churches," but they reminded the "Reverend and beloved" at Lynn that "wee have beene taught and verily beleeve the civil and eclesiastical power may very wel consist, and that no cause is so purely eclesiastical but the civil power may in its way deale therein." Eschewing any "eclesiasticisme"—the doctrine "that the civil magistrate hath eclesiastical power"—they nonetheless emphasized their obligation to "take cognizance and give judgment in eclesiastical cause, not in a church but civil way." In other words, magistrates would not meddle with purely doctrinal matters, but they would take note of matters touching civil concerns. "The God of order guide all our administration," they concluded, "to his glory and the peace and edification of his people." They then unanimously accepted the jury's verdict, and in September the Court of Assistants affirmed their judgment on appeal.[20]

These two cases were not isolated ones. Despite the reversal of Symonds's decision, the county court was assuming a new role in relation to the Essex churches. Excluding prosecutions for moral infractions or breach of the Sabbath (either working or nonattendance at worship) because those are at most only implicit challenges to the church, an examination of the court's activity in suppressing explicit challenges to the authority of the church or congregation reveals a marked change in as short a period as that between 1650 and the 1680s. In the first fifteen years of the court's existence (1636–50) it heard fifteen cases in which defendants were charged with challenging the authority of the minister or the congregation. Because each congregation could discipline only

20. Howe, *Readings in American Legal History*, pp. 133–37. *Assts. Rec.* 3:137.

professing members, it had to enlist the aid of the magistrates against those who were not in full communion. But in the last fifteen years of the court's existence under the Old Charter (1670–84), a different pattern appeared. More cases were brought involving challenges to the church or its minister (thirty-five), but in twelve of these the problem concerned an irreconcilable dispute among the members themselves, often focusing on a minister who had become a symbol of one faction or another. Unable to function as the harmonious units intended in 1629, many Essex congregations fell prey to the very "suspitions [and] backbyteings" that the 1629 Salem covenant had forsworn.

At the root of congregational dissension was the inability to sustain the ideal of unanimity, in either theory or practice, in decision making. Unanimity conduces to compromise and consensus, but by midcentury it was becoming more difficult to attain. Members divided into factions, and those in the majority began to insist that majority will was legitimate and should prevail—even over the will of the minister. At one time, the voice of the minister could be relied upon to harmonize divergent interests, but by the latter part of the century the clergy were proving unable to exert the strong moral leadership necessary to mediate conflict and impose order.[21]

One of the clergy's most obvious sources of vulnerability and weakness was their financial dependence. Massachusetts law guaranteed support of all pastors, but it specified that this money be assessed and collected by town officials.[22] The minister received an annual stipend, therefore, voted by a town meeting whose membership included non-communicants. Typically, he was voted in the latter decades of the century an amount ranging from fifty to one hundred pounds per year; part of it (usually a third or a fourth) was paid in cash, but the bulk was given as merchantable grain. It was also customary for him to receive firewood.[23] In the earliest years of settlement this maintenance of ministers was supplied by voluntary contribution. Because this system was replaced by the more fixed "stinting" of a salary as required by law, it might appear that the clergy gained a substantial measure of security by these new arrangements.[24]

21. The best example of the clash between majoritarianism and the authority of a minister occurred at Newbury, with the Reverend Thomas Parker. It is well described by Hall in *Faithful Shepherd*, pp. 212–14.

22. See the revised statute of 1654, *Col. Laws 1660–72*, pp. 148–49.

23. See, for example, the arrangements made by the town of Wenham with Joseph Gerrish in 1673, described in John Langdon Sibley, *Biographical Sketches of Graduates of Harvard University in Cambridge, Massachusetts*, 2:299–300. Freemanship was not required for participation in town meetings.

24. Hall, *Faithful Shepherd*, chap. 6. Hall admits that there were occasional refusals to pay ministerial rates, but he views the system as one that worked well.

In reality they obtained considerably less, for at least in Essex the congregations were able to retain control in one way or another. The control that an Essex minister first felt exerted upon him was the probationary nature of his position on being "settled." Strictly speaking, he was not yet entitled to call himself a minister; although he held a university degree, he still had to be ordained by a congregation. Ordination could follow his arrival very promptly, but in many cases it took years. William Hubbard and John Richardson waited two years at Ipswich and Newbury, respectively, while Joseph Capen preached three years at Topsfield and James Alling five years at Salisbury before being ordained. In some cases men preached even before a parish was officially established and legally entitled to ordain them. Zechariah Symmes, Jr., served at Bradford on a year-to-year basis from 1668 until a church was formally gathered there in 1683, and Samuel Cheever stood in a similar position at Marblehead from 1668 to 1684.[25] Even after ordination, a minister's tenure was uncertain. Thomas Wells was ordained at Amesbury in 1672, but the church made no permanent commitment to him for twenty years. At any time a congregation might decide to end support of its pastor and ask him to leave. Topsfield, for example, discharged Thomas Gilbert in 1671 and his successor Jeremiah Hobart in 1680. Lynn and Rowley also discharged ministers in the late seventeenth century, while Salem Village outdid them all with its notorious treatment of clergymen.[26]

Once a relatively fixed tenure had been established, it was still possible to exert great pressure on a minister by manipulating the pay he received. Neither compensation for expenses nor salaries were permanently set, and towns might reward their ministers by adjusting either sum. Samuel Phillips, while assistant to Ezekiel Rogers, was voted between fifty and ninety pounds yearly, depending on expenses. Surviving records indicate that maintenance increases were by no means automatic or routine. John Emerson, Zechariah Symmes, Jr., and Joseph Gerrish, who were all popular in their towns, did receive substantial raises, but others did not. Jeremiah Shepard was voted a fixed salary, but his congregation retained the old practice of making contributions when it saw fit to do so.[27] A more subtle means of keeping influence over a minister's financial condition was to vary the proportion of cash and "country pay"

25. Sibley, *Harvard Graduates*, 1:54–62, 491–92; 3:173–74. Harold F. Worthley, *Records of the Particular (Congregational) Churches of Massachusetts, Gathered 1620–1805*, pp. 346–47, 408–10.

26. Worthley, *Records of (Congregational) Churches*, pp. 171–73, 333–35, 622–23; Sibley, *Harvard Graduates*, 2:268–70.

27. Sibley, *Harvard Graduates*, 1:221–28, 485–87, 489–94; 2:299–301; Alonzo Lewis and J. R. Newhall, *History of Lynn Including Lynnfield, Saugus, Swampscott, and Nahant*, 1:277.

(goods) he was given. Cash was more desirable, of course: in 1681 Joseph Capen was offered seventy-five pounds in country pay or sixty-five pounds including twenty pounds in cash, and he chose the latter. If a town favored its minister, it might reward him with an increased proportion of cash. John Emerson of Gloucester, for example, obtained steady increases during his tenure there. Although his salary remained at the sixty-five pounds voted at his arrival, he began to receive a larger amount in cash. His first payments were all country pay, but in 1672 he was receiving one-eighth in money, and finally one-fourth.[28]

Dependence on an uncertain salary was a serious weakness, for there was no requirement that ministers be given any property as freehold. First-generation ministers had received property through their status as initial settlers and grantee-proprietors; but by the second generation this practice became less common and a town could withhold such a grant, preventing the minister from accumulating the security afforded by owning real estate. Unless a minister was able to maintain the favor of his town meeting, it was unlikely that he would get a freehold. John Emerson at Gloucester and Joseph Gerrish at Wenham were successful in this, but many others were not. In Topsfield, Jeremiah Hobart revealed the pressures and anxieties suffered by ministers when he stalked out of the town meeting, frustrated from waiting, hoping, and haggling over possession of the parsonage. At home he made his opinion of the building and the selectmen better known: "I would that parsonage were afire," he commented, "and som of them in it."[29]

With the outward security of their contractual maintenance severely limited in practice, ministers found the power of their positions eroding, too. Many found it difficult to gain and keep favor with all groups and not to offend those laymen who held power over their jobs and salaries. It always had been easy to offend opinions in sectarian Massachusetts, and with the Restoration the volatile conditions did not end. Thomas Parker angered several parishioners in Newbury and was criticized for his Presbyterian sympathies in 1672, while Thomas Gilbert caused problems with too vehement an attack on Stuart "Idolatry and Superstition" in 1666.[30] James Allen of Boston turned to this problem in his election sermon of 1679. After exhorting his listeners to "value Ministry, and the faithful ministers, esteem them as Covenant blessings," he decried the

28. Sibley, *Harvard Graduates*, 1:485–87.

29. Ibid., 2:299–301. Petition of Thomas Putnam et al. [1683], EP 39:81–82. Presentment of Jeremiah Hobart [1680], EP 32:142–43.

30. Complaints against Lomas and Adams [1672], IpMbk. 1666–82, May term #89, #90. Complaint against Thomas Gilbert [1666], EP 12:145. See also the prosecution of Gilbert for his speeches against the king that same year, EP 11:89.

treatment inflicted on them. No longer were ministers fully able to exert leadership, because there was no longer "a people ready to receive what should be made known to them." Instead, he lamented, the New England clergy had been subjected to "outward Temptations to please men" by their uncertain tenures and the fiscal discretion of town meetings.[31]

The financial uncertainties of the clergy in Essex produced numerous legal conflicts between insistent or embattled ministers and their reluctant, hostile, or parsimonious townsmen. One man in Salem, brought before the court upon complaint by the town constable for refusing to pay rates and resisting distraint of his property, protested that as a non-member of the church he owed nothing to the support of its two ministers. As he said in his own defense, "if ever he dealt with John Higginson or Nickolas Nois [Noyse] he would pay them, but he never dealt with them for anything."[32]

Resistance to paying the ministers' rate, like tax evasion in any society, was not uncommon in Essex,[33] but it took on a more serious, collective form when town meetings attempted to escape the financial responsibilities of maintaining a minister. The disputes at Salem Village have dominated historical attention and have been portrayed as a unique backdrop—and hence plausible cause—of the later witchcraft accusations, but they were not at all unique. Newbury experienced a comparably disruptive dispute in 1671, and in 1677 Rowley also subjected its ministers to treatment that would have been unthinkable forty years earlier.[34]

The Rowley dispute came to the attention of the county court at its April term in 1677, when three "complaints" were made. The first was brought by Jonathan Platts against the "Reverend Teacher" Samuel Phillips for accusing him and other townsmen of cheating on the collection of his pay and for calling Platts a "scoffer, an Ishmaelite, and persecutor of God's people." Phillips had made his remarks after the town meeting raised the price of corn paid to the town to satisfy the ministers' rates. Though the General Court had set the price at eight groats (2s.8d.) per bushel, the town set it at three shillings, thereby reducing the actual amount of corn paid by the inhabitants. The effect was to lower the stipend paid to both Phillips, the teaching minister, and Jeremiah Shepard, the preacher. But Phillips objected first; born in Essex, England, in 1625, he was part of the founding generation and was conditioned to

---

31. James Allen, *New-England's Choicest Blessing*, pp. 7, 11.
32. Dunton v. Neale [1685], EP 44:69–70, and execution at EP 46:143.
33. Stevens v. Very, and Stevens v. Duncan [1673], EP 20:125, for example.
34. Platts v. Pickard [1677], EP 26:63–67. Nelson v. Phillips [1677], EP 26:68. See also the difficulties at Beverly, in Petition of Jeremiah Hubbard [1672], EP 19:6.

expect that deference be paid to him, as well as a salary commensurate with his standing as a leader of the errand into the wilderness. It was thus not surprising that he erupted in anger and indignation when the town cut his salary through a stratagem and when the deacon came to report to him that the corn being paid in as rates was not fit for consumption even by hogs. He had become, as one supporter told the court, the recipient of "dirt and reproaches on one whom they [his antagonists] and we ought to honor."[35]

Platts withdrew his action against Phillips, but his brother Samuel Platts and two other selectmen, Richard Holmes and Daniel Wicom, refused to withdraw their own "Complaint, or Complaints," against John Pickard, another selectman. Pickard had accused the three complainants of betraying their trust to the town and acting contrary to its wishes at a town meeting in 1676. The dispute was a tangled and bitter one. Whatever their opinion of Phillips, the three complainants supported Shepard against Pickard and a majority of the town meeting who sought to remove him. To circumvent the majority of the meeting that opposed Shepard, Wicom had called for a vote to be taken on the subject of continuing Shepard's tenure and arranged "that all that are for Mr Shepard preaching a monthly lecture stay in the house and all that are against it go out of doors." These directions were intended to assure an accurate count of each side, but instead confusion followed. "[W]e understood not which way it went," deposed Constable Jeremiah Elsweth, who added that "nether was it declard nor recorded nor desired to be recorded." Apparently Wicom and his allied selectmen treated those remaining—Shepard's supporters—as a rump meeting and accepted their vote as a legal town vote. Since the matter had come before the court not by any writ, but by "complaint," the court felt free to say that both sides had acted irregularly, to advise them to "be more modest and peaceable," and to order them "for the present" to pay their own court costs.[36]

The third case grew out of another outburst by Phillips, who was reluctant to sue his opponents despite their taunts that the only way he would gain satisfaction would be to "win it by law." Phillips preferred to use his pulpit to denounce Philip Nelson, a leader of the opposition, as being the "principall cause of those unhappie divisions," and of breaking the fifth, eighth, and ninth commandments. Nelson thereupon entered his own "complaint" at the court against Phillips for making false accusations, although he apologized to the court for having "presumed to

35. Platts v. Phillips [1677], EP 26:61–62.
36. Platts v. Pickard. The background of this case was presented as testimony in Shepard v. Tenney [1677], EP 27:2.

trespas so much upon your patience." Nevertheless, before answering Phillips's accusations he explained his need to

> make my adress to your Honors here in, which if you shall so farr entertaine, as to vout-safe an hearinge of, I hope my innocencie will challenge a vindication and I shall not thinke my aims wholy lost, perhaps I may seeme to some to pass the bounds of christian modesty in presentinge this my complaint against an elder of a Church, and one that I stand related unto by church covenant but such is your wisdome, that you can, and your honorable affection to peace and justice, that I doubt not but you will heare with patience this my complaint especially if you consider how I am enforced to it by daily threats to be dealt with as an offender at home, whereby I may at last come to be deprived of the communion of Gods saints, and sweete and comfortable enjoyment of God in all his holy ordinances.[37]

Again the court had to deal with a civil challenge to a church censure—or, in this case, to the threat of a censure. Phillips's supporters countered Nelson's complaint by asserting that Nelson "is in no necesity to make aplication to civill autority," and they protested that it was "Iregular that in stead of a christian answer which hath bene long waited for he should make an acusation to this honoured court." But Nelson directed his complaint to a body he addressed as "patrons of peace, and favourers of justice." To Nelson it was essential that he have the right to defend his liberties in a court of law, and he echoed Samuel Symonds (one of the judges hearing these cases) by adding his confident hope that "justiss will take place without respect of persons"—that is, that the ministry would occupy no special position before the law. The court answered the complaint by admonishing both sides: it implied a limit to the force and nature of the ministry's power to censure by saying that Phillips "had used too high expressions" against Nelson and also that "in the main Mr. Nellson had transgressed the rule" of the congregation. After setting these important bounds on the internal conduct of congregational affairs, the court ordered Nelson to pay costs and give Phillips "due satticefaction."[38]

Besides the general need for judicial intervention seen in these three cases, the differing responses of Phillips and Shepard are noteworthy. Phillips tried, but failed, to command deference by virtue of his clerical standing. In contrast to his older colleague, Shepard—born in Cambridge, Massachusetts, in 1648—was at age twenty-nine part of a different generation. Unwilling to rely solely on his status and its traditional power to humble or persuade his opponents, he was not reluctant to sue them: at the next term of the court at Ipswich in September he brought

37. Nelson v. Phillips.
38. Ibid.

an action on the case for the nonpayment of his stipend. One reason for bringing the action was the failure of an arbitration attempt made in his unresolved dispute with the town meeting. Five ministers had served as arbitrators, and they had reported to both sides on 4 November 1675 their hope "that upon mutual forbereing and for guiding each other in love you may retaine the spirit of unity of spirit in the bond of peace and returne to the injoyment of communion with crist and one another in all his ordenances." It also had been their recommendation that the town hold another meeting to vote on Shepard's stipend, but it was at that meeting that Wicom had thrown the issue into further confusion by accepting the vote of the rump meeting. Shepard trusted neither arbitration nor another tumultous town meeting, for emotions had become so heated that no money at all was being collected. At the court term of April 1677, however, the jury returned a verdict for him, awarding him the fifty pounds he claimed, and the Court of Assistants later admonished his opponents for trying to overturn the decision by an appeal. Shepard ultimately accepted twenty pounds before leaving to preach at Chebacco parish.[39]

In the twenty years since Symonds had given his opinion in *Giddings* v. *Brown*, the new attitude he expressed regarding the role of law in society had become generally accepted in Essex. Symonds had made the point that no person should lose his property except by an express law of the General Court. That in itself was not a new idea, for it had been set forth in the *Body of Liberties* of 1641. But when that code had been drafted, the guarantee of life, property, and good name against "colour of Law or countenence of Authoritie" had been inserted as protection against the discretionary power of the magistracy.[40] Symonds's use of the principle had been new because he applied it against the church and the town. By the time of the Rowley church dispute, his novel formulation of the idea had become more commonly accepted: magistracy was no longer an object of potential distrust but had become a source of protection. As Philip Nelson had said in his complaint, the magistrates were "no other then fathers in our Commonwealth." This general principle of the court as guarantor of personal liberties had been expressed in the complaint by the three selectmen. It was the magistracy to whom these people were turning for the regulation of their society and to litigation as a means of defending their property or reputations.

People also turned to the court for the enforcement of church con-

---

39. Sibley, *Harvard Graduates*, 2:267–79.

40. Farrand, *Laws and Liberties*, p. A2. On the effort to curb the magistracy through codification, see Robert E. Wall, *Massachusetts Bay*, pp. 17–22; and Edmund S. Morgan, *The Puritan Dilemma*, pp. 166–73.

tractual obligations. At Salem Village this factor played an important part in the most famous ministerial controversy in seventeenth-century Essex, that between the parish trustees (led by Thomas, Nathaniel, and John Putnam) and the Reverend George Burroughs. Many issues clouded this dispute, but in general they reveal the low state to which many clergymen had sunk by the end of that century. As has been demonstrated in other congregations, the maintenance arrangements between the parish and the minister were the basic instrument by which he was kept under its strict control. Burroughs had been forced to accept only £60 yearly after being promised £93.6s. in February 1680, but he had been willing to accept the lower amount in order to obtain the assurance of a permanent settlement.[41]

By 1683, however, Burroughs had not received that assurance, and he left the Village suddenly. To the trustees, this was a breach of his contractual obligations, and they immediately petitioned the county court to force him to adhere to those duties. To Burroughs, on the other hand, the trustees were violating the spirit of their arrangement no matter what its explicit, legal terms were. He had accepted his sixty pounds, he said, but "All is to be understood so long as I have gospel incuragement," by which he meant support of his ministry and a measure of security in his tenure. Gaining neither of these, he had expressed his dissatisfaction and the intention to resign his pulpit.

Burroughs had had to flee secretly because his efforts at informally "issueing things in peace, and parting in love" had been dashed when John and Thomas Putnam had had his body attached by *capias* after he could show no property to be attached when sued by them in two actions of debt. The details of those cases, concerning debts Burroughs owed for his wife's funeral, are well known,[42] but it is worth emphasizing that the trustees were using the court to hold a minister accountable to precise contractual terms. Of course, the Putnams were a notoriously litigious family, and Nathaniel's clever "kites-tayle" land claim against the Endecotts was another exaggerated example of the litigation that was becoming common in the county. Though exaggerated and somewhat of a caricature of the more general reality, the actions of the Putnams nonetheless serve to illustrate the contours of that reality.[43]

The difficulties that Essex ministers had with their congregations

41. These contractual arrangements are fully presented in Petition of Thomas Putnam et al. [1683], EP 39:81–82.

42. Charles W. Upham, *Salem Witchcraft*, 1:257–63. Putnam v. Burroughs [2 actions, 1683], EP 39:104–5.

43. This dispute followed a similar one there between the trustees and Joseph Bailey, which Sibley discusses and calls "the best picture anywhere to be found of a first-rate parish controversy of the olden times" (*Harvard Graduates*, 2:291–99).

aggravated their relations with nonmembers, too, for financial insecurity drove many ministers into the general competition for economic advancement. John Rogers and John Ward, for example, supplemented their incomes with the fees from medical practice, while Jeremiah Shepard and Edward Payson augmented theirs by teaching school.[44] John Emerson became quite an entrepreneur by putting to use the lessons he had learned as a baker's son. He plunged into milling enterprises and became the owner of three of Gloucester's largest mills. He also expanded the real estate holdings he inherited and was able to present his daughter with a handsome dowry of one hundred pounds.[45] Others turned to the business of investing their modest earnings in land. But in doing so they paid a high price in diminished prestige. When a pastor was also a competitor for scarce and valuable land resources, he no longer stood quite so high in one's estimation and became a potential target of resentment and jealousy. One Salem communicant, for instance, felt impelled to swear out a warrant for the arrest of Gilbert Tapley in 1678 when the latter suggested slanderously that his pastor harbored unscrupulous designs on a parcel of land in Salem.[46]

Many other Essex ministers dabbled in real estate speculation and that, together with their other money-making efforts, caused them sometimes to be accused of hypocrisy or avarice. John Higginson, called an "oppressor of the poor" by two Quakers, was also accused of lying about the amount of country pay he had received in 1674.[47] In Lynn it was said that one constable deliberately collected more rates than had been assessed in order to "steale enough to maintain Joseph Whiting."[48] It is thus not difficult to understand why, in this general context, an Ipswich man laughed in church one Sunday when William Hubbard preached that "the good a christian desired ded not lie in lands and great farmes but in the lit and countinance of gods favioure."[49]

The ministers of course used the court to defend their reputations, but once they had compromised with worldliness, nonpastoral enter-

---

44. Sibley, *Harvard Graduates*, 1:166–67; 2:272, 514–15. Frederick Lewis Weis, *The Colonial Clergy and the Colonial Churches of New England*, p. 214. John Woodbridge, who had preached at Andover and Newbury, abandoned the ministry for a career in politics, and in 1682 he wrote a pamphlet on the economic benefits of a bank. See his *Severals Relating to a Fund*.

45. Sibley, *Harvard Graduates*, 1:485–86.

46. Warrant for Gilbert Tapley [1678], EP 30:83. See also the dispute over land held by Antipas Newman in Wenham, in Newman v. Read [1677], EP 26:44–48.

47. Warrant for Thomas Vealey and Charles Hill [1678], EP 30:83. Complaint against Guppy [1674], SaMbk. 1667–79, June term #46, #64.

48. Complaint against Hannah Diven [1681], EP 36:8–9.

49. Presentment of Thomas Baker [1678], EP 28:52. Hubbard was to take sides as a witness in a land cause in 1692. Knight v. Knight, EP 52:6.

prises, and litigation, they discovered that they became vulnerable in court, too. Thomas Gilbert of Topsfield learned this lesson painfully in 1670, when seven members of his congregation presented him for being "overtaken with drink." They told the court—and all the spectators present—how during a service he had repeated himself several times, lisped, and lost his place before angrily running out of the meetinghouse without giving a final benediction. The description of his behavior at dinner after the sacrament was still more embarrassing. Gilbert, one woman testified, took a healthy draft of wine "and emedatly upon this I did see Mr Gilbert['s] eyes groe very dim and he did sinke doune in his chare Lening bake and after he had sat a while hee tooke his psalme books to sing . . . after the same maner as hee did in the pulpit Clepping his words very short so as I could not understand him. As soon as dener was done," she concluded, "my sister Perkins and I went to tother rome and presantly we hard him vomit." Gilbert and several friends maintained that he suffered from a chronic "distemper," but any authority he possessed in Topsfield was shattered. His sermon against the legal harassment of ministers only caused his opponents to bring him to court again, and he was soon discharged.[50]

The appearance of ministers in court was both symptom and cause of their loss of influence. Lacking other means of disciplining affronts to their dignity and authority, members of the Essex clergy had to sue at law. John Hale was forced to present three women of Beverly for wreaking "revengeful" mischief on his cattle and for killing a cow in 1679, for example.[51] The courts, however, were a dubious ally of the clergy and might be used just as effectively against them. When Samuel Phillips, who had had a very unhappy encounter in court in 1677, referred to judges in a fit of temper as "tormenters" who possessed the power of "the swords poynt," he was giving grudging acknowledgment to the replacement of one instrument of social control by another after half a century's exposure to conditions in the New World.[52]

While some ministers such as Gilbert were bemoaning that fact, others were learning to accept it and were even giving it their explicit support. They did so because of their growing recognition that the godly commonwealth had to be a peaceable commonwealth and that "the gift of Christ's peace" often required defending through litigation. To John

50. Complaints against Thomas Gilbert [1670], EP 15:129, and [1671], EP 17: 45–46.
51. Presentment of Elizabeth Johnson [1679], EP 31:7, and SaMbk. 1667–79, Apr. term #51. See also Complaint against Samuel Weed, *Dalton Records*, 6:428; and Complaint against John Pearce [1680], EP 31:112.
52. Complaint against Samuel Phillips [1679], EP 31:19.

Higginson, minister at Salem, both spiritual and secular legacies had to be defended. "You must do as those that have a rich Legacy bequeathed to them," he counseled; "if they meet with any difficulty they put their case in Suit, they sue for their own at court."[53]

Many laymen were also giving ample evidence of the importance with which they regarded their laws and the right to sue in court to defend them. Essexmen still made reference to the Bible in their petitions and depositions, but they made increasingly frequent reference to the colony's code of law and the principles articulated there. The most commonly cited point was the protection against loss of life, property, or reputation from "colour of Law or countenance of Authoritie." This guarantee, which was a preamble to the *Body of Liberties*, to the *Laws and Liberties*, and to the revised codes of 1660 and 1672, was to assure "the free fruition of such Liberties, Immunities, Priviledges, as Humanity, Civillity and Christianity call for, as due to every Man in his Place and Proportion, without Impeachment and Infringement . . . [which are] the Tranquility and Stability of Churches and Common-wealth." Cited simply as "Pagge the first"—from its location in those codes—this statement was a way of invoking the general prescriptive rights accumulated in the course of the colony's development, as well as liberties associated in their minds with the Civil War struggle against the Stuarts.[54]

Yet explicit insistence that "every Free subject have liberty to pet[ition]" was not the only way in which the central role of the law was being demonstrated.[55] In literally dozens of cases, people in Essex were demonstrating their strong implicit preference for legal forms and procedures over those of the interdependent local community. One of the most important and frequently used methods of conflict resolution in Essex towns had been local arbitration, in which people with a disagreement chose "honest" and "indifferent" men to mediate and settle the matter. Used often and effectively in the early years of settlement, arbitration had offered a large degree of finality—not one case of failed arbitration had to be settled at the county court before 1649.[56] Yet more and more cases came to the attention of the court after that date, and between 1672 and 1692 the court had to end forty-five disputes after arbitration had been tried unsuccessfully.

The failure of arbitration was a failure of the local community, for

53. John Higginson, *Our Dying Saviour's Legacy of Peace to His Disciples in a Troublesome World*, p. 95.

54. See, for example, Putnam v. Pease [1674], IpMbk. 1666–82, Mar. term #5, #45.

55. Petition of Newbury residents [1654], EP 2:150–52.

56. Brigham v. Payne [1649], IpMbk. 1646–66, Mar. term #11. Dane v. Gould [1649], ibid., #10. Gillman v. Coffin [1649], NorMbk. 1648–78, Oct. term.

arbitration was preeminently a local matter. The parties in the dispute, as well as their chosen arbitrators, were almost invariably from the same neighborhood or town. By choosing "indifferent" men, people at that time did not intend to select arbitrators who were unfamiliar with the issue at hand; "indifferent" merely meant that someone was not financially interested in the outcome. As in the manorial or communal "juries," arbitrators were chosen because they were well acquainted with the facts of the problem, and great efforts were made to find men who were familiar with the dispute. Though each party could—and did—choose someone partial to his cause, his opponent had the right to reject that choice. Such objections were rarely raised, but routine provision was made to "choose a third man" if a deadlock ensued. Together, these three (or five, if two were chosen by each side at first) would arrive at a decision and require the opposing parties to adhere to it on penalty of forfeiting a large "bond of arbitration," sometimes amounting to several hundred pounds.[57]

The emphasis on choosing local people familiar with the dispute is illustrated in table 1. As can be seen, fifteen of the twenty towns and

TABLE 1. Unsuccessful Arbitration Attempts Resulting in Litigation at the Essex County Court, 1672–1692 (in chronological order)

Residence of Plaintiff	Residence of Defendant	Residences of Arbitrators
Lynn	Lynn	?
Salem	?	?
Rowley	Rowley	?
Lynn	Topsfield and Lynn	Salem
Marblehead	Marblehead	?
Marblehead	Marblehead	Marblehead (3)
Salem	Salem	Salem; Salem or Wenham
Lynn	Lynn	?
Ipswich	Ipswich	Topsfield (2); Ipswich
Newbury	Newbury	Newbury; Haverhill; Ipswich
Rowley	?	Rowley (3)
Newbury	Newbury	Newbury; Rowley
Beverly	Beverly	Salem
Exeter	Exeter	?
Ipswich	Newbury	Ipswich; Newbury (2)
Hampton	Hampton	York or Exeter
Marblehead	Marblehead	Marblehead; Salem (3)

57. Pickton v. Corning [1676], EP 24:128–29. Nealand v. Kemboll [1681], IpMbk. 1666–82, Sept. term #13.

TABLE 1, *continued*

Residence of Plaintiff	Residence of Defendant	Residences of Arbitrators
Salisbury	Salisbury	Salisbury
Ipswich	Ipswich	Ipswich
Salem	?	Salem (3)
Salem	Newbury	Marblehead (4)* Salem (5); Wenham; Ipswich (3); Salem or Marblehead
Ipswich	Ipswich	Ipswich (3)
Rowley	Newbury	Rowley (3)
Lynn	Ipswich	Lynn (2)**
Ipswich	Ipswich	?
Salem	Salem	Salem (2)
Ipswich	Ipswich	Ipswich (2)
Newbury	Newbury	Newbury (2)
Newbury	Newbury	Newbury; ?
Haverhill	Haverhill	?
Ipswich	Wenham	Ipswich
Newbury	Newbury	Newbury (2); Salem (ex-Newbury)
Haverhill	Haverhill	?
Lynn	Lynn	Lynn (Selectmen)
Lynn	Lynn	Lynn (2)
Ipswich	Hog Island	?
Topsfield	Ipswich	Rowley; Wenham
Lynn	Lynn	Lynn; Salem; Marblehead
Ipswich	Ipswich	Ipswich (3)
Salem	Salem	Salem (2)
Beverly	Beverly	?
Lynn	Lynn	?
Ipswich	Ipswich	?
Bradford	Boxford	?
Beverly	Beverly	?

*Over land in Marblehead.
**Over a mill in Lynn.

parishes in Essex County were faced with unsuccessful arbitration attempts that came to court. In the vast majority of cases, the arbitrators were local men or persons acquainted with the facts. In 1678, for example, a Marblehead commonage dispute was referred to four men—one from that town and three from Salem. Naming three Salemites was not an attempt to find impartial outsiders, however. Rather, because Marblehead had been set off from Salem in 1649, longtime residents of the land-granting town of Salem could be relied upon to know about the establishment of the Marblehead commonage system.[58] In another case, a dispute apparently between men of Ipswich and Topsfield (with arbitrators from the former), the Topsfield resident had become a "resident" of that town only when a border realignment between towns changed his address. He refused to accept the change and considered himself still part of the Ipswich community.[59]

Arbitration also relied on the suasion of the community for enforcement, and parties sometimes chose men in a position to exert pressure on their opponents. When Richard Kent of Newbury had a land disagreement with Richard Dole and Henry Jacques of Rowley over property in Rowley, he chose as his arbitrators men from that town and not from his own. In the first place, their opinions would carry greater weight among the Rowley community in the settlement than that of outsiders from Newbury.[60] It could also be expected, however, that they would be able to detect his opponents' noncompliance with the decision and as fellow townsmen exert pressure on them to honor the pact.[61]

Community arbitration had been an essential method of assuring stability and promoting neighborliness in Puritan Essex. Both parties shared the costs of settlement and posted bonds guaranteeing future amicability. They had to promise, as two Marblehead brothers-in-law did in 1673, "that they would live peaceably and quietly, and whoever should be the occasion of future trouble should forfeit 40 li." If either believed that the other was violating the agreement to live "peaceably," the entire matter could be reopened. Whatever the previous decision of the arbitrators, the newly aggrieved party was entitled to claim the pledged amount.[62]

This procedure was able to continue as an effective conflict resolution device in Essex, however, only as long as economic and social conditions did not overwhelm certain inherent deficiencies. Second-generation Essex residents were no less concerned with community harmony than their parents had been, but they recognized that the new realities of the

58. Devorix v. Merritt [1678], EP 28:67.
59. Nealand v. Kemboll [1681]. See also Dudley v. Gillman [1678], NorMbk. 1672–81, p. 82; and Fellowes v. Browne [1679], ibid., p. 98.
60. Dole v. Kent [1681], EP 36:42–51, with map at p. 46.
61. For example, Cross v. March [1677], EP 26:94.
62. Smith v. Rowland [1673], EP 19:146–49. In this case, Captain John Smith was told by the arbitrators to return the item in dispute to Richard Rowland, but two years later Rowland antagonized him over another issue and Smith brought suit; he did not recover the £40, but he was awarded an anchor, three pairs of sea boots, and some cloth.

late seventeenth century demanded a system more effective than arbitration. Though two men might desire sincerely to "run the line between them that they might live like Christians," they might discover that their neighbors refused to allow arbitrators even to measure the land in controversy for fear that their property, too, would be jeopardized. Once a decision was made, moreover, people wanted assurance that it would take effect promptly and continue in force. However, the refusal of a single arbitrator to accept a majority decision was sufficient to ruin a settlement, as it did in Ipswich when the other mediators finally "went away saying that they would not meddle with it any more."[63] In such situations, where "the great endeavors of friends to persuade peace proved altogether fruitless," litigation offered obvious advantages as a system of creating and maintaining order so that neighbors could "live in peace and love . . . as their relation and duty required." As never before, losing parties simply refused to accept the decisions of their neighbors. Some would merely refuse to sign the bond guaranteeing the agreement, but more commonly they rendered the community's efforts null either by refusing to submit their problem to arbitrators or by disavowing their decision.[64] By contrast, a *capias* attaching one's property or person could not be ignored; failure to appear in court produced a judgment by default and the attachment of the goods meant that satisfaction could be obtained through a writ of execution.

The availability of precise forms was another advantage of litigation, since they imposed a measure of explicit precision where arbitration, especially later in the century, was becoming less precise. In the early years of the colony, people with disagreements sought men whose formal training offered an expertise in drawing up formal agreements, whether bonds, contracts, or land conveyances. Thomas Lechford, for instance, made a living in Boston for several years by drafting such documents, many of which were arbitration bonds. To the north in Essex, there were also men educated in England who possessed this expertise. But as they died off, they were succeeded by a less skilled generation. Superficially, as well as in substance, the degeneration of skills is obvious in the records: not only did their penmanship drift from the standard forms of orthography into a barely legible scrawl, but the provisions of the agreements they drew up also drifted into imprecision. In England at this time, arbitration was becoming more standardized, and in 1647 John March wrote a treatise on the subject because "submission to Arbitrements were

63. Johnson v. Herriman [1684], EP 42:101–6. Nealand v. Kemboll [1681]; and Nealand v. Kemboll [1682], EP 38:114–18.
64. Smith v. Rowland. Foulsham v. Gillman [1676], *Dalton Records*, 6:209. On unwillingness to post bond, see Farrington v. Graves [1682], EP 37:134. On disavowal of the decision, see Clement v. March [1684], EP 41:106.

never more in use then in these times" to avoid the high costs of the royal courts.[65] On the other hand, justice was not as expensive in Massachusetts,[66] and arbitration—besides not being much of a savings in costs—developed none of the standardized rules that English arbitrators were applying.

In Lynn a brickmaker and a merchant discovered this weakness in 1679 when their arbitrators brought in a decision concerning their disagreement. Although the merchant, Matthew Farrington, won the award, he found that practical considerations made it impossible to accept on the terms provided. When he repudiated the decision the brickmaker, Henry Stacy, sued him in an action of debt.[67] Farrington's attorney, Anthony Checkley, explained that the system of arbitration was too inexact to be of any use in a debt case between businessmen. "Uncertainty is the Cause of Diferences," he told the court, and "Diferences are the matter of Arbitrants and Awards. Where diferences are not Sertainly determined their is noe award—This award is unsertaine in Severall Respects," he explained, "and leaves the parties in greater diference then they was in before the Arbitration and hath not determined any one thing that is submitted." His client was to receive bricks in satisfaction of the debt, he said, and the arbitral agreement "must Relate to the quantity and quality of the Bricks—and to the payment for the Same." However, "the Award Soe Called doeth not make Certaine how many Bricks Nor what Kind of Bricks." To a merchant it was necessary to know exactly what he might expect to receive; given the state of the award, he had little idea of what he had "won," if anything. The award said nothing as to "How much, in what Speties, and at what time." The arbitrators had specified only that "he may take the Kilne of Nine Arches, Excepting those that Henry Stacy hath already taken out and he to take no more Bricks but of them Nine Arches. Now," Checkley continued, "whether their be left five thousand, ten thousand, or one hundred thousand, or whether merchantable or Refuse by the award is uncertaine." The arbitrators also had awarded seven pounds in cash to Farrington, but as Checkley pointed out, "Againe as to the payment for the Same, [it] is altogether unsertaine. What money must the seven pounds be paid in, whether New England money or England money?"[68]

When the three arbitrators had met at the "Signe of the Anchor"

---

65. John March, *Actions for Slaunder . . . to which is added Awards or Arbitrements.* Arbitration was "well developed" and common in England; see M. J. Ingram, "Law and Disorder in Early Seventeenth-Century Wiltshire," pp. 125–26.

66. Fees were set by law; they are enumerated in *Col. Laws 1672–86*, pp. 2, 130. Generally, they amounted to 20 shillings. Though hardly inexpensive, these fees were considerably less than those in the English royal courts.

67. Stacy v. Farrington [1689], EP 48:49–51.

68. Ibid.

tavern in Lynn, they believed, as they wrote in their report, that they had made a "full and finall Determination of the said Differense According to our best Understanding and Judgment." Unfortunately, their "best Understanding and Judgment" were unequal to the task before them. As Checkley said repeatedly in his argument, "the parties [are] in greater diferenses then was before." In general, arbitration as it was practiced in Essex no longer could "Answer the End, viz, to deside diference; but on the contrary it makes diference."[69]

The problem here, as in many other instances of failed arbitration, was inexactness, a difficulty that could sometimes cause humorous evasions of the intent of the effort. When arbitrators decided that a Newbury feltmaker should confess his error in saying that a local cooper had told a hundred lies, the feltmaker apologized by saying, "I am sore [sorry] I wais so positife in the sorten number that I charget him with." The loophole was closed when the cooper sued him for defamation.[70]

In sharp contrast to the uncertainty and imprecision inherent in arbitration, the writ system offered many advantages to a less than highly skilled population. The legal forms used at the Essex court were not always the proper ones, strictly speaking—men sued in "trespass upon the case" when they should have used trespass, or they sued over the forfeiture of arbitration bonds in actions of case when debt was appropriate.[71] But the writs they used, although they contained none of the formulary allegations of proper English writs, nonetheless embodied certain required steps that directed the procedures taken. A writ of attachment was based on the amount of damages alleged and thus told the constable (to whom it was directed in Essex) how much property to attach. In his declaration the plaintiff had to describe the precise nature of the damages alleged. Defendants then had to submit written answers, which often included depositions taken from witnesses in their support. The court did not follow the rules of common law pleading that distinguished between general and special pleading and thus governed the type of evidence that could be put in,[72] but the requirement for written evidence provided some control over the proceedings. Moreover, the giving of a written deposition tended to elicit more precise descriptions of the

69. Ibid. In his concluding argument, Checkley cited "March his tretice of arbitram[en]ts." Jury found for the defendant and awarded him costs of court.

70. Merrick v. Atkinson [1683], EP 39:50.

71. Nealand v. Kemboll [1681], for using case in a bond forfeiture. On the use of case against an official, rather than trespass as was standard in England, see Howe's description of Giddings v. Browne in *Readings in American Legal History*, p. 232.

72. Double pleading, as this was known, became common again only at the end of the eighteenth century and was confirmed by statute in 1836 with "An Act to Abolish Special Pleading in Civil Actions," *Massachusetts Laws*, 1836, c. 273.

facts. The court's judgments were usually worded much more precisely than an arbitration award, and the writ of execution was a carefully drawn order to the marshal giving him precise directions on what to seize.

The supplanting of arbitration by litigation was a tribute to the important social function of the county legal system as a uniform and unitary source of authority in Massachusetts. In contrast to the parallel English situation, this fact was a novel characteristic of colonial law. In England, the court to which an aggrieved party looked for satisfaction was not always easy to identify. Although it was a fairly straightforward question, for example, between King's Bench, Common Pleas, and Exchequer, it was not so simple on the local level, where a man's status or residence often created overlapping jurisdictions. This problem, in fact, was a major reason that arbitration was such a common practice in late medieval Europe. The unitary Massachusetts county court system, however, stood in plain contrast to the English system of local justice.[73]

This relative simplicity enabled the Massachusetts courts to make a powerful contribution to social stability. Not only did they offer a degree of certainty and a competence far exceeding local conflict resolution procedures, but they also served as a reliable and publicly accessible repository for all settlements. Arbitration agreements were customarily decided in private and recorded on only one sheet of paper, a practice that led to further conflict when someone "unjustly carried away a Bond of arbitration with an Award annexed thereunto."[74] The court, by contrast, announced its judgment publicly and then "let the origenall remaine wher it is customary for all writengs that have beene used in courts untill this day." The terms of the judgment, people knew, were a "declaration to the world and future ages."[75]

Social factors, too, undermined the effectiveness and legitimacy of arbitration, for it was a procedure presupposing membership in a community. A man submitting to it needed acquaintances to appear for him, and the community needed persons whose pressures would be respected by the parties to assure their adherence to the agreement. However,

73. Marc Bloch, *Feudal Society*, 2:359. Mark DeWolfe Howe poses a revealing question to be asked of a litigant in any society: "Under what law are you living?" Because sensitive imperial and political considerations would have made any Bay Colony resident wary of such a question, perhaps a better one would have been "Under what courts are you living?" In comparison to his English counterpart, a litigant would have answered with simple brevity. Howe poses his question and discusses the varied English background in "The Sources of Law in Colonial Massachusetts."

74. Hathorne v. Ingols [1691], EP 50:100. See also Browne v. Hichin [1685], IpMbk. 1686–92, Mar. term #4, and, in review, Sept. term #8.

75. Browne v. Hichin. Petition of Nathaniel and Thomas Wade [1684], EP 41: 51–61.

nonresidents or people otherwise "outside" the community sometimes discovered difficulties in the system. Familiarity with the facts and partiality to one's position were valued and necessary qualities in the procedure, but outsiders were not always able to find men with those qualities to take their position in an arbitration. For example, John Griffin of Bradford forced his neighbor Robert Hasseltine to sue him in 1674 when Griffin could find no one in the town to support his position. In dispute was the sufficiency of Hasseltine's fences, and several persons had been asked to appraise the damage done by Griffin's hogs to Hasseltine's crops. Their decision was to allow the latter's demand for damages, but Griffin objected that all of the "prizers" were related to Hasseltine. Moreover, Griffin could obtain no objective decision from Bradford town officials: one fence-viewer was Hasseltine's son-in-law and the other was his nephew. Griffin, an outsider to this closed network of local association, was asking the court to intervene and protect rights he believed were jeopardized by biased town procedures.[76]

Griffin's plight was shared by men in other Essex towns; just as the Salem resident who explained that "he had no friend in Salem but the honored Court," Griffin had discovered that rights were no longer implicitly understood or adequately guaranteed by local institutions and community pressures.[77] Instead, they had to be explicitly demanded, litigiously defended, and judicially protected. John Whittier of Haverhill aptly summed up this new attitude of personal responsibility in 1684 when rejecting an offer of arbitration. Defending his refusal to submit to community mediation, he told his neighbors, "Evory man must mind [i.e., attend to] his oune busnis."[78]

76. Griffin v. Hasseltine [1674], EP 21:2–6 (on appeal from a magistrate sitting out of sessions). For Haverhill, see Johnson v. Herriman [1684], 42:101–6.
77. Presentment of Edmond Bridges [1678], EP 30:21, 35, 96.
78. Whittier v. Swan [1684], IpMbk. 1682–92, Mar. term #21.

5 The Court and the Community

Law in a Postrevolutionary Puritan Society

Many persons in Essex continued to use arbitration, and doubtless many of them found it adequate to their needs. So, too, did many attempt to continue the Puritan tradition of neighborly watchfulness and regulation of personal behavior, for it, too, was a legacy of the small, interdependent community. But Puritan meddling in the affairs of others might also generate tensions, and it was not unusual for people to leave their nucleated villages and migrate to outlying areas to escape these problems. Historians generally have interpreted the scattering of settlements as an economic impulse (to cultivate larger farms) or as an attempt to duplicate the patterns of closed-field agriculture.[1] These were certainly the major reasons behind the mobility, but the desire to escape the watchfulness and exacerbated tensions of the small Puritan community must be considered, too. Such irritating situations prompted one man in Gloucester to announce in 1656 "that if his wife was of his mind he would set his house on fire and run away by the light, and the Devil should take the farm; and that he would live no longer among such a company of hell hounds." Another man, living in Salem, finally decided after much contention with his neighbors "to Remove, Sell his house, and build further for the injoyment of peace."[2] But removal was not always possible, especially as land became more scarce, and litigation came to serve the same end. Going to court—whether as complainant in a criminal proceeding or as plaintiff in a civil action—not only restrained emotions; it also helped to establish standards of behavior by defining what was acceptable behavior in the intimate, densely populated community where close and repeated contact caused many problems among neighbors. Through the court, people in Essex actually redefined and attached new

---

1. William Bradford was the first historian to equate "scattering" with the "weakening" of society in New England when he lamented in 1632 that families were leaving behind the stability and enforced discipline of nucleated village life in order to cultivate larger, isolated farm lots (*Of Plymouth Plantation, 1620–1647*, p. 253).

2. Presentment of Row [1656], EMbk. 1655–66, June term #42. Maule v. Derby [1686], EP 46:38–41.

values to their concept of neighborliness. In doing so, they made the legal system an essential part of their local communities.

The idealized town plans of the founders did not reckon with New World agricultural realities. One of the first problems they encountered was the need to increase their meager supply of livestock without delay and, accordingly, to permit cattle to wander about in order to breed as quickly as possible. While English owners were reluctant to allow their cattle to roam freely and produce inferior offspring through indiscriminate breeding, the earliest Massachusetts farmers were less concerned with the quality of their livestock than with a rapid increase in numbers. Roaming livestock, therefore, were a common and tolerated fact of village life, despite requirements that they be tended by a town herder.[3]

The new agricultural reality was soon reflected in the reversal of traditional ideas about fencing obligations. Because English agricultural practices placed more value on the close regulation of animals, a livestock owner bore a certain responsibility to keep his animals under control. As a result, English trespass law made him liable for damages in some situations; if, for example, he allowed them to stray from well-known, customary cattle paths and to trespass, he had to pay damages regardless of how carelessly his neighbor's crops were fenced.[4] This qualification disappeared in Massachusetts, where all responsibility was placed on the man tilling the soil. Farmers were ordered to fence their cornfields sufficiently to keep out cattle and swine, and no damages were recoverable if this requirement was not met.[5]

But the General Court did not specify the type of fences required and in 1633 ordered only that the "inhabitants of the towne" determine if, in their opinion, fences were "insufficient."[6] Essex townsmen discharged their responsibility by allowing a variety of fencing methods. Salem, for example, in 1637 ordered that "all our fences formerly made shalbe

3. *Col. Laws 1672–86*, p. 18. The General Court did not attempt to improve the breeding of horses by restricting their movement until 1668. *Col. Laws 1660–72*, pp. 243–44. William B. Weeden, *Economic and Social History of New England*, 1:64–66. The use of alewives as fertilizer, in addition, reduced dependency on manure and lessened the need for Essex farmers to confine their livestock to fallow plots in order to fertilize the land.

4. W. S. Holdsworth, *A History of English Law*, 3:378–79. "Contributory negligence" did not evolve at common law until the nineteenth century, and thus situations existed that qualified the common law requirement of protecting oneself and one's property. Ibid., 8:459.

5. The only exceptions to this rule were unyoked swine, swine and calves under a year old, and "unruly cattle which will not be restrained by ordinary fences" (*Mass. Rec.* 1:215; *Col. Laws 1660–72*, p. 132 [1642]). The colony's fencing laws can be found in *Mass. Rec.* 1:106, 215, 241, 333; 2:15, 39; 3:241.

6. *Mass. Rec.* 1:106. See also Max Farrand, ed., *The Laws and Liberties of Massachusetts*, p. 6 (1643, 1647).

sufficientlie repaired by the last of this first month [March], with either post and raile or bond with poles or laths on each side within a foote and a halfe of the Topp, *or some other way so sufficientlie*."[7] Despite many town bylaws in existence for the maintenance of fences, however, the General Court in 1653 was still receiving "information of many inconveniencyes and differences by meanes of deficient fences," and it had to order yet again that selectmen make and enforce "wholsom orders" on fencing.[8] Apparently, the construction of fences depended in large measure on the feelings of particular neighbors as to their need and desirability. As with formal determination of boundaries and titles, people in early Essex were sometimes very lax about enclosing their tillage land or about maintaining adequate pales once their borders were set out.

This failure to impose order in the first generation produced serious problems for the second. Town officials, no longer able to escape their responsibilities, encountered stiff resistance to their efforts. Many times their attempts to redress the lack of regulation met with open hostility, and they had to obtain support from the courts to do their jobs. As had occurred in England, constables were sometimes assaulted when trying to do their duty and found it difficult to enlist the aid of bystanders when it was needed.[9] In part, town officials were treated this way because of their low status; men of substance were rarely chosen to serve as constables and a Lynn man described them as "sorry or pittiful fellowes."[10] Additionally, some town officers were resented because of their partiality. Jeremiah Rogers of Salem, for instance, resisted a hayward's order because he believed that the official was enforcing a rule that he had never enforced against his own father-in-law.[11]

It fell to the courts, therefore, to establish standards of fencing to be followed by everyone and to determine, when necessary, that someone's "swine came in through the fence now in controversy, there being a pitiful hedge, which is no fence by law."[12] Without the courts to intervene, violence often erupted between neighbors. In Rowley in 1682, for instance, a bull belonging to Ebenezer Brown ate half a bushel of corn from the nearby Boynton planting field. Boynton saw the animal in his

7. Salem Records, *EIHC* 9:40 (emphasis added).

8. *Mass. Rec.* 3:319. Salisbury issued six orders for fence maintenance between 1643 and 1647. Salisbury Records, pp. 83, 86, 88–89, 103, 107, 115.

9. For assaults on town officials, see Presentments of Plum [1675], SaMbk. 1667–79, July term #60; Lee [1677], IpMbk. 1666–82, Mar. term #62, #63; and Welch [1678], SaMbk. 1667–79, June term #49. For refusal to assist, see Presentment of Pudeater [1677], EP 26:130.

10. Selectmen of Lynn v. Kirtland [1686], EP 46:94.

11. Rogers v. Bullock [1678], EP 30:101.

12. Perkins v. Clarke [1680], EP 32:78–81.

crops and took the bull into his barn. When Brown came to retrieve the bull, however, Goodwife Boynton stood before the barn and barred his way. Because relations always had been amicable between the Browns and the Boyntons regardless of the state of their fences, Ebenezer wanted to know why she acted so. "I must not trust anybody but old Goodman Browne," she replied. Ebenezer was enraged and retorted, "My word is as good as my fathers; I am as Good a man as my father." With Goodwife Boynton still barring the way, Brown pushed aside the ladders blocking his way and one of them fell on the woman.[13]

To avoid encounters of this sort, many people instead went directly to the court to recover damages. Walter Wright of Andover suspected trouble if he tried to settle informally the matter of damages done in his cornfield by a neighbor's horse. He therefore set the damages done by the animal at forty shillings, an amount that was the statutory minimum jurisdiction of the county court. With corn valued at only three shillings per bushel, it was unlikely that the horse had eaten that much (more than thirteen bushels). Wright's neighbor William Chandler knew this, and he contemptuously answered that the damage "was more like to be forty lyes" than forty shillings. Wright, however, wanted to settle the matter in court, where accumulated neighborhood resentments would not be allowed to erupt into violence. It was a wise but futile attempt: Chandler's retort elicited an insult from Wright, Chandler leaped and seized him, and Wright finally stabbed Chandler.[14]

Wright's desire to avoid violence was shared by many in Essex who found that "speaking in a friendly way . . . about mending [a] fence" produced only assaults or brusque, hostile replies. With town officials subject to these pressures, too, and unable to overcome them, the county court proved useful. In fact, litigation at the county court was so attractive in comparison to local settlement that people frequently bypassed their local "commissioners to end small causes" as well as their resident magistrates and brought their disputes directly to the county court where they could have a trial by a jury drawn from all over the county. From 1672 to 1684, when the legal system was disrupted by the Dominion of New England, over one hundred petty cases of bad fences—completely unrelated to questions of title—were brought to the county court by actions of trespass.[15]

The historian has no way of knowing how many neighbors contin-

13. Complaint against Ebenezer Brown [1682], EP 37:73. See also Boarman v. Perkins [1692], EP 52:126–33; and Hunt v. Perkins [1692], ibid., pp. 121–25.

14. Complaint against Walter Wright [1678], IpMbk. 1666–82. Nov. term #36. Col. Laws 1672–86, pp. 20–21.

15. Town selectmen were empowered to hear "small causes" to which magistrates were parties. Col. Laws 1672–86, pp. 20–21. For the precise powers of commissioners and magistrates out of session, see ibid., pp. 11, 27, 58, 81, 133, 154.

ued quietly to employ "friendly speaking" with success, but in the latter decades of the century the court was called upon with increasing frequency to handle such minor cases of trespassing animals or of assault by neighbors. Essex neighbors went to the county court despite the statutory requirement that many of these cases be handled by the commissioners or a resident magistrate. Occasionally, people went to the trouble of inflating the damages sought to more than forty shillings,[16] but the court routinely accepted cases that did not meet the statutory minimum and were, moreover, purely intratown matters.[17] Twenty-six of the forty-nine cases in which Salem residents were involved in 1683 did not concern people from other towns. In one of them, moreover, the plaintiff ignored the Salem session of the court and went to the Ipswich session, where Salem men were prohibited by law from sitting as jurors.[18]

Unfenced meadow and upland were not the only sources of tension in the small Essex community, for intensified social contacts increased sexual tensions. The lack of marriage partners might have been a minor contributing factor, but even in 1642 Governor Bradford bemoaned in Plymouth that there was "not only incontinency between persons unmarried, . . . but some married persons also."[19] Indeed, fornication was common in Essex, and sexual advances by married men caused no little discomfort to women there. Hannah Wooden of Wenham told the court of such an instance when Mordecai Larcum had escorted her home. Larcum kissed her and threatened to "have my maden head," but she broke away and called him "an ugly beast to talk so, [for] had he not got a wife of his owne." Larcum, however, "said twas no matter," because an unhappy marriage had prompted his advances. He told his wife that "hee would never lye with her any more" and had turned to the women in his immediate circle of acquaintance for gratification. Apparently, walking them home after local gatherings was his favorite tactic, for another woman allegedly had been approached in that manner; Larcum was said to have pulled her to the ground, and "his briches were down" before she could struggle free.[20]

16. Keazer v. Haven [1682], EP 37:38–42.
17. See, for example, Perkins v. Clarke [1680], EP 32:78–81, for six bushels of corn as damages; corn was priced at three shillings per bushel. In addition to the damages awarded, it is important to note that the court ordered Clarke to fence his land as had been agreed when he purchased it.
18. Pilgrim v. Corwin [1683], EP 40:15. On jurors, *Mass. Rec.* 1:325.
19. Edmund S. Morgan alludes to the absence of marriage partners in "The Puritans and Sex," p. 595. Bradford believed that unusually strict observation and prosecution were the major reasons for such a large number of reported offenses (*Plymouth Plantation*, pp. 316–17).
20. Complaint against Mordecai Larcum [1692], EP 52:91–97. The unhappy marriage was frequently given as an excuse for illicit sexual activity by married persons. Puritan

Promiscuity in Essex communities fit a pattern resulting from the circumstances of village life, where the close and repeated contacts of daily routines created sexual temptations and opportunities. In Ipswich, for instance, Sarah Roe was unhappy with her husband William, a mariner. When a neighbor called on Sarah one day when William was at sea, she saw another neighbor, John Leigh, in bed with her. Leigh's nearness to the Roe home had given him many occasions to visit Sarah; one witness told the court, as an example, how Sarah and John met in Leigh's meadow after Sarah had been gathering gooseberries. It was so common for them to meet in the course of their chores that it was easy to add one more activity to the routine without arousing suspicion. Moreover, the frequency of routine contact with Leigh was a source of temptation during the long periods when her husband was at sea.[21] In a maritime town, such absences were a considerable source of problems. In 1678, for example, Bethiah Gatchell was presented for bearing two children while her husband was on an extended voyage to the West Indies. As the father of the children, Bethiah named her husband's brother.[22]

Of course, women were not always responsive to sexual advances, but living and working in such proximity made them impossible to avoid and created many tensions. In Rowley in the 1670s, Margaret Tophet had no interest at all in Samuel Mighill; but Mighill was interested in her and she had no way of evading the social contacts that enabled him to annoy her. In one instance Samuel approached her while they were threshing in a barn, and in another he was so bold as to proposition her when he and his wife were visiting at the house where Margaret was a servant. It was finally necessary for her to present him to the court as a means of stopping his "lascivious behavior."[23]

In a society where persons were brought into such contact by marriage ties, close quarters,[24] or the routines of daily life,[25] intolerable

---

emphasis on marital and sexual compatibility, it may have been hoped, might excuse their behavior somewhat and lead the magistrate to impose less harsh penalties. On the ideal of marital compatibility, see Morgan, "Puritans and Sex," p. 593.

21. Presentment of John Leigh [1673], EP 19:104–6. See also Presentment of Waite [1683], IpMbk. 1682–92, Apr. term #48, for an instance of a woman's meeting her lover in a brewhouse; Presentment of Rayment [1679], SaMbk. 1667–79, June term #68, in an orchard; Presentment of James Creeke [1682], EP 37:86–89, for numerous other possibilities.

22. Complaint against Bethiah Gatchell [1678], EP 30:43.

23. Presentment of Samuel Mighill [1674], IpMbk. 1666–82, Mar. term #68.

24. The intimacy and antagonism produced by close quarters in households is one subject of John Demos, A Little Commonwealth. See also David H. Flaherty, Privacy in Colonial New England, pp. 45–84.

25. Bathing, for instance, was commonly in the nude in village streams or ponds. For the consternation this caused in Rowley, see Presentment of Mary Leonard [1674], SaMbk. 1667–79, June term #43.

tensions were created by an attempted seduction or by desires that could not be gratified. Closeness, rather than establishing a social framework to suppress or ease these tensions, therefore actually served to intensify them. In Salem Village in 1672, in fact, proximity and family ties almost prevented the solution of a very disturbing situation. The source of the problem was the behavior of John Smith, who approached the wife of Lot Killam and "offered her abuse." She rejected this sexual advance and told her husband, who spoke to Smith and warned him away from her. But the next object of Smith's desires was his own sister-in-law, Elizabeth Goodell, and the problem was not as easily resolved when *she* tried to stop his advances. To be sure, she was deeply offended by his attempts and believed that "the language John Smith used to me and the Actions were such as most tend to the way of his calling in dealing with Cattel." Smith was persistent, however. His first advance had been while working in the swamp near the Goodell house; he had asked Elizabeth for a light for his pipe and suggested that she "tarry and smoke" with him. From his manner of asking, Elizabeth knew what he meant, and she ran away from him; but it was not easy to avoid her brother-in-law. While Smith's wife was lying in after giving birth (and Smith was prevented from having sexual relations with her), he even tried to seduce Elizabeth while she was visiting the new mother.[26]

Tensions became unbearable as concern for family harmony forced Elizabeth to suppress her complaints. "What a sad life I should have had with my Husbands relations," she later explained, if the subject were broached to her husband and family resolution attempted. Elizabeth grew so filled with anger and frustration at one point that she "was like to have broken her brother [-in-law] Smith's head with the ladle" she had nearby. Moreover, neighbors were beginning to gossip about the relationship, an issue that, she said, "had come to the mouths of such talkers as have perverted the truth and made the matter appere far worse than it ever was, to my great Scandall and reproach."[27]

Whatever wishes existed for continuing the close relationship among the several households of the family, there was an even greater need for an openly asserted distance between them to remove the source of the sexual tensions and silence the harmful rumors. Social bounds—just as agricultural ones—had to be established and enforced. To that end, Elizabeth finally had to take legal action and "acquaint Major Hathorne with it." Judge Hathorne ended the problem by ordering Smith to be whipped before the Salem meeting.[28]

26. Complaints against John Smith and Elizabeth Goodell [1672], EP 18:117–20.
27. Ibid.
28. Ibid. Among the many witnesses in support of Goodell against Smith's notorious

The court served an important role in situations such as Elizabeth's, or others where "privet healing" failed. It offered wives a way of stopping their husbands' extramarital activity when their own efforts—even one woman's "breaking her husband's head with a quart pot and otherwise abusing him"—failed.[29] A single magistrate sitting out of sessions might order a man who had made unwanted advances never to go near a particular woman unless accompanied by his wife,[30] or the full court might require a man to post a heavy bond to assure his future good behavior toward a woman.[31] Additionally, the courts permitted people publicly to clear their reputations of false and harmful gossip. Proof could be demanded before magistrates, a jury, and spectators, and the court order could make a gossip confess his error and stop spreading stories.[32]

In the life of the neighborhood, then, the legal system helped ease tensions arising from proximity and intensified social contacts, and prevented them from becoming more serious problems to community harmony. But the role of the court was not only negative; that is, it did more than simply restrain people by punishing them or enjoining certain forms of unacceptable behavior. The measure of its importance in the community is suggested by the fact that it was also integrative. In that way, it made a positive contribution to local stability by facilitating an offender's reintegration into society. Indeed, the narrower the power and importance of the Congregational church in a society becoming more sectarian, the more important the function of the court system: the court's authority was not limited to professing church members, nor did it have to rely on the willingness of wayward members to present themselves before it for punishment.[33]

Public confession and penitence in church, of course, were tradi-

---

lechery was Mary Carty, whose testimony revealed another problem of proximity in the Essex community—the need to share a horse as transportation. Mary related Elizabeth's earlier complaint to her that she had had to ride the same horse home with Smith and that he "proferred to putt his hands under her Apron and with that she Jumpt from behind him and ran away so he Jumpt off from his horse and ran and caught her and putt his hands up under her cloaths into her body and said she had something in her twatt."

29. Warrant for John Davis [1680], EP 34:93.
30. Complaint against Harris [1674], SaMbk. 1667–79, June term #67.
31. Complaint against Severans [1673], NorMbk. 1672–81, p. 29. See also Complaint against Ford and Clenton [1677], EP 27:103–4.
32. Confession of John Poland [1679], IpMbk. 1666–82, Sept. term #15. Complaint against Larcum. Presentment of James Creeke. Complaints against John Davis and wife [1680], EP 37:5–9. Atkinson v. Ackerman [1686], EP 46:3–10. In this last case a man who was already convicted of a paternity charge went back to court to reopen the case. He was so unnerved by the repeated taunts of the mother and others in Newbury that he hoped to clear his reputation in a new trial.
33. Emphasizing the role of the church is Emil Oberholzer, Jr., *Delinquent Saints*.

tional Puritan methods of regaining acceptance in a group after acting contrary to its norms, and it was hoped that anyone excommunicated by a congregation would soon make a repentant confession of guilt and request readmission. In Salem at least, the ineffectiveness of this system became apparent by the 1660s. Five members were excommunicated in 1661, and it was not until 1664 that another, Samuel Archer, Sr., suffered that punishment after being convicted by the court for drunkenness and showing "no signe of repentance." Two years later Joseph Williams and John Archer were excommunicated, but neither appeared before the congregation to hear the charges or the vote and neither responded by making a quick repentance or application for readmission. The congregation apparently had higher hopes for Williams than for Archer, and it voted to give him more time. Williams took two and a half years before making an attempt at repentance in 1669, and he was readmitted "though his confession was more dry and more generall than was to be desired." His behavior was, nonetheless, becoming more typical of those who were disciplined by the Salem church, which had to record that it was willing "to accept a low degree of penitentiall confession" in such a situation. With only a single exception from that date until Rebecca Nurse and Giles Corey were excommunicated after their witchcraft convictions in 1692, the five persons excommunicated already had separated themselves from the congregation, and none of them gave any hint of a desire to be readmitted. Joseph Phipeny, for example, had stopped attending church in 1674 "upon a difference between him and Brother Henry Skerry," and two years later he was finally excommunicated after giving "very perverse answers to the Brethren that were sent from the church to him, and utterly refusing so much as to come to Church meeting." Nathaniel Peas was excommunicated in 1675 for nonattendance, while Moses Eborn and his wife, who were censured by civil authorities in 1675 for premarital fornication, simply refused to come to church for ecclesiastical discipline and were excommunicated. As the position of the church in the larger community shrank, its integrative role declined proportionately. Repudiated by many of the persons it tried to discipline, the church could do little more than it did in 1688 when Jacob Allen and his wife became Quakers. John Corwin, Samuel Gardner, and Benjamin Gerrish went to them as "Messengers" "to require them to come to the Elders and to the Church to give an Account and to return from their evil way," but the Allens "utterly refused to come to the Church." The minister, Nicholas Noyes, then went directly to "Admonish them to repent from these Scriptures," but also to no avail.[34]

34. Richard D. Pierce, ed., *Records of the First Church in Salem, Massachusetts,* *1629–1736,* pp. 100, 111, 122, 133, 134, 140, 167.

By contrast, the court at this same time was beginning to assume some of the integrative role that the church was losing: offenders accomplished their readmission to society after violating rules by bringing complaints or appearing as witnesses against someone else for offenses of which they had been convicted in the past. By making such an accusation, the offender was acknowledging that his own behavior had been deviant and that he was now accepting society's standards. The legal form of the presentment, therefore, was in some respects taking the place of the ecclesiastical form of repentance; in addition, the former offender was now plainly acting in behalf of the community and no longer against it. These accusations did not have to be directed at one's initial accuser, as was Nathaniel Leonard's charge against a woman who had accused him of lewd behavior. Persons convicted of sexual offenses, therefore, might atone by presenting any such offender to the court. For the same reason, a convicted thief might testify in court about another man suspected of stealing sheep,[35] but the process seems to have been used most often in offenses of a sexual nature. Josiah Clark, for instance, had been charged with the paternity support of Sarah Warr's child; the year after he became free of those costs he was part of a group taking exception to Sarah Roe's affair with John Leigh.[36]

While the church was losing much of its authority and influence to the legal system, the neighborly regulation of private behavior also appears to have been weakening in the second half of the seventeenth century; in fact, persons attempting to admonish neighbors often met brazen resistance to their efforts in the latter years of the century.[37] In the earlier decades it was assumed that proximity of residence facilitated neighborly watchfulness and that each person would take on the responsibility of exerting pressure on his or her neighbor to pursue a life of morality and rectitude. To be sure, many persons who were the objects of such censures resented or resisted them, and legal institutions were required to support such efforts to impose discipline. Nevertheless, collective discipline was part of the communal paradigm of Massachusetts society—to William Hubbard, recalling it in 1682, it had been viewed as "the foundation or the studs to support and conjoin the parts of a building." This view had changed by 1682, although it was a change that is

---

35. Presentment of Thomas Knowlton [1673], IpMbk. 1666–82, Mar. term #30; and Presentment against Leycros and Gregory [1673], ibid., #63.

36. Presentment of John Leigh [1673], EP 19:104–6.

37. See, for example, one woman's "continuing in bead with [her lover] and not withdrawing from him" when caught in the act and reproved by a neighbor. Presentments of Hanna Acey and Caleb Boynton [1690], EP 49:118.

hard to demonstrate because of a basic methodological problem of not knowing how well or how frequently the old system continued to work. Like arbitration, neighborly admonition was intended to keep a dispute out of court, and the only surviving evidence is those efforts that failed. Indeed, measuring the changes that overtook neighborly watchfulness is harder than measuring those that overtook arbitration. When an arbitration agreement failed, that fact was usually included in the plaintiff's declaration or in his writ seeking forfeiture of the arbitration bond. Such easily quantifiable evidence is harder to obtain for attempts at neighborly watchfulness, however. It is not unusual to find reference in the records to an unsuccessful "private meeting with others for conference and prayer," but not all cases arising from such failures contain that information. Instead, the historian has to seek data implicit in court testimony. Nevertheless, where numbers cannot be produced with any confidence that they are representative enough to afford a valid quantitative comparison between chronological periods, there is much suggestive evidence of a qualitative nature. One example of such evidence indicating the perceived advantage of legal institutions over less formal neighborhood pressures occurred in Haverhill in 1682. Fearing that her husband was going to kill her, Elizabeth Ela ran to a county magistrate, Captain Nathaniel Saltonstall, for aid. Finding that he was not at home, she ran to the home of a neighbor, William White. White, however, did not even allow her in the door, answering only, "Alass, poore woman, I am sorry for you." Elizabeth was desperate and threatened, "If you will not entertaine mee and lett mee abide in your house I will lie in the street in the snow, and if I perish, my blood be upon your head." When White suggested that she see a magistrate, she told him that that was impossible. As she related in court, "The Captaine was not at home and the Constable and Grandjuryman were so far of[f] that shee was not able to goe to them."[38]

Reluctant to act by himself, White persuaded another neighbor, Andrew Greley, to go with him to Ela to stop the man from beating his wife. White's initial reluctance had been a wise response, for Ela greeted them with a torrent of abuse and the threat that "he would get even with" White and "humble" him. To Ela, White's intervention showed him to be a "pimping knave" and a "meddling knave." "Very high in his expression," Ela told his neighbor to go home and manage his own affairs because "I knu how to order mine before you knu mee." Ela went on in his tirade against White, "I hate you. I do hope to have a time to

38. William Hubbard, *A General History of New England from the Discovery to MDCLXXX*, p. 114. Confession of Robert Swan [1685], EP 45:121. Complaint against Daniel Ela [1682], EP 37:67–68.

requite you for your kindness. Also hee said he was Lord paramount in his owne house, hee might doe or say what he would and none should controule him." Ela was correct; "in his owne house" none of his neighbors could "controule" him. The court could, however, and it fined him forty shillings when his neighbors entered their complaint against him. It is noteworthy that Elizabeth tried to obtain the aid of a magistrate first, and when the case came to court she apologized for eliciting the aid of neighbors.[39]

Other cases suggest that the authority and effectiveness of neighbors to control personal conduct had been eroded in the half century of settlement in Essex. In Newbury, for instance, William Fanning and his wife lived such a dissipated life that one neighbor confessed his inability to "Imaggin how the said Fanning can Live at that Rate as he dos." The Fannings consistently missed church and quarreled drunkenly with each other. Nevertheless, their neighbors left them alone after one attempt to calm things had proved to be a mistake: Fanning brandished an axe at his incautious critic and "did swear god dam you and called him sun of a hoer and many such ugly names." For some time after this incident, his neighbors tolerated his wild private behavior. It was only when the Fannings began to "live unquietly with thir neighbors" and to disturb *them* that direct action was again attempted. The immediate occasion was another fight between the Fannings. But this time Mrs. Fanning staggered into a neighbor's house with her throat cut, and it was decided that someone should "part them from fiting." Captain John March finally brought a complaint to the county court, but the charge was neither battery nor attempted murder. Rather, the community objected that the Fannings were now encouraging their servants, as well as the servants of others, to engage in thievery. Only at that point was it regarded as necessary—or wise—for the neighbors to intervene. Until then, his axe-wielding threats were viewed as more dangerous than his private conduct, which affected none of them.[40]

In Salem Village in 1685 the neighbors of Edward Bishop twice demonstrated how the court was needed to impose order in a community when the intervention of neighbors was being challenged. The Bishops, "against the counsel and approbation of their near neighbors," were allowing drunk and disorderly behavior at their ordinary. Bishop's children and servants were wild, and even on the Sabbath they performed "lewd and uncivil carriages to their neighbors." One neighbor told the court that he and his family "lived in danger of their lives and loss of

---

39. Complaint against Ela.
40. Complaint against William Fanning [1691], EP 50:57–59.

what they possess by Bishop's family on account of their revengeful, threatening words" when asked to be more peaceable. Giving up all hope of private suasion, the community "up at the ffarmes" got the court to revoke Bishop's liquor license. In spite of that, Bishop continued his unneighborly behavior until at last he was brought before a grand jury; for good measure and the establishment of peace, the children and servants were also summoned.[41]

The failure of effective social discipline by means of informal local pressures was another example of how the ideal of the stable, interdependent community that could regulate itself collectively was becoming less of a reality. Neighbors were growing reluctant to meddle in the affairs of others unless the peace or safety of the community was directly threatened by antisocial behavior such as Fanning's or Bishop's. The public safety of the community was thus one of the few issues that justified pressure by neighbors on one another. A man in Salisbury, for example, was taken to task by his neighbors for leaving his house too soon after suffering from smallpox. His potentially infectious state justified their actions, and the court admonished him for his angry retort to them.[42]

Both the court and the general public appear to have made the same distinction between the public and private consequences of behavior when dealing with sexual offenses, too. Evidence submitted in prosecutions of sexual transgressions virtually never contained information gained by prying or intentional snooping. In only 2 of the 534 prosecutions between 1672 and 1692 was such evidence given. In one, an employee was intentionally spying on his employer with the ulterior motive of discrediting him in order to force the revocation of the man's liquor license so that *he* could assume it.[43] In the other case, the defendant was able to present a witness for "heaving the door off the hinge of the [defendant's] dwelling house . . . at about ten or eleven of the clock at night" in order to catch him in the act.[44]

File papers that do exist for the other cases reveal that sexual offenses came to official attention mainly for two reasons: when a woman complained about a man's "lewd behavior" toward her or when an

41. Presentments of Edward Bishop [1685], EP 44:116; 45:45.
42. Complaint against Jonathan Allin [1679], NorMbk. 1672–81, p. 103.
43. Complaint against Moore [1688], EP 47:123–24. Petition of John Loder [1688], EP 48:16.
44. Presentment of Clement Coldam [1673], EP 20:131. Witnessing the act of fornication appears to have been necessary to prove the offense unless a pregnancy occurred. However, Coldam could have presented the two for what was called "suspicion of uncleanness" merely on the basis of what he had seen before. His preference for the harsher charge is noteworthy in light of the disapproval shown for his actions.

illegitimate birth forced the community to take notice and demand support from the father so that they, as ratepayers, would not have to maintain the child. In cases not leading to a pregnancy, the offense was noticed only as a result of unavoidable or accidental discovery in the small community, such as an unmarried couple setting up residence together or cases of public kissing.[45]

Changes such as these reflected a major development in Puritan social thought that, after two generations, the county's clergy was articulating into a new social ideology. From their origins in Tudor England, Puritan ideas about society had emphasized order and stability, with discipline relying upon "suspicion and mutual surveillance." Whether this mutual watchfulness would be implemented by civil or congregational authority, Puritans resorted first to the "brotherly admonition" as their basic instrument of enforcing social control. The need to assure collective order was firmly grounded in theology, for the spiritually "elect" Puritan community also rested on a social covenant with God embracing all people living in their society. Puritans might inveigh against the "civil man" who had only the outward signs of inward grace, but they at least preferred his presence among them to that of the man who lived contrary to accepted standards, whom they were to pursue and correct.[46] Such active eradication of private evils was essential because the transgressions of even a few would jeopardize the status of the entire group in God's eyes. It was thus the obligation of every member to be watchful for disorder and divergence from the path of righteous behavior. "Whatever sins come within his reach," Thomas Hooker had instructed the Puritan who wished to preserve the social covenant, "he labors the removal of them, out of the familyes where he dwells, out of the plantations where he lives, out of the companies and occasions, with whom he hath occasion to meet and *meddle at any time.*"[47]

The generation that succeeded Hooker viewed the maintenance of social order very differently. At least in Essex, more frequent criticism was now directed at those who would "meddle at any time" in the private affairs of others in order to root out all forms of ungodly conduct. Quite to the contrary of Hooker, most people now believed—and their magistrates and ministers told them, too—that such intrusions served only to create more disorder.

Major General Daniel Denison of Ipswich was in a position to com-

---

45. Presentment of Nathaniel Carrill and the widow Wilson [1683], EP 40:101.

46. For a description of the "civil man," see Edmund S. Morgan, *The Puritan Family*, p. 1. On the social covenant, see Perry Miller, *The New England Mind*, 1:398–409.

47. Thomas Hooker, *The Application of Redemption*, p. 684, quoted by Morgan, *Puritan Family*, p. 6 (emphasis added).

ment on this change, and he gave it his strong approval. Denison had arrived in Massachusetts as a young man in 1631, but he did not become a judge of the Essex County court until 1651 when he succeeded to John Endecott's seat.[48] He was, therefore, as much a member of the second generation in Essex, and from this vantage point he was able to recognize the clash of new social ideals with the lingering remnants of the old in the mid-seventeenth century. Shortly before his death in 1682 he wrote *Irenicon*, a long tract whose purpose was set forth in its subtitle, *A Salve for New-Englands Sore*. Among the major causes of trouble, Denison listed the "Censoriousness" still characterizing many people, and he severely criticized this zealotry in pursuit of a godly community. "Why do we lay out our perdues, and set our Sentinels upon others, and keep no guard upon our own quarters?" he asked. In a notable allusion to the problems of neighborly relations in an agrarian society, Denison told his readers that they "complain of the ill husbandry of our own Neighbours, [with] our own Fields lying unfenced and overgrown with weeds." His counsel to the well-meaning Puritan was to refrain from meddling and brotherly watchfulness: wise men will "very hardly be drawn to make or intermeddle in a Fray," he advised, "lest they get a broken head for their pains."[49]

Denison's friend, the Reverend William Hubbard of Ipswich, made the same analysis and suggestions. He too recognized the difficulty of attempting to apply traditional neighborly admonitions in second-generation Essex. "Let men take heed how they pass rash censures upon others," he wrote in his *General History*, "lest unawares they read their own destiny in pronouncing sentence upon their neighbours." Although Reverend Hubbard had seen fewer cases of broken heads than had Judge Denison, he had seen how neighborly mediation and reprimands had caused bad feeling and counter accusations.[50] To Hubbard, Essex people would do well to heed the lesson illustrated by the downfall of Josiah, who "failed in the point of this Wisdom, about the medling with a controversie which did little or nothing concern him at that time. For he that medleth with a strife, that doth not belong unto him, as Solomon tells us, doth but hold a Dog by the ears, whom he can neither detain, nor let go without great danger to himself."[51]

Like Denison, Hubbard was describing a social ethic for a post-

---

48. Daniel Denison Slade, *Major Daniel Denison*, p. 1.
49. Daniel Denison, *Irenicon, or a Salve for New-Englands Sore*, pp. 198–99, 209–10.
50. Hubbard, *History of New England*, p. 643. Compare this position with the opinion expressed by the Salem church in 1638 over John Humfrey, in this volume, chap. 2, n. 35.
51. William Hubbard, *The Benefit of a Well-Ordered Conversation*, pp. 46–47.

revolutionary Puritan society. "Good order" always had been a Puritan goal, but it had been subordinated to the quest for a millennially pure communal society, at least in theory. To Denison and Hubbard in the latter part of the seventeenth century, "good order"—outward, civil behavior—was now of equal importance. Hubbard was speaking to a deep and widespread sentiment when he observed, "It is not the hot, fiery, curst tempers in a place, that will maintain and keep up the purity of Religion, and good order, so well as that which proceeds from men of sedate, composed, and even tempers."[52] Hubbard, too, turned to an agrarian metaphor to suggest that the best way to "keep up" a well-ordered society was by erecting adequate fences in social relationships as well as in farming situations. He warned those who objected to this system of social boundaries to "take heed lest by removing stones [they] themselves be hurt thereby, and lest a serpent bite them while they are breaking *the hedge that should secure others' liberties*." Hubbard's literary device placed the protection of liberty and social peace in the maintenance of adequate institutionalized fences within the community. Where earlier Puritans had thought of the "hedge" mainly as an external barrier shielding the purified and interdependent Puritan community from outside corruptions, Hubbard's generation was beginning to think of the "hedge" in a new, additional sense—as affording internal protection as well. "[T]o fling a stone" in brotherly criticism of a neighbor, they were coming to admit, meant the removal of a stone from a fence and constituted a dangerous social breach that an earlier generation of Puritans had, in theory at least, tolerated. No member of those earlier generations, it is likely, ever enjoyed being censured, and doubtless most of them resented it. But such intrusions into their behavior had had official support in sermons and tracts. Now, that support was gone in Essex and with it the public toleration of those who continued to make the effort.[53]

The contrasting ideals of the two generations were, moreover, explicitly acknowledged when the first generation was compared to the second. Whatever the reality had been in the 1630s, ministers of the second generation like William Stoughton correctly perceived that the ideal of the founders had been one in which "God sifted a whole Nation that he might send Choice Grain over into this wilderness"—that is, that the founders had attempted to establish a society of visible saints whose common assumptions, interests, and goals would prevail unchallenged.[54]

52. Ibid., p. 40.

53. Hubbard, *History of New England*, p. xiv (emphasis added). On the earlier concept of the hedge, see Peter N. Carroll, *Puritanism and the Wilderness*, pp. 16–25.

54. William Stoughton's famous remark appears in his *New England's True Interest*, cited by Miller, *New England Mind*, 2:135.

By contrast, the inescapable reality of the second generation made such a hope untenable, for separation of the righteous and the reprobate was no longer a realistic goal. Wave upon wave of immigration—as well as an order from Charles II—now made it impossible to persecute those of different beliefs as easily as the Quakers had been punished. Just as important, parents saw that their own children could not profess the vital conversion experiences that had been necessary for membership in an elect commonwealth.[55]

Saint and sinner now had to live in the same society. "Alas," wrote Cotton Mather, "they live near together; they live close by one another; they live in the same *Neighbourhood*."[56] Mather, who made this observation in 1720 in a eulogy to the Reverend Joseph Gerrish of Wenham, described how even in that small hinterland village the interconnections and complexities of society required a new social ethic. Gerrish had been minister at Wenham since 1675; the town "under his Conduct became above thrice as Big, as he found it, at his first coming to them." With that increase of population came a spiritually diverse community including both "the children of God" and the "children of the Devil." While Mather knew that "there shall be a Separation made between them in Another World," he observed, "In this [world] they might be intermixed with one another. The Wheat must have the Tares growing in it, until the Harvest, which is to be at the End of the World." Mather's eulogy praised Gerrish for achieving a "well ordered" society with a diverse populace between 1675 and 1720; describing Gerrish and Wenham, Mather virtually equated the good Puritan with the good neighbor. "If you will be righteous," Mather instructed, "then think, 'Who are my Neighbours?' And think, 'What shall I do for my Neighbours?' If you would be Excellent Christians, prove it by being Excellent Neighbours."[57]

The "civil man," once the object of harsh denunciation in the first generation, had become an acceptable—even laudable—member of the second and third. In his place as an object of resentment and a source of tension was the censorious meddler who pried into the private affairs of neighbors in order to ferret out deviance. Many who objected to this type of intrusion believed, as did Daniel Ela, that in their own homes they were not disrupting the peace of the community. Even if the intruder was a town official, in fact, Essex aversion to meddling had grown so great

55. David D. Hall, *The Faithful Shepherd*, pp. 199–202. On the specific question of the relative "decline" of piety, see Robert G. Pope, "New England versus the New England Mind," pp. 95–108.

56. Cotton Mather, *Detur Dignori*, p. 2.

57. Ibid., pp. 2, 10, 24–26. For more information on Gerrish, see John Langdon Sibley, *Biographical Sketches of Graduates of Harvard University in Cambridge, Massachusetts*, 2:299–304.

that he might become a target of violence or be taken to court for his "vexing" intrusions. Robert Sweet and Thomas Weymouth learned this painfully in 1682. As watchmen one night they told John Gatchell and his two sons to put out their lights and go to bed, but they were assaulted for their efforts. According to one son, the Gatchells were merely "talk-ing in our own house and wee allwayes spake Loude because my father Is harde of heareing." They defended their action on the grounds that the intrusion was unwarranted—that it was, in effect, social trespass. Before hitting the watchmen, Joseph Gatchell had asked them to leave and confine their efforts to their proper sphere: "You may goe aboute your busnes Into the Kings high way."[58]

The presentment of town scolds betokened this new attitude toward neighborly admonitions and surveillance. Nathan Webster of Bradford was abrasively active in bringing accusations to the grand jury for the petty transgressions of his neighbors, but in 1682 he found the situation reversed when they took him to court. The actual charge was the killing of a tame deer, but his neighbors admitted that they were only taking revenge on him for meddling in their private lives. "He disgrast us openly in the face of the cuntry," John Tenney confessed, "and we cannot beare to be disgraced by him, but what we doe, we doe to humble him." Webster, for instance, had presented "benjamin kimball for cursing and would not put it up [i.e., drop the matter]" when asked to do so. Al-though the courts were the forum for his activities, Webster's zealous enforcement of his own outdated conception of the social order was so disruptive that he was creating more community disharmony than he thought he was halting. As Tenney so accurately remarked, the issue had become one in which "the plaister be as bigg as the sore."[59]

In the years after midcentury the leaders of the Bay Colony worked to impose order upon a society in the process of becoming mature. Par-ticularly after the crisis of King Philip's War, laws were issued from the General Court to strengthen existing legislation and to regulate matters that never before had required its attention. Panicked by a war that it re-garded as a visitation of God's disfavor on a sinful society, the legislature even revived the ancient post of tithingman to enforce its new laws among "the Ten Families of their Neighbours" and "diligently to inspect the manner of all disorderly persons."[60] But the impact of such hasty—

58. Complaint against Joseph Gatchell [1682], EP 38:75–76.
59. Presentment of Nathan Webster [1682], EP 37:101–5. In Salem Phillip Crom-well suffered a like fate for presenting drunkenness at the county court. See Presentment of Joy [1673], EP 20:78; and Presentment of Phillip Cromwell [1678], EP 29:55.
60. On the "Provoking Evils" that resulted in statutory action, see Col. Laws 1672–86, pp. 233, 249–50, 294, 305, 342.

and backward-looking—statutes was minimal and ephemeral. Of greater fundamental and long-term significance were those actions of private individuals to regulate their own local communities and to redefine their relationships with one another. Basic questions about community life were confronted and answered. Through the complaints people brought to court and through the standards that juries and judges applied, a new concept of the "well-ordered" society emerged, but only slowly, as judgments in hundreds of cases sketched in the contours of acceptable behavior. Having been molded over time, however, the final product had a firm grounding, socially as well as legally.

6 Challenges to the Law

The Conflict of Legal
and Extralegal Methods of Social Control

The Reverend William Hubbard was able to view the evolution of law, religion, and society from an unusually well-balanced perspective. His education at Harvard College, where he was a member of its first graduating class, included aspects of secular law as well as divine law. But it was in his personal experience that law and religion were especially commingled. In 1638 his father (also named William) was elected an associate judge of the Ipswich court, and in 1658 the younger William accepted a call to be minister of the Ipswich church; for four years father and son served as magistrate and minister for their town. Judge Hubbard moved to Boston in 1662, but his experiences had demonstrated to Reverend Hubbard the importance of the legal system in bringing order to Essex society.[1]

As a minister, the younger William Hubbard was not unaware that many people nevertheless regarded the legal system as unchristian. He perceived that abuses of the legal system by some of the more litigious men in the county—including members of the Wainwright family of Ipswich—had produced among others a resentment of courts, lawyers, and magistrates. Many men, these critics felt, were putting the system to uses that ran contrary to the accepted principle that "where Order prevails, Beauty shines forth." Hubbard, like others who emphasized the ordering function of law in Massachusetts society, compared the legal system to the necessary fences or walls that regulated community life. However, he also cautioned moderation in its application when he discussed the magistrate's role in a 1676 tract dedicated to Governor John Leverett: "*Duro con duro non sat bon muro*, say the Italians; *a firm wall will not be made up of hard stones*, without the mixture of some more yielding matter to cement them together." Those who pushed the law to "hard" extremes, he perceived, were repudiating the "Christian charity"

---

1. Frederick Lewis Weis, *The Colonial Clergy and the Colonial Churches of New England*, pp. 112–13. John Langdon Sibley, *Biographical Sketches of Graduates of Harvard University in Cambridge, Massachusetts*, 1:54–62.

that must not be ignored in any society. Excessively aggressive litigiousness was part of "that spirit of Covetousness and inordinate love of the world" that "makes them able to devour widdows houses, yet never say it is enough. They that first came hither for Gospel could not well tell what to doe with more Land then a small number of acres," Hubbard observed, "yet now men more easily swallow down so many hundreds and are not satisfied." By seeking to revive dormant claims and gain land through litigation, for example, or by suing to recover money due upon accounts open to dispute, many in Essex were failing to recognize the need for "moderation . . . in things of a civil nature," as "many times the rigorous exaction of the strict letter of the rule of Justice, proves unjust in the issue."[2]

Such "unjust" results were socially harmful because "hard and severe" actions would many times "beget more obstinacy in their Adversaries." The "obstinacy" he had seen was a deep-rooted hostility that many of these "Adversaries" harbored toward a legal system they regarded as excessively rigid and impersonal. Hubbard understood how important it was that "the Law . . . is an heart without affection, a mind without passion, a treasurer to keep what we have, and a steward to distribute what we ought to have," but he had seen, too, how this lack of "affection" and "passion" was sometimes used as a means of exploiting others. Magistrates thus had a vital responsibility to see that the law was used "as men use to doe with the herb Bazil, which being gently stroked, yields a pleasant savour, but being pressed, sends forth an unsavoury smell." Unjust application of the law, he warned, produces disorder where it should promote order and "converts the meanes applyed for the remedy to increase the malady." Worse yet, it was producing hostility to the legal system and causing Englishmen to "turn Indians, that they might be revenged of their Brethren."[3]

The polarization against which Hubbard warned was between those who relied upon strict legal forms to regulate society and those who opposed the law as unchristian, and it overlay more fundamental polarizations in Puritan society. As a minister, Hubbard was well aware of the tension inherent in nonseparating Congregationalism. On the one hand, Congregationalism had formal rules of church government, and even the path toward final sanctification was a well-defined, step-by-step process. On the other, there existed a more radical antinomian strain emphasizing what Perry Miller has called the "infallibility of the spirit." According to Thomas Shepard's attack on that position, it would "deny use of the Law

2. William Hubbard, *The Happiness of a People in the Wisdome of their Rulers Directing*, pp. 8, 30, 58–59.
3. Ibid., pp. 30, 44, 56–58.

to any that are in Christ"—"Law" in the sense of the Decalogue as well as civil codes and church rules. To the Antinomian, the term "legal" was an opprobrious one, suggesting rigid adherence to human contrivances that obscured the way to the truth of God's will. John Cotton, for example, had objected when Anne Hutchinson piously dismissed the Christian's "daily and hearty performance of holy duties" as "a legal business." Although Hutchinson and her followers had been punished—and many banished—in 1637, the specter of antinomianism never disappeared from Essex. Later, the related heresy of Quakerism with its doctrine of the "inner light" kept many of these ideas present in the society despite the fierce measures taken by legal authorities to banish such dangerous threats to the secular and ecclesiastical orders.[4]

In the courtroom Hubbard had perceived a similar polarization. All institutions of social control inevitably arouse resentment; by their very nature they exert force that is rarely appreciated by those on whom it falls, and when that force is regarded as illegitimate it is particularly onerous. To Hubbard, as to many of those who felt the weight of that control, its unjust application was comparable to the naked piracy of the hated "Turk," the very image of evil incarnate in seventeenth-century Massachusetts. Most obviously, the "Turk" suggested ostentatious cruelty and the war against Christianity still being waged on the fringes of Europe. Another image, however, was more apparent to the Essex population, whose trade was expanding into Mediterranean waters during this period and whose property was being stolen from them by brazen Turkish pirates.[5] Hubbard, of course, had warned against excessive legalism, but he had done so partly in order to warn against provoking the opposite extreme of behavior among people who evaded all legally constituted forms of authority in the county.[6] Such people regarded litigation only as a method of self-aggrandizement and a tool of unfair advantage. To them, the court was nothing more than an oppressively technical institution that served merely to defeat informal or communal methods of regulating their communities. Anthony Crosbie of Rowley, for example, made these criticisms over the refusal of the merchant John Tod to submit their disagreement over accounts to arbitration by "men indifferently chosen." In a long letter to "Marchant Tod" about the dispute,

4. Perry Miller, *The New England Mind*, 1:74.
5. On the general image of the "Turk," see Bernard Bailyn, *Ideological Origins of the American Revolution*, p. 63n. On Essex merchants' problems with Turkish piracy, see Sidney Perley, *The History of Salem, Massachusetts*, 3:296. A royalist opponent would also refer to the New England legal systems in 1692 as arbitrary and "Turkish" (Gershom Bulkeley, *Will and Doom or the Miseries of Connecticut by and Under an Usurped and Arbitrary Power*, p. 192).
6. Hubbard, *Happiness*, pp. 57–58.

he complained of the costs of litigation and accused his adversary, "[Y]ou pretend Christianitie, but how it apeareth when no course will serve but Law I leave it. If you will not accept what I now offer, pray Consider the dishoner we have brought to god, offence to his people, distraction to ouer selves and families." With litigation inescapable, he hoped that it would be conducted at least "in a more Cristian maner by bringing the naked truth to light instead of false glosses formerlie used" in their previous legal encounter in 1667.[7]

Protests of this sort were not entirely unjustified, for abuses did occasionally threaten to betray justice. Family matters, for instance, could be decided on grounds that were technical rather than reflective of family sentiment; one's own clothing might even be attached—improperly— "under pretense of law," as one irritated defendant expressed it.[8] Such rigidities or irregularities were rare, but when they did occur resentment was aroused that litigation was "knavish" or involved the "use of any trick at law" to wrong one's neighbor. One successful plaintiff, it was charged, had "gotten an advantage because of the unjust course of Law" and was using it "with a great deale of rigor." Hardship was caused by insistence on strict formality in a lending and borrowing society, particularly because borrowers rarely requested written acknowledgment of repayment. Generally, this posed no problem—one man estimated that 90 percent of the population ignored obtaining such acknowledgment—but it occasionally did create suffering. One debtor's unhappy experience indicated the potential danger of the system: his creditor had "sued him from Corte to Corte . . . till he had undon him and made him so poore that hee brot him from selcke that he wore, that he had insted tharof nothing bout pached Clothes and Stockings [worn] out at the heels." As a result, persons might appear in court to prevent the "trouble" of a potential lawsuit. As Ephraim Severans explained in 1673, he went to court and "gave his oath to secure himself" from a threatened defamation suit. So perfunctory was this tactic of simply filing a sworn statement with the court that Severans later made "a sport and game" of it; but he was not, in fact, sued as a result.[9]

As abettors of the injustices that occurred, attorneys were logical targets of criticism. Their position always had been a dubious one in Massachusetts, and from Thomas Lechford onward they were the object of legislation to prevent their subverting the course of justice. The difficulties of transportation, however, prevented many litigants from ap-

7. Crosbie v. Tod [1667], EP 12:46. Tod v. Crosbie [1670], EP 15:88.
8. Cannon v. Hunniwell [1678], EP 30:63.
9. Petition of John Atkinson [1683], EP 37:78, 85. Affidavit of Joseph Peasly [1673], NorWbk, p. 96.

pearing personally at court and made it necessary to permit persons familiar with legal procedure to represent those who were unable to appear at Salem or Ipswich. Once the strictures and prejudices against pleading another's case were ended, litigants could choose skillful attorneys to defend their interests. In Essex there was no lack of men willing to collect a fee for appearing in court as advocate of someone else's position—regardless of its merit—but their actions did not go without challenge or protest. The Reverend Samuel Phillips, himself an unhappy victim in several actions, publicly censured a parisioner in 1679 for defending an openly blasphemous person and for entering an action against the blasphemer's accuser. In a sermon he suggested that "aturneys and advocates" were guilty of complicity in sin for defending it and taking "pleasure in evill actions of others." To Phillips the trial had been a miscarriage of justice, and he protested to Daniel Denison. The magistrate, however, was bound by his commission to hear all pleas and actions. Although Denison suspected that some of the statements made in the case were untrue, he confessed, "I must give men their oathes when they com to be sworn, because of my place."[10]

Opponents of law in seventeenth-century Essex had two choices: to submit to litigation under protest or to evade it by taking the law into their own hands. Many obviously accepted the former, but such was the depth of conviction and emotion among others that submission was impossible and they employed a variety of extralegal countermeasures to enforce their own contrary set of beliefs. These forms of behavior were antithetical to the new social ideology emerging in the county, and when such actions were employed against law or legal institutions the confrontation might be intense enough to provoke excesses from both sides. While those using the court might attach the person of a debtor and then allow him to languish in gaol until he satisfied an obligation, their opponents might, in Hubbard's words, "turn Indians, that they might be revenged of their Brethren"; that is, opponents of law and legal institutions were not reluctant to commit clandestine acts of violence against a rival's property or to threaten him with bodily harm, even through malefic magic.[11]

The justification for extralegal activity was a traditional Puritan

10. Complaint against Samuel Phillips [1679], EP 31:19. For one instance of a lawyer's being criticized for taking a position he knew to be wrong, see Knight v. Leach [1680], EP 33:125–40.

11. See, for example, one man's success at intimidating another and for a time preventing his court testimony by instilling the fear that his mill dam and fences would be destroyed (Complaint against Sarah Bowd [1683], EP 40:58–60). See also Complaints against John Collier [1684], EP 42:23, 27–41; and Presentment of John Roberts [1673], EP 19:106.

argument; indeed, some of the protests had an explicitly religious—often chiliastic—tone. Jeremiah Watts, a Salem Village potter, wrote to his minister that the effort of establishing the Village could not be "accomplisht in A way of god when brother is against brother and neighbours against neighbours all quarrelling and smitting one another." Watts blamed the courts for encouraging conflict. "Will a Righous and holy god owne contention and strife?" he asked. Answering his own question, he took a strong antinomian position. "[W]e need not to chuse magistrats to Rull." Instead, he offered that all problems be solved "by setting forward private Christian meetting amongst us that we may come together for to know one anothers sperits."[12]

Watts was admonished for his remarks, but others were equally firm and expressive in their assertion that conscience took precedence over the findings and orders of the court. Robert Swan of Haverhill epitomized this attitude when he spoke at town meeting "in a tumultuous and seditious maner, openly opposing them that pleaded for the Law of the Country to be observed and abetting them that did oppose and act contrary to the Law." Swan did not deny saying that "men were led about by the Lawes like a Company of Puppy-dogs," but he insisted that "at present I am not yet convicted in my own conscience of anything criminal."[13] When threatened with court action, men such as Swan could retaliate with threats of their own to forestall it. Swan in particular was a master of extralegal tactics, and when he became involved in a dispute with the litigious Wainwright brothers their clash was so bitter that one observer remarked, "Ay, the Devill and the Turk are at war together."[14] The Wainwrights, who were merchants doing business in Haverhill and Ipswich, had sued Swan several times for money due on obligations that the farmer believed unjustifiable. To Swan, the two merchants "were a Couple of Cheating Knaves, that they had used him in nothing but vexatious Suits and had recovered Judgment against him, when and in which actions he owed them nothing, and as for Simon Wainwright he said he was a Rogue, and like Ahab Coveting Naboth's vineyard, and said I owed him money upon book, the which I tendered him, and he would not receive, but he seekes to ruine me, for he would have my living." Swan, in fact, was so suspicious of the legal system that he accused a magistrate of complicity. "Carrett-head," he claimed, referring to the

12. Complaint against Jeremiah Watts [1682], EP 37:97. Watts also attacked "pulpit preaching" and demanded the right of every person to "witness against Antichrist." He asserted, "I am singled out alone to give my testimony for Christ discovering Antichrists marks," and he predicted that the existing courts and churches "will not stand before a Just and holy god."

13. Complaint against Robert Swan [1686], EP 45:121–24.

14. Wainwright v. Swan [1690], EP 48:88–99.

red-haired Nathaniel Saltonstall, did "uphold him [Wainwright] in all his roguery." Swan's allusion to Ahab and Naboth was to an episode in the Bible where the courts were employed to deprive a man of his land. Ahab, by scheming to acquire a tract of land adjacent to his palace, was doing something that many litigious farmers in Essex (such as Nathaniel Putnam in Salem) were attempting. This high-handed use of the legal system to accomplish an unjust goal seemed to Swan to be just what the Wainwrights were now trying to do against him.[15]

In fear of losing his estate, Swan turned to a method that he had employed before with considerable success—the threat and performance of malicious mischief. Without speaking directly to Wainwright, Swan let it be known to others in the community "that he and his would be revenge[d] of Simon Wainwright for his suing of him to Salem Court, which he called Roguery." Swan, related a witness, had told him that "it was great injustice that the Court had at Salem done him in . . . but yet replyed and said it over and over, that he would find out a way to be revengeful of said Simon." Swan's malicious mischief was a matter of notoriety in Haverhill. In the past he had "spoiled" the livestock of several of his neighbors and had gained possession of some adjacent land when he "had routed and hunted two [claimants] off of itt." By making and carrying out threats of property destruction, he had been able to force two neighbors to move and to accede to his claim to the land. "[N]o man that should live there should Keep any Creatures," another witness recalled Swan as boasting, "for he would kill them." For good measure, he also had destroyed a load of hay by throwing off its cover and allowing it to get soaked by a rainstorm. Swan, however, outdid himself for Wainwright. Besides threatening the man's servants and killing his sheep and a horse, Swan and his sons tore down Wainwright's fences. They then turned to the merchant's large orchard. With the help of his two sons and a third boy, Swan pulled down 146 apple trees. Responding swiftly, Wainwright entered a complaint with Saltonstall against Swan, "a person not unlikely to doe such villanous acts, he being accustomed to the same."[16]

Swan's violent actions contrasted sharply with the legal actions employed by the Wainwrights. Although Swan's tactics were particularly extensive in scope, they were the usual course of action taken by opponents of the legal system in the county. Their malicious mischief was not

15. Ibid. For Ahab's denunciation by the prophet Elijah and his punishment by God, see 1 Kings 21. R. H. Tawney, *The Agrarian Problem in the Sixteenth Century*, p. 148, alludes to Ahab as "the father of enclosers."

16. Wainwright v. Swan. This was not the only episode in which a litigious Wainwright suffered malicious revenge. See also the reference in Dennis v. Brown [1691], EP 50:107.

an irrational, sudden outburst born of frustration and rage, but part of a calculated strategy of veiled threat, secret violence, and adamant refusal to confess. Feeling no contrition for actions that they believed justified, mischief makers might stand silent and deny all connection with the crime. William Beale, for instance, was confronted by his neighbors and simply refused to acknowledge their presence. Asked sarcastically if he was hard of hearing, Beale answered, "I dont heare. I am deafe." In this manner he successfully evaded the question they were asking him. They were forced, as a result, to take him to court and present him for the only thing they could prove—telling the willful lie that he was deaf.[17]

The prospect of mayhem or violence was thus a source of no little fear among all but the most powerful officeholders in the county. The magistracy, which had broad discretionary powers available to it for summary retaliation, appears to have been unthreatened by extralegal mischief; but it was not unusual for virtually any other type of person planning to take legal action at a future quarterly term of the court to fear that "it should not be long before his house should be burned or his cattle knocked in the head" to persuade him not to obtain a writ. "Marchant Tod," for instance, told the court that his opponents in a civil dispute "were constantly plotting at the ordinary as is well known to many in Rowley, so that he had to secure the services of [attorney] Goodman Pickard" to bring Crosbie before the court and make him post bond for his future good behavior.[18] For people like Tod, the Essex county court was a vital source of protection and the legal system a means of combating the threat of mayhem. The law allowed them to strike back at mischief makers, in fact, in a way that confirmed their opponents' claims about unfair legal practices—the making of excessively harsh or even phony criminal complaints to the court. Perhaps the most extreme—and certainly the most bizarre—example of the false or vexatious charge was made in 1686 by Sara Ackerman after John Atkinson pushed and shoved her. To retaliate, she claimed that she had been pregnant when Atkinson pushed her and that he had caused her pregnancy spontaneously to abort. To prove this, she took an emetic and then beat herself in the stomach; after vomiting she showed her neighbors a sheep fetus that she said was her own miscarried child. Fortunately, one of the neighbors told the court of her ploy, and Atkinson, though brought to trial, was acquitted.[19]

The gap continually widened throughout the seventeenth century.

17. Presentment of William Beale [1677], EP 26:138.
18. Complaint against Cross et al. [1668], EP 13:123–31. Crosbie v. Tod [1667], EP 12:46.
19. Complaint against John Atkinson [1686], EP 46:117–21.

While the general trend was toward acceptance and diffusion of the new sense of neighborly responsibility, in many other people the new community standards and obligations produced only a hostile reaction. The need to maintain legally sufficient fences, for example, provoked among some in Essex County the vicious response of maiming trespassing animals. Rather than perform the difficult but necessary labor of fence mending to assure good neighborliness, these people would, by contrast, drive off wandering livestock with dogs.[20] While one might merely "trim" (cut the hair from) a horse to warn its owner,[21] another might drive it into a river and force it to stay there until it tired and drowned.[22] Still others simply cornered the animal and clubbed it, or shot it to death.[23] The maiming of livestock was a substitute for the well-known legal responsibilities of neighborly relations in an agrarian community; it was not merely a supplement to them, for the people who inflicted cruelty on animals were shown in court to have neglected their fences. Impounding animals was a well-known and common procedure, too, but such people also avoided that means of regulating their relationships.[24] Instead, they would make the effort of "spoiling" the livestock—sometimes going beyond that to assault its owner as well. Violence and mischief, on the one hand, and the maintenance of legally sufficient fences and the use of legal impoundment, on the other, were mutually exclusive forms of community regulation. Different types of people employed each of these forms, and the two existed uneasily together.[25]

Physical violence and vandalism, however, were not the only measures employed in the simmering disputes within Essex communities. One widely used technique was not physical but was spiritual or psychological—the threat of applying malefic magic. Invoking the devil as an ally in petty jealousies and conflicts was not uncommon, for it was merely another extralegal weapon available to those who challenged the established form of law and authority in Essex County. Cotton Mather, in fact, linked witchcraft with clandestine attacks on neighbors and masters in 1689. Like Hubbard and Denison, Mather also used the agrarian

20. For example, Perkins v. Green [1679], *Dalton Records*, 7:273.
21. Complaint against Stevens and Foster [1677], EP 26:49–50.
22. Presentment of George Jacobs, Jr. [1674], SaMbk. 1667–79, Nov. term #33.
23. Complaint against Elizabeth Johnson [1679], EP 31:7. Legg v. Bowen [1677], EP 26:79. Complaint against Lee [1689], EP 48:22–26.
24. The steps to be followed in impoundment are set forth in *Col. Laws 1672–86*, pp. 124–25.
25. For an assault on an animal's owner as well as the beast, see Complaint against Samuel Lomas [1680], EP 32:136–37. On the mutual exclusivity of these two forms of behavior (legal and extralegal) see pp. 154–57 of this volume.

metaphor of the protecting fence to describe how closely related witch-craft was to mischievous behavior: "hellish *Witches*," he wrote in his *Memorable Providences*, "are permitted to break through the *Hedge* which our *Heavenly Father* has made about them that seek Him." The en-closing hedge was symbolic of the new social order, but there were still "people among us who do *secretly* and *frequently* those things that have a sort of *Witchcraft* in them." His allusions were not obscure, for he named "*foul-mouthed* men [who] shall *wish harm* unto their Neighbors"; these were men who "hurt the *souls* of their Neighbors by the Venome of their Evil Communication" or their "slandrous Defamation."[26]

It was a sentiment shared by many in Essex who feared the clan-destine violence of recalcitrant neighbors who would call their enemies "damned toads" and threaten "that the devil would have them." Al-though the outburst of 1692 that made Salem synonymous with witch-craft in American culture was spectacular in its magnitude and tragedy, it was not the first instance in which people in Essex either used themselves or suspected their neighbors of using magical, satanic forces in their daily lives. Suspicions were common in that society, but very few practitioners —real or reputed—were prosecuted for such activity until 1692. In fact, only one Essex resident was convicted of the crime before that date: in 1680 Elizabeth Morse of Newbury was found guilty of "familiarity with the divil" and imprisoned for a year.[27] Moreover, virtually the only indications that exist for the prevalence of witchcraft belief are the refer-ences made to such beliefs in other court testimony. A long-standing dispute might come to court as a civil suit for damages suffered by defamation or an assault, but deponents would refer to witchcraft suspi-cions in their description of the backgrounds to the litigation. There is thus far more evidence of witchcraft's being suspected than there is of its prosecution. One apparent exception was the presentment of Margaret Giffards for suspicion of witchcraft in 1680. When she failed to appear in court at Salem she was ordered to be at its next session in Ipswich; her accuser appeared there, but Margaret did not, and the matter was not heard of again.[28]

Whether people made witchcraft accusations only as a way of bring-ing disgrace upon their neighbors or, in fact, out of a real fear that they were being harmed remains an open question.[29] But recent evidence

26. Cotton Mather, *Memorable Providences, Relating to Witchcraft and Possessions*, p. 54; and "A Discourse on Witchcraft," pp. 13, 24, 25.

27. *Assts. Rec.* 1:159.

28. Complaint against Margaret Giffards [1680], EP 33:111.

29. The distinction is very important, for accusations by alleged victims serve a very different function from that of a person's actually trying to use magical forces or threaten-

makes it appear likely that many persons in seventeenth-century Essex did attempt to use supernatural power to effect specific goals.[30] Whatever the actual extent to which such tactics were really tried, some believed in their effectiveness and often claimed supernatural explanations for mysterious occurrences in their rural society. Indeed, the line between suspicious physical mischief and supernatural mischief was a narrow and blurred one that meant little to contemporary Essex residents. Samuel Pippen of Ipswich, engaged in a land dispute with his neighbor, spread the rumor that he was going to destroy all the timber on the lot in question, "for he was resolved to make a devil of Benjamin Marshall." Thomas Wells of Chebacco parish was more explicit in linking magic, mischief, and opposition to the legal system when he sought to intimidate his litigious adversaries with the claim that he "can set spelles and Rases the Divell, hee affirming himselfe to be an artise." Seeing that court action was inescapable, he "did say in a threttning way that thare was somthing aworking that would tak afect." Although asked to dine with his brother (who was among those opposing him), Thomas replied, "Noe, for if I cant have your good will except I be a servant to the Devill I care not." To Thomas, "our Coartes at Ipswich was all one [with] the Inquishon howse in spayen." A corrupt institution—the magistrates "cayer not so Longue as they can feast ther fat gotes"—the legal system was to be opposed with any available tool, and he was quite proficient at threatening malefic magic against its employment. Thomas's hostility to the legal system and his threatening witchcraft were not a random combination of sentiments in Essex society. Seen together, they are noteworthy for suggesting that witchcraft was an alternative form of social control in the community, a body of forces that existed outside and opposed to the legal system.[31]

Once statements of this sort were made and personal harm was suffered, it was only a short step to believing that the Devil was actually participating. Martha and Giles Corey, it was believed, were invoking the Devil's aid when they reacted to the presentments made against them in 1678. The Coreys suffered no little annoyance from these actions, brought by their neighbors after Giles had argued over a pair of fetters for a horse and after Martha had accused a neighbor of milking the Corey cows. As Martha petitioned when brought to court for cursing and swearing, she and Giles were being presented and "unjustly molested

---

ing to do so. Nevertheless, in Essex accusations by victims were generally directed at the same type of persons who claimed to be using witchcraft. For exceptions to this, see pp. 152–53, 178–79 of this volume.

30. This point is the subject of Chadwick Hansen, *Witchcraft at Salem*.

31. Complaint against Cross et al. This phenomenon is very well described by E. E. Evans-Pritchard, *Witchcraft, Oracles, and Magic among the Azande*, pp. 107–10.

by some of our neighbors to our great damage and defamation, our case havinge ben heard and Judgment given, our innocency appearinge we ar clearly acquitted of such accusations as were unjustly layd to our charge. . . . The cause of this trouble doth originally arise out of mere prejudice." She protested that the present accusations were contrived out of issues that had ended "above a yeare since," and that only "malignant malice" had produced the present "false accusations."[32] Feeling so strongly that her neighbors were unjustly vexing her in court, in fact, she snapped at her opponents, "The divell take you." This last remark, however, was taken seriously by Mary Gloyd, the woman she had accused of milking her cows, and when the case came to court Mary had an interesting tale to tell. Shortly after Martha's outburst, Mary was, in fact, in the milking yard, and she heard the sound of horses running toward her. Unable to see any horses, Mary left the yard to investigate further but still found none. Despite a natural explanation by a neighbor—that there was always a troop of horse in the area—Mary Gloyd had believed Martha Corey's remark to be an actual threat and believed she had been menaced by spectral horses. Aware that a person in Martha's position would be prone to employ malefic magic and convinced of its effectiveness, Mary had imagined her supernatural retribution to take a form closely reflecting the issues of the dispute—the unfettered horses and the milking yard.[33] No prosecution for witchcraft ensued, but the tensions revealed by the conflict remained and would later take the form of witchcraft suspicions once again.

Witchcraft, whether actually attempted or only threatened, was widely enough believed in that it might be used against any form of generally accepted authority in the community. In his "Discourse on Witchcraft" Cotton Mather dealt with this use of witchcraft and observed, "When persons are *discontented* with their own state; when persons through discontent at their own *Poverty*, or at their *Misery*, shall alwaies murmuring and repining at the Providence of God, the *Devils* do then invite them to an Agreement."[34] The function of magic in reversing the existing structure of power and obligation served particularly well against household government, as children, servants, and disaffected wives were able to use the threat or complaint of witchcraft to alleviate harsh working conditions or to intimidate those in power. In English folk culture, elaborate rituals had existed for the purpose of temporarily easing the rigors of subordination to authority but at the same time not threatening them permanently. The old "Hock Tuesday" ceremony, for

32. Complaints against Corey [1678], EP 30:36–42.
33. Ibid. Not coincidentally, the spirits were said to have appeared when the afflicted person should have been hard at work.
34. Mather, "Discourse," p. 23.

instance, allowed women to tie up and mock their menfolk and thereby served "to reverse temporarily the inequalities existing between married men and women through the medium of conflict." Ritual "role reversals" of this sort were of declining importance in England by this time, but there continued to be a need for them in Massachusetts. However, Puritanism in Massachusetts had strengthened existing patterns of authority through the courts and church, while successfully abolishing all public folk ceremonies, including those that served important social functions. The destruction of Thomas Morton's maypole is the most famous example of this process, but it has distracted attention from the more private manifestations of folk practice that continued and could not be rooted out. The use of magic was one such practice, and because of its nonthreatening, ameliorative function its occasional discovery did not produce prosecutions, convictions, and executions.[35] Until the crisis of the Intercharter period, magic was tolerated as a harmless outlet for domestic and community tensions.

The identification of witchcraft with servile resistance has been overlooked as an important facet of witchcraft in Essex, not only in the famous episode of 1692 but also in that society in earlier years. Indeed, the most recent and insightful study of the 1692 phenomenon emphasizes the opposite—i.e., that persons living according to a "subsistence, peasant-based economy" resented and feared the "mercantile capitalism" of others in the town of Salem and that the former used witchcraft accusations against the latter as an outlet for hatred of such objectionable changes. According to that study, Cotton Mather's reference to witches as people "discontented" at their "Poverty" and "Misery" was actually a way of identifying witches as "prospering and upwardly mobile people" whose success aroused fear and envy and led to their being seen as satanists.[36] It is beyond dispute that there were connections between the accusations of 1692 and preexisting group tensions in Salem Village and Town, just as it is clear that witchcraft accusations in any society can serve to achieve an idealized social order. However, Mather's identification of witchcraft with discontent over "Poverty" and "Misery"

35. This ameliorative function has been observed in many different societies. See I. M. Lewis, "A Structural Approach to Witchcraft and Spirit Possession," pp. 293–309. Role reversals are dealt with more directly by Max Gluckman, *Custom and Conflict in Africa*, pp. 109–32. On Hock Tuesday, see Charles Phythian-Adams, "The Communal Year at Coventry, 1450–1550," pp. 57–85.

36. Paul Boyer and Stephen Nissenbaum, *Salem Possessed*, pp. 26n, 80–109. The authors, who try to make the outburst an attack on new wealth and economic trends, significantly concede that most of their examples of accused "persons of quality" were not formally charged, "much less executed" (ibid., p. 33). It is more revealing, however, to examine those who were actually tried, condemned, and executed; for it was their behavior and character that most threatened society.

may also be interpreted literally; that is, that he meant precisely what he said and that witchcraft was a tool of the poor and those in servile or subordinate positions. Such a literal reading is not only more logical; it is also supported by the specific facts obtaining in Essex at that time and by the larger context of seventeenth-century folk practice in England and America.

In Essex, Massachusetts, apprehension and suspicion about the likely practitioners of the black art appear to have closely resembled the pattern seen in Essex, England, where the needy—and especially the elderly among them—were the frequent objects of witchcraft accusations. This was so, according to a careful and perceptive study, in part because the failure of local institutions of charity and poor relief during a time of economic and social change was placing an unaccustomed strain on local communities to maintain the poor and aged. Witchcraft accusations against these groups therefore eased the guilt of no longer supporting them adequately and contributed to a new definition of neighborliness to replace that of the old mutually dependent community.[37] Such seems to have been an important element of witchcraft accusations—whether prosecuted or not—in Essex, Massachusetts, as well. In the twenty years of court activity before 1692 there are recorded forty instances of epithets referring to someone's "devilish" behavior or to him or her as, for instance, an "old devil" or "blare-eyed witch." These were recorded, generally, in actions of defamation or complaints of assault concerning the objects of such remarks, and they reveal a remarkable consistency. In only one of the forty cases—a reference to a "devilish" lying merchant— was any identification made between commerce or economic prosperity and the use of magic. The well-to-do simply had no need to use magic, as it served no necessary function for them. As a result, the community had little reason to suspect them of using it; conversely, people had considerable reason to suspect those who were hungry, needy, or subordinate of resorting to witchcraft in order to better their situation. Cotton Mather made this identification explicitly, and it was a commonly held belief in the county. When Thomas Knowlton stole a sack of meal, therefore, it was not simply rhetoric when people called him "divil, imp, hell hound, and a limb of the divil."[38]

The widespread identification of witchcraft as illegitimate force or authority is seen in the other thirty-nine instances where reference was made to the devil or magic, for in them a distinct pattern can be discerned

37. The English situation is described by A. D. J. Macfarlane, *Witchcraft in Tudor and Stuart England*.

38. Complaint against Thomas Knowlton [1673], IpMbk. 1666–82, Mar. term #30.

that suggests that "devilish" behavior had a rather definite meaning in Essex County. In eight of the thirty-nine, the poor, elderly, or widowed were the objects of the term. Perhaps the best example is William Pinson's reference to Thomas Robbins as a "grand old divell" in 1685. Robbins was aged and blind, and Pinson had been appointed trustee of his estate so that Robbins and his aged wife might be cared for in their declining years. Pinson, however, felt that the trusteeship was more onerous to him than he had anticipated, and he resented the obligations of time and money it involved. He became abusive to Robbins and finally decided to try ending the relationship. One day he allegedly swung a pitchfork close to Robbins's nose, threatening, "Ah, Rascoll, you are a cross grand old divell, Ile dispose of this Estate and thee too this weeke." In another seven instances, the identification was made between the devil and gossip or meddlesomeness, as when someone who rebuked another for his behavior was said to be acting devilishly. Two examples occurred regarding sexual advances as being prompted by the devil, three were linked to excesses of parental or familial pressure, and three more to opposition to litigation. Six outbursts concerned religious disagreements, where the implication was that another's religious practices were "the way to hell," as one person described them.[39] One reference cannot be determined.

Domestic relations were the area in which the function of witchcraft was best applied, however, as demonstrated by the remaining nine instances of devilish identification. Servants frequently referred to the devil to escape a work obligation or to break an unfavorable indenture. The William Morse household in Newbury is a good example of this process at work. John Stiles, a servant, was unhappy working for Morse and constantly used "idle words" with his master. To gain his freedom from the indenture that bound him, Stiles acted in collusion with Caleb Powell, a mariner, to convince the Morses that he was bewitched; only by leaving the household and living under Powell's tutelage could the spell be broken, they said. Morse was convinced of Stiles's possession by spirits, or at least that Powell was using magic and "molesting" his household: shoes flew across rooms, items disappeared, animals entered his locked house at night, barn doors mysteriously opened, and Stiles claimed that he was unable to read his prayers on the Sabbath because the Devil would not permit him to do so. In reality, Stiles was deceiving his master —one neighbor testified that she saw him throw a shoe while Morse was praying—and Powell fed the belief in witchcraft by boasting of his

39. On the elderly, see Robbins v. Pinson [1688], EP 44:76–83. On family matters, see Complaint against Elizabeth Perkins [1681], IpMbk. 1666–82, Mar. term #23. On religion, see Complaint against Mary Hammond [1682], EP 38:58.

knowledge of the "black art," a skill he said he had learned while *he* was a servant.[40]

Whether Morse believed that his house was afflicted by spirits is not certain, but he did know that his authority over Stiles was under attack. His response was to seek support from the county court, and he accused Powell of witchcraft in 1680. Once witnesses exposed the deception, however, the court did not have to punish Powell, declaring him guilty only of "suspicion of witchcraft" and assessing costs. Nevertheless, the court had demonstrated the effectiveness of the legal system as a supplement to familial authority, and it had shorn one artful servant of a powerful method of resistance.

An allegation of witchcraft was thus congruent with the social tensions existing between masters and their subordinates, and it could be used periodically to ease the rigidities of that relationship. For example, in 1674 Christopher Browne, a Beverly fisherman, "reported that he had been treated or discoursing with one whom he pretended to be the devil, who came like a gentleman urging him to bind himself as a servant to him." Browne's purpose—to suggest that he had a choice of masters and was not utterly dependent on his current, worldly master—was transparent to the court, and he was "dismissed for the present, his discourse seeming inconsistent with truth."[41]

Black servants, too, found claims of satanic artifice a useful tactic. Along with Indians they occupied the lowest social stratum in Essex and were most subject to the harshness of a subordinate position. Any assertion of defiance would be met by stern discipline—often at the hands of the court—but they found that claims of supernatural possession gave them a small measure of relief. "Wonn, John Ingerson's negro," accused Bridget Oliver in 1679 of harassing him with apparitions and, significantly, making it impossible for him to do his assigned chores: on one occasion his horse ran uncontrollably into a swamp, from which he had to fetch it; and another time Goody Oliver's apparition came to the hayhouse and he had to chase it away with a pitchfork.[42]

The conflict between magic and legitimate authority was most pronounced when witchcraft was used to abet criminal activity. Margaret

40. Complaint against Caleb Powell [1680], EP 32:130–33. One witness said that he "heard Calleb Powell say that he thought by Astrologie, and I think he said by astronmie too with it, hee could find out whither or no ther wear diabolicall meanes used about the said mors his trouble and that the said caleb said he thougt to try to find it out." See also Presentment of John Stiles [1680], EP 33:26.

41. Presentment of Christopher Browne [1674], SaMbk. 1667–79, Nov. term.

42. Presentment of Bridget Oliver [1679], EP 34:114. Bridget later remarried and was known as Bridget Bishop in 1692. See also Presentment of Elizabeth Iago [1676], EP 24:122.

Lord, a servant in the household of the Reverend John Hale in Beverly, used the threat of malefic magic to steal from her master and others in the neighborhood. Hale's young daughter Rebecca knew of these crimes, but as Rebecca finally told the court in 1678, "I have known of the naughty doings of our maid marget lord a great while but I was afraid to tell my mother of them least marget should kill me, for shee threatened Iff I told of her tricks shee would burn mee with a marking Iron and that shee kept a rope in the hay to hang mee with Iff I told. . . . She threatened to burn Sara [Roots, another girl aware of the thefts] with the fire pan heating of it in the fire. She said she had a book in which shee Could read and call [the] divell to kill Sarah." Margaret not only kept Sarah silent, too, but she also had the girl run errands for her and promised that "Iff Sara would doe what shee bade hir, the devill should not ketch hir." To reinforce her claim of supernatural powers, Margaret told Hale's children that her sorcery had killed many people in the community and that she was thinking of killing their mother soon. Despite these terrifying and incriminating statements, no witchcraft trial resulted, and only those persons who had purchased the stolen goods were punished by the court.[43]

One of the more delicate situations in the Essex household was the pattern of problems arising from sexual tensions, particularly those between masters and their young female servants. As in all records of sexual encounters, it is difficult to determine from the evidence if a master had been forward, if the servant had been seductive to advance her position in the household, or if no contact at all had taken place and the accusation was groundless. In any case, a great deal of uneasiness about such relationships seems to have existed, and when the court heard cases arising from them, significant facts about authority and the use of witchcraft accusations become apparent from the evidence.

The Nathaniel Leonard household may suggest how these tangled affairs sometimes operated. Hana Downing was Leonard's servant, and she continually bothered him about her chores. He finally told her "to attend to her duty" and had to box her ears for her disobedience. It is possible that she was retaliating when she spread stories about his sexual advances and those of his son Samuel. Leonard was upset by these stories and sued for defamation, "I being a singell man [i.e., a widower], *my fortten would be levelled with her owne*, which we trust shall prove is very mene."[44]

The significance of Leonard's reaction—a countercharge of insubor-

<hr />

43. Presentment of William Hoar et al. [1678], EP 29:7–24. See also Presentment of John Stiles; he, too, was engaging in thievery, but he was referring to witchcraft in a different way to cover the crime; that is, he was blaming the losses on some type of demonic activity beyond his control.

44. Emphasis added. Leonard v. Downing [1674], EP 21:71.

dinate behavior and a defamation suit—is the light it sheds on domestic relations and the employment of certain tactics to evade authority or to reverse existing patterns of dominance. Like accusations of witchcraft, the charge of a grave moral offense was a powerful weapon of weaker members of society against those holding power over them, for they could allege that such power was being exercised in a way that violated the legal bounds of master-servant relations. A servant could not simply allege that she was being worked too hard, for the court was reluctant to meddle in matters of household employment; but she could allege that the master was acting improperly by making sexual demands on her. Such demands, like extreme cruelty or satanic powers, were unacceptable (and illegal) forms of coercion that contravened the community's officially sanctioned patterns of authority. In many ways presaging the witchcraft accusations of 1692, young Hannah Harvie accused her master of seducing her early that year. Hannah, the daughter of Peter Harvie of Salem, was working for a family in Wenham, but she visited her friends in Salem on 8 February 1692, just as the suspicious practices of the Samuel Parris household were coming to light.[45] Any link between Hannah and the girls at Salem Village is impossible to discover, but the parallel function of their accusations is noteworthy. Each brought the accused down to a status equal to that of the servants. Leonard was very conscious of the equalizing function of Hana Downing's accusation ("my fortten would be levelled with her own"), and the connection between sexual accusations and those of witchcraft thus can be seen in the assumption held in both situations that the victimized girls were menaced by someone (the Devil or a master) who was somehow trying to possess them against their wills through illegitimate powers. The naming of a dominant individual in the household as a "devil" or "old wizard" thus allowed the subordinate individual to claim enchantment as an excuse for her own behavior or to repudiate the authority of the other person as satanic and illegitimate. For example, a wife who complained that "shee had lived twenty years a maid and then her mother had married her to a fooll" called her unwanted husband a "Devill." The epithet "devil" was not used indiscriminately, therefore, and was frequently employed to describe the illegitimate exercise of personal or extralegal power over a servant or other subordinate individual such as a wife or child.[46]

People in Essex seemed unconcerned about witchcraft because it only ameliorated the rigors of authority patterns and did not threaten

45. Complaint against Mordecai Larcum [1692], EP 52:91–97. The "afflicted" girls who produced the first witchcraft accusations of 1692 had been gathering at the home of the Reverend Samuel Parris. Charles W. Upham, *Salem Witchcraft*, 2:2–12.

46. Perkins v. Perkins [1687], EP 47:48–50. Such accusations explain why some persons of higher status were named in 1692; but the issue was structural and had little to do with resentment of aspiring capitalism.

seriously to overwhelm them; it was only one of the various types of extralegal mischief practiced in the county by a small and annoying—but not yet threatening—group of people there. These opponents of law and authority were well known by their neighbors, for they were repeatedly at odds with authority and were immediately suspected when animals were "spoiled," fences wrecked, or crops destroyed. They were people who, like Robert Swan, repudiated the litigious habits of the general community and responded to lawsuits with the threat or act of retributive violence.

Litigation and extralegal force were, to a striking degree, mutually exclusive categories of behavior. The court profiles of litigious people rarely include appearances to answer charges of violence or evidence that they committed violent acts; by contrast, those of mischief makers show few court proceedings initiated by them. The preferences of Richard Lee, "Chebacco yeoman," are typical and illustrative. Four times between 1672 and 1684 other men used the courts against him. However, when a neighbor's horse entered his pasture in 1689, Lee did not impound it or sue for damages; instead, he shot the animal dead. Although he could not have been unaware of either impounding procedures or the legal recovery of trespass damages, he did not want to use the courts and instead employed an extralegal technique. After shooting the horse, in fact, he boasted that the court would have difficulty convicting anyone of the crime.[47]

A statistical representation demonstrates the degree to which these two views regarding the legal system had become polarized by the latter part of the seventeenth century in Essex County. Obviously, statistics in the social sciences are valuable only in the light of understanding that human attitudes and behavior do not fall neatly into any two categories, but rather span a broad spectrum of complex and ambiguous categories. Nevertheless, some attempt can be made to measure the degree of difference between groups. One method is to construct a court "career" or "profile" of each individual or of a valid sample of individuals.[48] A person's court "career" can be defined as the history of his direct participation in the legal system, as either plaintiff, defendant, criminal complainant, or witness. From that profile, one can identify the nature of the appearances as "legalist" or "extralegalist." "Legalist" refers to a per-

47. Higginson v. Lee [two actions, 1672], EP 18:116. Davis v. Lee [1676], IpMbk. 1666–82, Mar. term #10. Wainwright v. Chubb [1684], EP 41:89. Presentment of Richard and Thomas Lee [1689], EP 48:22–26.
48. On degrees of difference, see V. O. Key, Jr., *A Primer of Statistics for Political Scientists*, p. 108. On the ways of assuring a "valid sample," see Margaret Hagood, *Statistics for Sociologists*, pp. 405–7.

son's using the court system in preference to other methods of conflict resolution or social control available in order to accomplish a specific goal. For example, a man might make a complaint to the court about a neighbor's behavior rather than confer with him informally or seek neighborly mediation; use the court to try title to land rather than negotiate; bring a domestic matter to court rather than resolve it within the household or family; petition the court to settle a matter among neighbors rather than deal with it collectively; repudiate an arbitration agreement; seek to recover money for goods sold and delivered or for a sum borrowed by suing for it without attempting arbitration; or complain about or be a victim of mischievous destruction of property. Alternatively, "extralegal" behavior includes being a defendant in a criminal case;[49] being a defendant in an action for civil damages due for committing malicious destruction of property such as arson or "trimming" a horse, or for acts of goal-directed malice such as gossip or public humiliation; being a vagrant warned out of town; or seeking to obstruct justice, as in beating someone who was impounding one's livestock, or in trying to prevent someone from testifying in court.

Various statistical methods exist for quantifying the degree of difference between groups or the strength of association between different factors. But the simplest and most effective way is to identify court appearances according to the preceding two categories and then to analyze whether the two different groups of activity appear together in each individual's "career." If so, what proportion of his contacts with the legal system fit one category or the other? The results of such a classification of "careers" of a 1-in-5 sample drawn alphabetically from the 2,834 adult males who had some direct contact with the county legal system from March term 1672 to (but not including) the witchcraft trials in 1692 confirm this polarization.[50]

Of the sample population of 566 men, 207 (or 37 percent) appeared in court only once; 63 of the 207 appeared as "extralegalist," while 144 of them were "legalist." This group of 207 was dropped (because a single appearance cannot be tested for consistency), and the profiles of the

49. This excludes prosecution for premarital fornication, for in some cases such a presentment was a way in which a couple could expiate their sin and clear the way for the infant's baptism. As a result, such a prosecution was a way of employing the court for a specific goal and did not necessarily evidence hostility to law.

50. Key, *Primer*, chap. 4. Women were excluded simply because their legal status was so different. Though Puritan Essex widened the scope of woman's legal capacities, it was still a circumscribed role. This factor would bias any sample attempting to draw conclusions about the types of legal activity of the population in general. It is noteworthy and not coincidental, however, that women could not use the courts as freely as men could and that women constituted the vast majority of those accused of practicing witchcraft in Essex.

TABLE 2. Court Profiles of a Sample Population of Adult Males Who Had More than One Contact with the County Legal System, 1672–1692

Percentage of Appearances that Are Legalist in Each Profile	Number of Men	Percentage
0	34	9.5
1–10	0	0
11–20	4	1.1
21–30	3	0.8
31–40	16	4.5
41–50	28	7.8
51–60	6	1.7
61–70	14	3.9
71–80	13	3.6
81–90	16	4.5
91–99	9	2.5
100	216	60.2
Total	359	100.1

remaining 359 who appeared more than once are shown in table 2. Over 60 percent of the men (216) have profiles that are 100 percent legalist; that is, whether they came to court twice or more than twenty times (and the average is slightly over four appearances) their activity was legalist each time. Conversely, 34 of the 359, or 9.5 percent, never exhibited legalist behavior, but always extralegalist. Appearing an average of 2.6 times, these men spoiled cattle, threw down fences, committed assaults, became drunk and menacing, or threatened witchcraft. Altogether, almost 70 percent of those who had more than one direct contact with the legal system fall into these two mutually exclusive extremes. The distinction between the two types of behavior is more graphic if those men whose "careers" show percentages of over 70 percent or under 30 percent are added to the first two groups. When these groups are combined, 254, or almost 71 percent, fall into the more legalist group, and 41, or approximately 11 percent, into the opposite one, yielding a figure of 82 percent who appeared in court more than once as falling into one general pattern of behavior or the other. By contrast, the middle range of profiles (from 31 to 70 percent) included only 64 men, or just under 18 percent of the 359 men appearing more than once. The polarization would be still greater, and the middle ground further eroded, if two problems could be eliminated. First, it is impossible to distinguish between men with the same name; their legal "additions" of occupation and residence are not in all cases available, and many had the same occupation and lived in the same town. It is very likely, therefore, that in some cases two "careers" were combined under the name of one person, producing a blurring of two possibly distinct profiles. A second, though lesser, problem involves those men who were extralegalist at one point in their lives but who later became legalist; these were persons, as described earlier, who brought accusations to court against forms of behavior for which they themselves earlier had been punished, in a form of secular repentance.[51]

Nevertheless, the dichotomy is clear, as it was to residents of seventeenth-century Essex. They were aware that extralegal tactics as a form of social control were opposed to the legalistic foundations of their society and were (as these tactics have been shown to be in more recent societies) an extremely conservative reaction against the changes that had overtaken that society.[52] They knew that extralegal tactics might be used to prevent legal action or by a servant to escape a day's responsibilities. But the official authority of the powerful county courts could be relied upon to keep a situation from becoming uncontrollable and could prevent any permanent alteration of relationships. The law, it was recognized, stood as an effective barrier against such rebellious behavior. Even Cotton Mather used a legal metaphor to describe how witchcraft was to be handled: "There will be that clause in our Indictment, *They were moved by the Instigation of the Devil*."[53] With legal authority accessible and effective, the residents of Essex had no need to pay extraordinary attention to harmless or sporadic challenges—until 1692.

51. See p. 126, above. Combining two different persons into a single identity may very well explain the puzzling career of one (?) John Godfrey, who is the subject of John Demos, "John Godfrey and His Neighbors." Godfrey was a common surname in Essex, where we find reference to male Godfreys named Andrew, Francis, George, James, John, Peter, and William. It is quite possible that there was more than one "John Godfrey," and Demos admits several suggestions of uncertainty over John's identity at ibid., p. 244.

52. On the "conservative" nature of witchcraft when applied as a form of social control, see Macfarlane, *Witchcraft*, pp. 248–49.

53. Mather, "Discourse," p. 35.

7 Law, Magic, and Disorder

The Crisis of the Interregnum, 1684–1692

In 1684 the charter of "the Governor and Company of the Massachusetts Bay in New England" was annulled, and all privileges exercised by the colony's government were revoked.[1] Some in Massachusetts welcomed the revocation, while an intense minority mourned the passing of the Puritan experiment. Beyond these partisan reactions, however, a more pervasive general fear gripped the colony when it became apparent that the entire social, political, and economic order was threatened by the destruction of the legal and governmental institutions. When the General Court received unofficial news of the charter revocation in September 1684,[2] it therefore quickly drafted a letter to its agent in London, Robert Humfreys, suggesting a strategy for regaining the colony's liberties. While the court insisted on "the priviledge of Englishmen, that we should not be condemned unheard," it also revealed that it would make no attempt to prove that the peculiar Massachusetts legal practice conformed to the strict English forms—"which wee pretend not to a thorow acquaintance with." Instead, the legislature wrote to its "dread soveraigne" the following summer to explain that colonial practice had diverged from English ways only by mistake. Assuming an unaccustomed suppliant tone, the General Court pleaded ignorance: "Our remoteness from your majestys court, our wildernesse imployment, having inavoydably rendered us ignorant of many things in law, hath given an occasion for those errors, which, upon notice, we have endeavored the reforming of, and are not conscious to any wilfull administrations, derogatory to the honnour and interest of the croune. What errors, through inadvertency or humane fraylty, have binn committed by us," it petitioned, "we humbly implore your majesties gracious pardon of."[3]

The plan was a masterful one. Although the colony had admitted departing from English law, it was nevertheless asking "the continuance of those our liberties" and adopting various stratagems to preserve them.

1. The legal issues involved in the revocation are related by Michael G. Hall, *Edward Randolph and the American Colonies, 1676–1703*, pp. 79–83.
2. Viola F. Barnes, *The Dominion of New England*, p. 23n.
3. *Mass. Rec.* 5:458–59, 496.

Its first gesture was simply to ignore the dissolution of the government and to continue sessions of the General Court as though the charter were still in force. The deputies, conscious of the impending challenge to local legal procedure, acted to clarify and reassert those practices they knew to be inconsistent with English requirements. Land affairs were especially vulnerable, for Edward Randolph already had criticized their system for supposedly allowing title to squatters and doubt existed about the validity of grants made by town meetings that were not legal corporations and hence not authorized to grant land.[4]

In addition, the royal investigative commission of 1665 had criticized the colonial law of 1646 directing that escheats go to the Massachusetts treasury and had declared its opinion that escheats should go to the crown. Fearful of the consequences that might follow an insistence upon adherence to strict English forms for granting land, the legislature reconfirmed all existing grants in March 1685 to end, it was hoped, any confusion about their status "in the law."[5]

While a legislative committee was busy revising all colonial law the following spring—a task performed so earnestly that it took only three weeks—the deputies acted to make sure that the customary local legal remedies would be available in the counties even with the establishment of English common law courts. In gradually and imperceptibly assuming equity powers to deal with the novel economic and social necessities of New World life, Massachusetts county courts had gone beyond what they were authorized to exercise, since only the General Court, drawing upon its powers analogous to those of a borough court, possessed such powers.[6] It was essential, however, that county courts be given explicit authority to make equitable judgments, too. On 17 May 1685, therefore— eight months after learning that the charter was vacated—the General Court granted equity powers to all county courts. Although it was ratifying by statute what had been an unacknowledged reality for decades, the legislature continued to maintain the fiction that the county courts had not exercised equity powers in the past, explaining in the act, "it is found by experience that in many cases and controversys between partys, wherein there is matter of apparent equity, there hath been no way provided for reliefe against the rigour of the common law, but by application to the Generall Court." Similarly, the legislature tried to

---

4. See chap. 2 of this volume. For a similar concern in Connecticut, see Richard Bushman, *From Puritan to Yankee*, pp. 44–46.

5. *Mass. Rec.* 5:353–54, 470–71; 4 (pt. ii):212. *Col. Laws 1672–86*, p. 49.

6. See chap. 2 of this volume. For a good summary of equity powers as exercised by a colonial court authorized to employ them, see Carroll T. Bond, "Introduction to the Legal Procedure," pp. xxii–xxxi.

assure that all matters of inheritance would be decided in the counties by giving their courts "full power and authority (as the Ordinary in England)" to handle wills. Probate in England, of course, was not handled by the common law courts either.[7]

These were futile gestures. The legislature had no authority to meet, and the Dominion of New England regime worked to make its new legal system conform to English practice. Accordingly, it promptly passed its own judicature act. This act, too, provided for equitable determinations, but such were to be provided by a new court of chancery, a single high court for the entire colony and not a county equity court familiar with local practices and realities. Instead of being made up of local magistrates, their elected associates, and a freely chosen jury, the new court was "to be holden by the Governour or such person as he shall appoint to be Chancellor Assisted with 5 or more of the Councill who in this Court shall have the same power and Authority as masters of Chancery in England have or ought to have." Moreover, appeals had to be sent out of the colony, directly to the king and Privy Council.[8]

The removal of equity powers was but one facet of the fragmentation of the familiar, broadly competent, and unitary county judicial structure. The county inferior courts of common pleas that succeeded it were limited in probate matters and civil disputes to minor causes and shorn of all authority to decide freehold titles. A weak replacement for what people had come to employ as an essential mechanism of social and economic stability, the inferior courts were not even controlled locally but were now to be run by men appointed in Boston. So fearful and angered were the residents that a militia lieutenant in Topsfield threatened to use his company to "keep Salem court with the former Magistrates." Although several men in Ipswich would soon be punished for denying the Dominion's authority to tax, the lieutenant insisted "that he was under another government and did not know this government."[9]

Handling many of the causes formerly heard by the county courts was the new superior court system staffed by itinerant justices. While an advantage of the old legal system had been the objectivity of county magistrates removed from town jealousies, the Dominion jurists were more

7. Mass. Arch. 40:212–14. *Col. Laws 1672–86*, pp. 31–33.

8. Mass. Arch. 40:231–32; 126:247. Viola F. Barnes incorrectly states that "the court of chancery established under the new system was a continuation of the one established in Massachusetts for the first time in 1685" (*Dominion of New England*, pp. 107–8).

9. Mass. Arch. 126:250–57. Emory Washburn, *Sketches in the Judicial History of Massachusetts*, pp. 90–91, 105. The militia lieutenant, John Gould, was tried for speaking "Seditious and treasonable words" before a special court of oyer and terminer held at Boston on 19 August 1686 and was fined £100, ordered to serve six months in prison, and ordered to give £100 security bond for his future good behavior (SCJ, Aug. 1686).

than impartial third parties: they were strangers utterly unacquainted with the realities and litigation habits of the county. Although the superior court sat quarterly at Salem and Ipswich, county residents generally resented it and distrusted its unfamiliar judges who refused to admit "matters of Equity and a Consideration transcending all Ordinary Cases." Equally serious, according to charges leveled at the Edmund Andros regime after the Glorious Revolution, was their differing definition of the vital idea of "possession" regarding land: "The Enjoyment and Improvement of Lands not inclosed, and especially if lying in common amongst many was denied to be possession."[10]

It is a historical commonplace that Andros challenged the validity of existing town claims to common land within their borders, and his challenge to Lynn commonage is one of the better-known episodes of the Dominion years.[11] Unfortunately, such a cause célèbre has led historians to see the general problem of land claims as being only between the crown, on the one hand, and towns or individuals, on the other. But the records indicate that individual Essex landowners were not worried about crown challenges, and aside from making a belated effort to confirm purchases from the Indians, Essex landowners did not bother to confirm their individual Essex holdings with the crown: only two men, Philip Nelson of Rowley and John Small of Salem, requested title confirmation from the Dominion government for land within the county. Almost all the claims that were made involved grants in Maine, where titles were more threatened by the claim of Robert Mason to that region.[12]

On the other hand, an examination of records from the superior court for the Salem and Ipswich circuit—records up to now believed lost—reveals a great concern on the local level, too; specifically, this was the fear that land arrangements between individuals would be upset by a lack of familiar, easily conducted procedures of litigation to try title to land. These local fears were borne out, in fact, almost as soon as the new system took effect: when Salem's notorious "kites tayle" land dispute was retried at the first session of the new court system in September 1686, no equitable considerations concerning errors of town recording were permitted and Nathaniel Putnam's claim was upheld after it had been defeated twice under the Old Charter system.[13]

The Dominion jurists were well aware of local divergence from

10. William H. Whitmore, ed., *The Andros Tracts*, 1:243.
11. Barnes, *Dominion of New England*, pp. 189–91.
12. Mass Arch. 126:199; 127:236a, 239, 246, 254, 257, 258, 259, 278, 280; 128:22a, 103, 109, 128, 137, 146, 174, 189, 200, 277, 296; 129:6, 66, 67, 69, 71, 98, 99, 111, 112.
13. Nurse v. Endecott [1686], EP 46:31–36. The Essex records of the superior court, it seems, never before have been cited in any study of the Massachusetts legal system and are not listed in the standard work on the colony's records, Carroll D. Wright's *Report on the*

English ways. The Massachusetts legal system had not suffered from what Thomas Barnes calls the "chaos of the 1640's," nor from the reaction of the Restoration period. Indeed, much of the Stuart colonial policy in the latter years of the dynasty concerned the imposition of conformity upon a colonial system that had departed significantly from what those monarchs believed were the proper forms of government and law. The Dominion magistrates and officials—many of whom had been trained in England and appointed because of their reliability to follow Stuart policy—therefore announced their intention of reversing the independent development of Massachusetts law.[14]

The success of the Dominion's efforts to impose a conformity to the common law is apparent in those cases that survive in the records of the superior court at Salem and Ipswich. Common law forms are conspicuous by their presence; the fictitious parties John Doe and Richard Roe made their first Essex appearances in an ejectment case in 1686, for example.[15] Technical requirements of procedure were enforced, and proportionately twice as many actions were dismissed on technical grounds than ever before. From 1672 to 1683, a total of 104 out of 2,961 civil causes (an average of 3.5 percent yearly) were barred or abated for technical insufficiency of the writ. By comparison, 37 of the 527 actions brought to the superior and inferior courts from 1684 to 1688 (an average of 7 percent yearly) were ended for those reasons. Because towns were not corporations, their selectmen had to sue in their own names, and their actions were abated if they did not.[16] Essexmen were not accustomed to observing the strict requirements of entering a writ, and one plaintiff saw his writ abated, "the declaration and writt not agreeing and the place not being mentioned in the declaration where the Contract was made."[17] Perhaps the most obvious gauge of popular aversion to the new court system is the reduced number of cases brought to the superior and inferior courts in the Dominion years, as indicated in table 3. Even if the

---

Custody and Condition of the Public Records of Parishes, Towns, and Counties. These records, whose presumed disappearance has left a gap in Massachusetts history, can be found included in the manuscript records of the county court at EP 45:145 through EP 46:136. They encompass two terms of the superior court presided over by William Stoughton, John Usher, and Bartholomew Gedney at Ipswich, September 1686, and at Salem, November 1686.

14. Thomas G. Barnes, *Somerset, 1625–1640*, p. 198. Mass. Arch. 35:155, 190. Whitmore, *Andros Tracts*, 1:46.

15. Roe v. Doe, of the demise of Henry Rhodes [1686], EP 46:101–11. Court costs increased with the imposition of a 1-shilling fee for "taxing cost" and a greater insistence on the usage of recognizances, which had been required only in cases of appeal. Under the Dominion, they were also sometimes required of plaintiffs in original actions. Cross v. Manning [1689], EP 48:20–21.

16. Selectmen of Salem v. Shattock [1686], EP 46:89.

17. Dole v. Nichols [1686], EP 47:132–33.

TABLE 3. Civil Litigation before the Courts of Essex County, 1672–1689

Year	Cases	Year	Cases
1672	233	1681	134
1673	277	1682	156
1674	286	1683	149
1675	168	1684	189
1676	184	1685	109
1677	211	1686	125*
1678	244	1687	46*
1679	218	1688	58*
1680	174	1689	23*

*Figures from complete records of the inferior court and incomplete records of the superior court.

incompleteness of the superior court records is taken into account, the lower amount of litigation is apparent. Perhaps Essexmen were reluctant to argue their disputes according to unfamiliar common law procedures, or they may have been averse to the increased court costs of the new system. Whatever the reason, they appear to have been suppressing their conflicts.

One major explanation for the reduced use of litigation, for which demonstrable proof exists, is the composition of the new bench. Before the Dominion the Essex county court had had a fairly stable bench composed of men living in the county. Since 1680 it had generally been made up of Nathaniel Saltonstall of Haverhill, Daniel Denison of Ipswich, Robert Pike of Salisbury, Samuel Appleton of Lynn, and William Browne and Bartholomew Gedney of Salem. Gedney, Appleton, and Browne were carried over to assist at the superior court, and Daniel Epps of Ipswich and Richard Dummer of Newbury were added to it. Yet it was not these local men who caused problems, but rather the new judges who made their own wills prevail.[18]

John Usher, Joseph Dudley, and William Stoughton were the councillors presiding at Salem and Ipswich, with their clerk, the English-trained George Farwell. All of them were new to the county, and together they caused no little antagonism. One case from the Salem superior session of May 1686 was particularly outrageous. In January of that year Philip Nelson obtained a writ of ejectment against John Pearson, Sr., to try the title to four and a half acres of meadow and planting land and a half share of a grist mill, all in Rowley. When the case came before the

18. On the stability of membership on the Essex bench, see pp. 53–54 of this volume.

superior court, the jury decided in Pearson's favor. Dudley and Stoughton accepted the verdict, and Farwell recorded it. However, Farwell was also Nelson's attorney, and when Pearson and his attorney Daniel Wicom left the courtroom Farwell removed the trial from the record and entered a new action. Dudley then sent the jury out again, and upon their special verdict he made a new decision in Nelson's favor. Wicom had no success at reversing this decision at the next superior session and had to appeal to the governor and council, the highest tribunal in the colony. Because clerk Farwell was not present when Wicom asked for the appeal, Wicom had to travel to Boston to enter it. There he paid the necessary fees to Dudley, who assured him that the appeal was duly entered. But "instead of hearing when our case should have a hearing," wrote Wicom after the uprising of 1689, "the next news came marshall [Jeremiah] Neale with an execution, which execution was signed by Mr. Dudley."[19]

The presence of appointed officials beyond local control combined with the strict insistence of common law forms to make the once familiar and accessible system of local justice unrecognizable in Essex. Finally, the last means of popular influence that Essexmen had had was removed when the Old Charter practice of each town's electing freemen to sit as jurors was ended. Instead, the sheriff appointed jurors drawn from his own list of those men meeting the English property qualification. Although this method of selection did not, in practice, produce juries composed of men of a higher social stratum than before, it was perceived as the final step in removing the courts from the control that had existed earlier.[20] With less control over, or trust in, their legal system, the people of Essex no longer viewed the county court as an instrument of effective community order. Local tensions and problems that previously had been handled at the county court were left unresolved by the Dominion regime; the difficulties could not be transferred to the town meetings, either, because these bodies were now limited to a single meeting yearly, only for the purpose of electing officials.[21] Moreover, Essexmen soon discovered that without the old resident magistrates and commissioners they were plagued by the absence of legal authority within their towns. Poor relief had to be suspended in Haverhill, for example, where selectmen complained that "we have not power ourselves" to perform a func-

19. Mass. Arch. 35:137.

20. The economic standing of jurors was determined by locating those from Salem whose names appeared on the rate list of 1683. Resentment at being tried by jurors chosen by the Dominion officials ran high in Essex, where protest against the tax levies of the Andros regime was strongest. When John Wise and several other men from Ipswich refused to pay the taxes as not being voted by the taxpayers, they were taken to Boston for trial before a jury that, Wise said, had been specially "geathered up to Serve the present turne." For an account of this trial, see George Allan Cook, *John Wise, Early American Democrat*, pp. 50–57.

21. Barnes, *Dominion of New England*, pp. 95–96.

tion once discharged by those county officials. At Salem the situation was worse, as eighty impoverished Huguenots had arrived from France in 1686, placing a heavy strain on the already overtaxed institutions of poor relief. Many of these "Frenchmen" were supported by the generosity of the local Jersey community, but their arrival exacerbated existing ethnic frictions in the town at a time when its institutions of conflict resolution and social control were least able to contain them.[22]

These traumas of the Interregnum period were only partially eased after the Dominion's overthrow in 1689. Indeed, anxieties about the return of law and order to the colony were heightened by the outbreak of King William's War. To make matters worse, securing a new charter met with continual delays, and the leaders of the revolution were unsure about their legal position. Although the officials who had been ousted by Dudley in 1686 reentered office, they could not simply resume the old charter, for it had been annulled by the crown in 1684. The colony's individual towns assembled in a convention and insistently pressed for resumption in May 1689, but the assistants overruled their vote. Finally, the assistants did reestablish the charter in all but name and designated Simon Bradstreet as governor, saying on 25 May 1689 that their action was, in spite of its substance, *not* "an assumption of charter government." Permission finally reached Boston in August to continue the Bradstreet regime in office, but uncertainty—and even overt resistance—persisted, as everyone knew that it was only a provisional government headed by an aged, symbolic vestige of the Founding Generation.[23]

Immediate challenges greeted these halting efforts. Robert Calef, ever eager to criticize the Puritan leadership of the colony, mocked this uncertain situation as "between government and no government." Indeed, former supporters of the Dominion were not exaggerating when they said in 1690 that the lack of a stable and strong government was so serious that "the common people now wish Sir Edmund Andros were back again." Describing the current situation as "anarchy," a group of Anglicans pleaded with the Lords of Trade for a new government. More ominously, Edward Randolph wrote from the Boston gaol that the interim regime was hurriedly trying to attach legitimacy to itself and "had held a Court of Assistants, and has condemned a malefactor for breach of one of their capital laws. He was lately executed," Randolph claimed, "to frighten the people into submission."[24] The clash of popular distrust and weak provisional instruments of government was not restricted to

22. Petition of Haverhill Selectmen [1686], EP 45:113. David T. Konig, "A New Look at the Essex 'French,'" pp. 177–78.

23. John Gorham Palfrey, *History of New England*, 3:588–89; 4:24–28, 63.

24. Ibid., 4:25n. Benjamin Bullivant to the Lords of Trade, Boston, 27 and 28 May 1690, *CSP* 13:272–73. Francis Foxcroft and others to the Lords of Trade, Boston, Jan.

Boston, however, and may have been greater in areas far from the seat of power—such that there was any—in the capital. To the south in Plymouth, for example, the reconstituted Old Colony court of general sessions was at pains to reassert its authority beyond challenge, and when Robert Stanford made "aprobrious and contumelious speeches and actions before and towards the court," the justices there took the extreme and unusual step of having him "Comitted to prison during the pleasure of the Court."[25]

This fear for the security of the traditional system of social control was particularly intense in outlying northern areas, where the danger of French and Indian attack was greater. Residents in New Hampshire complained that the war against France had stripped them of protection and that the "self-styled Government of Massachusetts" had left them defenseless.[26] Hampton, once part of Essex, finally received nine pounds of powder after complaining that "Boston would tax them but not help them."[27] Indeed, Deputy Governor Thomas Danforth, in refusing to send aid to the people of Maine, only increased their sense of isolation when he allegedly told them "that Jesus Christ was King of earth as well as heaven, and that if Jesus Christ did not help them, he could not."[28]

Immediately to the south in Essex the situation was equally insecure, for the county was subject to Boston's authority and its troops and armaments could be taken for defense of the capital or for the expedition to Canada. When Captain John Alden arrived in Marblehead to requisition harbor cannon in the fall of 1690, the town drummer summoned sixty to seventy men who "gathered in a riotous and tumultuous manner" to stop him. Insisting on their own pressing needs, the men of Marblehead complained that they would "laye open to their Enemie" and sent Alden back to Boston empty-handed. This riot was only the second episode of collective violence in the history of the county. The other outbreak, significantly, also occurred at Marblehead during a time

---

1690, ibid. Edward Randolph to the Lords of Trade, Boston, 10 Jan. 1690, ibid., p. 205. Andros expressed an opinion similar to Randolph's on the need to intimidate the populace. Andros to the Lords of Trade, Boston, 27 May 1690, ibid., p. 271.

25. Manuscript recordbook of the Plymouth County Court of General Sessions of the Peace [Sept. 1691], p. 63. In Connecticut, Gershom Bulkeley also inveighed against the newly reconstituted governments and wrote that it was "not lawful" for colonists to submit to their "usurped and pretended power." He also attacked their deviation from the "common and statute laws of England" (*Will and Doom, or the Miseries of Connecticut by and Under an Usurped and Arbitrary Power*, pp. 86, 90–95).

26. Inhabitants of Great Island, New Hampshire, to the Lords of Trade, CSP, 13: 262–63. See also a letter from Thomas Newton, ibid., for the charge that "the Charter Government cares little for that country [Maine] or for the lives of the settlers, but only for smaller matters."

27. Ibid., 13:263.

28. Bullivant to Lords of Trade, 27 and 28 May 1690, CSP 13:272–73.

of similar fear: after a group of seamen had been killed by Indians during King Philip's War, several Indian captives were set upon and mutilated by an outraged mob of local women.[29]

Anxieties in Essex became more intense when an escaped slave was apprehended and revealed the plans for an insurrection. He said he was fleeing to join Isaac Morrill, a local Jerseyman who had persuaded him to organize the blacks and Indians of the area as part of a combined uprising and invasion against the English settlements. Morrill had made elaborate preparations, he continued, and had spied on military garrisons from Massachusetts Bay to New York. Moreover, other advance scouting had been made by two Frenchmen visiting Newbury under the pretense of buying corn. The local blacks and Indians were to be directed by Morrill, "a Frenchman" named George Major (or Moger or Mayo), and two others. Joined by five hundred Indians and three hundred French troops crossing the Merrimack, they would destroy Haverhill, Amesbury, and Newbury. The story was corroborated by another slave, Robert Negro. According to his story, Major was planning to lead the assault "upon the backside of the cuntry and distroy all the English and save none but the Negro and Indian Servants and that the French would come with vessells and lay at the harbour that none should escape." With this information exposed, previous suspicions became confirming proof. Elizabeth Moody told of seeing Morrill carry a gun while he "viewed" Major Robert Pike's garrison. Robert and Elizabeth Long added that they saw Morrill with a gun hidden under his coat, while Major Daniel Davison "and the gentlemen of Newbury" reported observing him inquiring about the number of men in another troop.[30]

It was not long before the fears of an anxious population began to manifest themselves as spectral antagonists whose form and behavior embodied their suspicions. By 1692, these fears sent sixty armed men into the woods around Gloucester to intercept a spectral force of French and Indians. One member of the defending party, revealing his anxieties about the Isaac Morrill plot, reported that he had chased "a man with a blue shirt, and bushy black hair." The invaders, however, were unharmed by gunfire and eluded the Essex patrol.[31]

At a loss to strike against such ominous external threats, the people of Essex in early 1692 were also fearful that they might not even be able to contain the forces of disorder within their society. There was but little hope that the old charter would be restored permanently and no guar-

29. Complaint against Legg [1690], EP 50:5–11. James Axtell, "The Vengeful Women of Marblehead," pp. 647–52.

30. Complaint against Isaac Morrill [1690], EP 49:56–58.

31. Cotton Mather, *Magnalia Christi Americana*, 2:620–23.

antee that the new charter would establish the effective courts upon which they always had relied. In the meantime, the county courts had only the dubious implied authority of an order-in-council. To meet the possible threat of a challenge to its legitimacy, the government in Boston had acted swiftly and severely in 1689—by condemning fourteen men to death. Only six other people—four whites and two blacks—had been condemned since the end of King Philip's War in 1676, and the sentences were unprecedented in Massachusetts judicial history. Although probably only two of the men were executed, the provisional government clearly had demonstrated its powers to all who would question them.[32]

This demonstration of judicial power was precisely the solution that the people and leaders of Essex chose in order to preserve their civil and social order in 1692, for they, too, were reacting to the general crisis of disorder in the Interregnum years. Cotton Mather, commenting in *The Present State of New England* in 1690, perceptively noted the fears of uncertainty and the pressures building to take things in hand. "[I]f our God will wrest America out of the Hands of its old Land-Lord, Satan, and give these utmost ends of the Earth to our Lord Jesus," he hoped, "then our present conflicts will shortly be blown over, and something better than, a Golden Age, will arrive to this place, and this perhaps before all of our First Planters are fallen asleep. Now," Mather pointed out by way of contrast, "Tis a dismal Uncertainty and Ambiguity that wee see ourselves placed in. Briefly, such is our case, That something must be done out of hand. And indeed, our All is at the Stake; we are beset with a Thousand perplexities and Entanglements."[33] The response in Essex was a logical application of a society's fundamental social ideology to a specific problem, for it was in terms of their legalist paradigm that they perceived their internal threats.

One of the first such threats they identified was a man speaking antinomian words in Amesbury, and on 19 February 1692 Joseph Large of that town was jailed for heresy. The defendant had said "that our authority (as they do act) do crusify christ afresh." The defendant claimed that the Bible "was not the living word" and that he had received such word "from the wittnes of god in his own hart." According to the magistrates at Ipswich who heard this case in March 1692, however, "the hart was Deceatfull [and] Despretly evel," and Large's ideas had to be punished harshly. Because the accused refused to recant and persisted in his opinion, the court meted out an unusually stiff sentence—a fine of fifty pounds or a whipping of thirty stripes.[34]

32. Palfrey, *History of New England*, 4:63. Assts. Rec., 1:198–99, 294–95, 303–4, 320–21, 357. Edwin Powers, *Crime and Punishment in Early Massachusetts*, p. 293.
33. Cotton Mather, *The Present State of New England*, p. 35.
34. Complaint against Joseph Large [1692], EP 52:101–3. Both the amount of the fine

In the same month that Joseph Large was punished in Ipswich, the court in Salem began examining people accused of practicing witchcraft. The decision to prosecute was, in itself, a significant departure from the previous responses to witchcraft, for it was not at all necessary for such suspicions to be heard by a court of law. Rather, other methods were available to control the Devil's mischief. Prayer and fasting might be attempted as a way of exorcising the evil spirit from the afflicted, and this was in fact tried by the Reverend Samuel Parris when he first became aware of the strange behavior of the young girls in his household. When this procedure proved unsuccessful, another technique available was the use of "white magic" that, it was believed, could counter the effects of black magic. Shortly after the girls began showing symptoms and before any accusations were made, an aunt of one of the afflicted prevailed on Parris's West Indian servant Tituba and her husband John Indian to bake a "witch cake," which was fed to a dog suspected as one of the witch's familiars. According to English custom, this concoction of ordinary meal and the urine of a victim was supposed to injure and thus reveal the witch responsible for the affliction.[35] But *The Urinary Experiment*," as Cotton Mather had called it in 1689, was merely "the Devils *Shield* against a Devils *Sword*," and "all communion with *Hell* is dangerous." Before the Salem Village congregation, in fact, Parris rebuked the instigator of the witch cake effort, protesting that it was wrong to be "going to the Devil for help against the Devil."[36] Cotton Mather was adamant that magical techniques of this sort were "altogether unwarrantable," and his father regarded them as "not a Divine but a Diabolical Gift." Increase Mather was more emphatic in his opposition to using "the Devils Sacraments or Institution," cautioning that "we ought not to practice witchcraft to discover witches, nor may we make use of a White healing Witch (as they call them) to find out a Black and Bloody one."[37]

The Mathers cast their analysis in theological terms, but the general population of Essex had its own secular ideology that led them to the

---

and the number of stripes were extraordinary for Essex. The court also punished a man with unusual severity in 1689 for telling a rate collector he was a "foole" for doing his duty "for there was noe law nor Government in the Country" (Complaint against Manning [1689], EP 48:56–58).

35. Charles W. Upham, *Salem Witchcraft*, 2:95–96. Chadwick Hansen, *Witchcraft at Salem*, p. 57. White magic was also used to cure a bewitched horse, although it was acknowledged to be "not lawful." Isaac Cummins related the effort to "take a pipe of tobacco and lite it and put it in to the fundement of the mare." To his surprise, "then thar arose a blaze from the pipe of tobaco which seemd to me to cover the butocks of the said mear" (*WRec.* 2:80–82).

36. Upham, *Salem Witchcraft*, 2:96. Cotton Mather, *Memorable Providences, Relating to Witchcraft and Possessions*, pp. 59–60.

37. Cotton Mather, *Wonders of the Invisible World*, p. 33. Increase Mather, *Cases of Conscience Concerning Evil Spirits Personating Men*, pp. 264–65.

same conclusion and toward a legalistic prosecution of an extralegal threat to society. Clifford Geertz explains this operation of ideology upon action: "Whatever ideologies may be—projections of unacknowledged fears, disguises for ulterior motives, phatic expressions of group solidarity—they are, most distinctively, maps of problematic social reality and matrices of collective conscience."[38] Making the legal system their matrix for coping with their highly "problematic social reality," the people of Essex insisted upon a legalistic prosecution of the witches in order to assert the unequivocal rule of legal authority against all types of extralegal force. Implicitly as well as explicitly, Essex accusers identified in the defendants the various types of extralegal behavior that they recognized as rebellious and disruptive of civil order as they wished it to be.

A powerful court of oyer and terminer was commissioned by the Governor, Sir William Phips, and his council on 2 June 1692, and it was to this tribunal that people turned. Only the legislature was empowered to create courts; but in the rush to prosecute, Phips yielded to pressure and established the special court without waiting for the newly authorized legislature to convene. With the old court system soon to expire and no new one yet established, this court was set up to deal exclusively with the witchcraft outbreak. Although it possessed broad powers of punishment, its jurisdiction was limited to witchcraft cases alone. Though some oyer and terminer courts, such as that held by William Stoughton and others at Boston in 1686, held general commissions and operated like courts of general gaol delivery, it was commonly understood in 1692 that the Salem court had been commissioned to deal only with witchcraft. This limitation appears to have had the ironic effect of intensifying the outbreak, for it encouraged many simmering local tensions to be cast in supernatural terms. If anyone in the county wished to use this prestigious court as an agency of resolving a conflict or preserving the peace, he had to present evidence of satanic collusion in his complaint or the court could not hear it. In fact, all of the court's indictments were drawn up in advance, with witchcraft specified in them; they only had to be dated and affixed with the names and residences of the witches and those on whom they had used magic. As a result, witchcraft accusations became a blanket formula (and temporarily the only available method) for protecting society from all forms of threat in the insecure days of 1692.[39]

The trials were to be a critical test of one system of social control

38. Clifford Geertz, "Ideology as a Cultural System," p. 63.

39. On Phips's view of the court's jurisdiction, see Sidney Perley, *The History of Salem, Massachusetts*, 3:294. The English background can be found in W. S. Holdsworth, *A History of English Law*, 1:274. On Stoughton's oyer and terminer court of 1686, see SCJ, Aug. 1686.

against another: of open, publicly acknowledged forms against covert ones. All aspects of procedure in the trials, therefore, were symbolic and important goals in themselves. Anthony Checkley was chosen as prosecutor, for he was the most active attorney in Essex; he had represented some of the most litigious people there—men like George Corwin, who was named as sheriff—and had argued forcefully and often for legal precision against informality and uncertainty. In applying the law to combat witchcraft, Checkley and the bench were at pains to reach for demonstrably legal devices. Unfortunately for those on trial, the courts never had prosecuted a serious outbreak of witchcraft before, and Chief Justice Stoughton, assisted by six other judges, had two courses open. On the one hand, they possessed general rules and guidelines set for capital crimes in the *Laws and Liberties*. On the other hand, they knew that there were clearly defined procedures that had been developed specifically for the grave problem at hand; namely, the well-established legal procedures of English witch-hunting and trial. These old methods had never been used in New England, but they were associated with the sole purpose of combating magic and for that reason contained an enormous advantage. Although Nathaniel Saltonstall objected to the use of these methods and resigned from the court, hundreds of Essex accusers had no misgivings and their actions supported the decision. Moreover, the judges—four of them from Boston—knew that their actions would be subject to scrutiny in England, and they carefully followed Stoughton and Checkley.[40]

Strict witch-hunting procedure permitted the court to rely on techniques that were of undoubted value in "proving" a case against a suspected witch. The court was directed by past witch trials to look for a witch's "teat" (any unusual mark on the body) and to accept a single witness's testimony rather than to require two witnesses for conviction. Central to these procedures, however, was the admission of evidence obtained from "spectral sources" such as apparitions seen by accusers. Admitting spectral evidence was accepted in English practice; but, more important to the judges and people at Salem, it stood as an assertion that outward appearances and the overt behavior of visible apparitions were more important than secret, invisible, or clandestine activities. This practice—the admission as evidence of acts committed by apparitions visible only to the victim—has been cited as the most irrational, uncontrollable, and barbaric aspect of the entire witchcraft episode. It has

40. For good examples of Checkley's familiarity with proper English legal procedure, see his arguments in Endicott v. Preston [1690], EP 49:135; Croad v. Price [1691], EP 51:122–28; Price v. Croad [1692], EP 52:71–73. For a description of English witch trial procedure, see C. L'Estrange Ewen, *Witch Hunting and Witch Trials*.

been singled out as conclusive proof that the judges, jury, and population were engaged in an orgy of superstition.[41] Indeed, opposition by the Mathers to its use has been offered as almost the only defense of those much-maligned divines and has been presented as proof of their enlightened thinking in an otherwise benighted episode.[42] In reality, Increase Mather attacked the acceptance of spectral evidence because it was too rationalistic; he refused to repudiate the mystery of the invisible world and therefore assumed a position that rested on a theological absolute—namely, that the horrors of Satan were beyond limit or comprehension. As a result, he was forced to maintain that the Devil could do anything at all despite empirical observation to the contrary; hence, the Devil could even possess an innocent and unwilling person and make that person's specter afflict someone. The court, on the other hand, maintained that the empirical perception of reality was most important; what was seen by the victim was what counted.[43] Moreover, admitting spectral evidence was firmly founded in law; it had been used since 1593 in England, and Chief Justice Holt permitted its use in two cases he heard in 1690 and 1695. During the Salem trials, in fact, Dalton's *Countrey Justice* was cited to support the admissibility of this kind of evidence.[44]

Torture, which Robert Calef and John Proctor alleged was also used in 1692 to obtain evidence, was an archaic but still accepted technique for extracting "proof" from heretics, and it met the needs of 1692 by bringing into the open those facts that, it was believed, were being kept purposely hidden by silence. In the past, James I had "warmly" recommended the use of torture in witchcraft trials, as had the Puritan divine William Perkins.[45] According to Calef and Proctor, the two men whose confessions were extracted by tying neck and heels together "till the blood was ready to come out of their Noses" were Richard Carrier and Andrew Carrier; Proctor's son, William, was tortured in this way, too, it was alleged, but he did not confess. Although ministers at Boston had cautioned against using anything "the lawfulness whereof may be doubted by the people of God," they referred the judges to the Puritan divines Perkins and Bernard, where support for the practice could be found.[46]

41. For example, it is misunderstood and made the object of ridicule in Marion Starkey, *The Devil in Massachusetts*, p. 54.

42. Kenneth B. Murdock, *Increase Mather, the Foremost American Puritan*, pp. 294–306.

43. On this point about spectral evidence, I am indebted to the excellent discussion of the Mathers' role in 1692 as analyzed by Robert Middlekauff, *The Mathers*, pp. 154–55.

44. On the legality of spectral evidence, see George L. Kittredge, *Witchcraft in Old and New England*, pp. 363–64, 593.

45. G. L. Burr, ed., *Narratives of the Witchcraft Cases, 1648–1706*, p. 363n.

46. Thomas Hutchinson, *History of the Colony and Province of Massachusetts Bay*,

The definition of witchcraft, moreover, was a legalistic one calculated to isolate all users of *any* forms of magic in the county. As Chief Justice Stoughton charged the jury in June 1692, it was not necessary to prove—much less believe—that the afflicted girls actually had suffered pain; that is, that they "were really pined or consumed" by direct, malefic bewitchment at the hands of the accused. All that was required for proof of witchcraft was a belief that the afflicted were the object of *any* type of magical action that incidentally brought such pains and contortions with it. "This, said he, is a pining and consuming in the sense of the law."[47] Stoughton's reference was to the statute of 1604 concerning witchcraft; according to that law, no harm (*maleficium*) need be inflicted. Consulting spirits "for any purpose," Coke explained, ". . . without any other act or thing" was a capital crime. It did not matter for what purposes persons used magic, for what was at stake was an entire system of law and authority that was being challenged by an utterly antithetical *method* of social control. Magic was, therefore, a secular heresy that had to be crushed, and four of the accused had, in fact, done nothing more than make a "covenant with the Evill Spirit, the Devill."[48] Even the use of witchcraft by the accused to cure the afflicted was considered prima facie evidence of guilt, for the ability to use magic in such a way was merely another extralegal form of control over someone else.[49]

Hostility to the colony's system of law, government, and authority was therefore punished harshly. Indeed, this was the single characteristic most commonly exhibited by those who were dealt with most severely by the court—that is, by those who were actually put to death. No one who behaved defiantly or impudently toward the court escaped with his or her life. By contrast, many other persons were also condemned, but never executed; significantly, none of these challenged the legitimacy of the

2:38. Robert Calef, "More Wonders of the Invisible World," p. 363. Upham, *Salem Witchcraft*, 2:311.

47. Calef, "More Wonders," p. 380n. Stoughton's charge to the jury is mentioned in Thomas Brattle, "Account of the Witchcraft," p. 77.

48. Coke describes the new statute (1 Jac. I, c. 12) in *The Third Part of the Institutes of the Laws of England*, pp. 43–47. Punishment was to be by hanging, which was the manner in which the condemned Essex witches were executed. Ironically, it might be argued that the hanging of the Essex witches was not, strictly speaking, proper; when it was proved that *maleficium* was used against a master or husband, the offender was guilty of petty treason, and punishment was to be death by burning. On this point, see A. D. J. Macfarlane, "Witchcraft in Tudor and Stuart England," p. 73. For an Essex witch hanged for having "bewitcht" her husband to death, see *WRec.* 1:140, examination of Bridget Bishop.

49. To a remarkable degree, the accusations made at the witches in 1692 resemble those made at the Antinomians fifty-five years earlier. Compare, for example, Cotton Mather's observations on devilish artifice (*Wonders*, pp. 174–98) with Winthrop's description of how the Antinomians subtly spread their influence among the people of the colony (John Winthrop, "A Short History of the Rise, reign, and ruine of the Antinomians, Familists, and Libertines," pp. 204–5).

court and each accepted its sentence without challenge. Several of those ultimately executed, moreover, had reputations of being hostile to the court system in the past. Susannah Martin and Wilmot Reed had such a history, while the son of George Jacobs had been accused in 1674 of drowning horses that had trespassed on his lot; significantly, the horse belonged to Nathaniel Putnam, head of the litigious Putnam family and a strong proponent of the witchcraft trials.[50]

But Martha and Giles Corey took the most dangerously defiant stand. Martha, whose defense usually has been overshadowed by her husband's behavior, was very explicit in her defiance of the law and her claim to be innocent in God's view. The views of the court did not trouble her, she said, because it was blind to the truth and "shee would open the eyes of the magistrates and ministers." Sensing the ominously antinomian implications, the judges concentrated on that statement and mentioned it several times during her examination. Her opposition to the trials and her refusal to confess finally sealed her doom. Her husband Giles stood mute and refused even to make a plea, but his action was not, as is often asserted, an attempt to preserve his estate. Rather, he was making a powerfully defiant gesture against the official, legal processes of the "Tryal by Jury" as they operated in the county. His refusal to make any type of open, public statement was the most blatant challenge to the methods and goals of the court, and he was subjected to *peine forte et dure* so that a plea might be obtained from him. Of course, Corey may have been refusing to plead as a way of saving his estate from confiscation after his conviction, but such is not necessarily true. Although some estates were confiscated, not all were, and John Proctor devised his estate by will in the belief that it would descend to his heirs.[51]

Proctor, like several others executed, made the literally fatal mistake of publicly criticizing the court. In a letter to five ministers written at Salem gaol, he maintained that the judges and juries were deluded by the Devil, and he complained that the court's "actions are very like the Popish cruelties." His attitude was apparent to the girls accusing him, for during the examination one of them described his specter as mocking the magistrates; she cried out, "There is Goodman Proctor in the magistrates lap." Susannah Martin not only denied the validity of spectral evidence,

---

50. Upham, *Salem Witchcraft*, 1:198 (Jacobs). *WRec.* 1:207–8 (Martin); 2:104–5 (Reed). Although Woodward's edited volumes are incomplete, they will be referred to for the convenience of the reader who wishes to consult them. Where he omits evidence, the complete typescripts (*WP*) will be cited.

51. Calef, "More Wonders," p. 367. For another instance of defying an effort at prosecution by remaining silent, see above, p. 143. G. H. Moore disputes the contention that the purpose was retention of his estate (*Final Notes on Witchcraft in Massachusetts*, pp. 40–59). Moore, as Hansen points out, erred in saying that no estates were confiscated (*Witchcraft at Salem*, pp. 198–99, 297n).

but she also laughed at the proceedings and described them as "such folly." Sarah Good, who was also hanged, "continued Rayling against the Magistrates" while being taken to gaol. "Her answers," recorded the court regarding her behavior before it, "were in a very wicked spit[e]full manner, reflecting and retorting against the authority with base and abusive words."[52]

By contrast, repentance and confession of witchcraft were tacit approval of the system, and no one who held to a confession was put to death. Though approximately fifty people admitted the practice of witchcraft, only five of them were condemned, and four of these (Abigail Hobbs, Anne Foster, Mary Lacey, and Rebecca Eames) were not executed. Only Samuel Wardwell was hanged—but he renounced his confession. By the end of the trials Dorcas Hoar stood as living demonstration of the functional significance of repentance and confession. In court three of the accusing girls had told of seeing the Devil tell her not to confess, for confession was acquiescence in the legal methods that the Devil opposed. Dorcas shouted at them, "Oh! You are liars and God will stop the mouth of liars," but she still refused to confess. Reprimanded "not to speak after this manner in the Court," she retorted, "I will speak the Truth as long as I live" and predicted that God would show the light to them. For her efforts the court sentenced her to death and told her, "This is unusual impudence to threaten before Authority." The day before her execution, however, she finally did confess and an order was quickly sent to the sheriff to save her life.[53] Martha Carrier, who had been executed a month earlier, would have done well to confess, too. Her son Richard had confessed under torture, but he was acquitted.[54]

Restoration Essex was especially sensitive to the threat of opposition to lawful authority, for a disturbing example of the difficulty of punishing it had occurred in the 1660s. This was the notorious episode of Joseph Porter, Jr., who had called his father "theife, lyar, and simple ape, shittabed" and had spoken his absolute contempt for duly constituted authority, of both household and government. Young Porter "did with an axe cutt downe his [father's] fence severall times and did set fire of a pyle of wood neere the dwelling house. . . . He called his mother Rambeggur, Gammar Shithouse, Gammar Pissehouse, Gammar Two Shoes. . . . He

52. Upham, *Salem Witchcraft*, 2:310–11. WRec. 1:64 (Proctor), 197 (Martin); 2:19 (Good).

53. WRec. 1:172–80 (Hobbs), 235–53 (How); 2:135–37 (Foster), 139–41 (Lacey), 144 (Eames), 146–48 (Wardwell). Hansen, *Witchcraft at Salem*, p. 194.

54. WRec. 2:54–68, 198–99. Sarah Loring Bailey, *Historical Sketches of Andover*, p. 200. The importance of the confession has been remarked upon by E. E. Evans-Pritchard as enabling both the accuser and the persons confessing to "live together as neighbours" in the future and be able to "cooperate in the life of the community" (*Witchcraft, Oracles, and Magic among the Azande*, p. 97).

reviled Master Hauthorne, one of the magistrates, calling him base, corrupt fellow, and said he cared not a tird for him." He was convicted of abusing his parents, and by Massachusetts law the court was empowered to sentence him to death. No one expected Porter to be executed under this peculiar statute, but the authority to do so was a potent assurance of the colony's legal powers. Porter's challenge to those powers, however, assumed greater seriousness in 1665 when a royal commission was sent to the colony to investigate departures from English laws. Porter appealed to the visitors, and they overturned the conviction as contrary to English practice. The reaction of the General Court at that time is noteworthy in light of fears in 1692 about similar English judicial interference with local efforts at social control: the royal action, it had said, was a "breach . . . in the wall of our government, [and] it would be an inlett of much trouble to us."[55] By insisting on strict legal forms in the witchcraft trials, however, there would be no such breach; opposition to authority would be handled with no fear of criticisms about improper proceedings.

During the prosecutions in 1692 witchcraft was described by the accusers in its common form as mischievous threats to avenge or forestall various types of court action in the past. After a "shining man" told her to report to Hathorne about John Willard's murders, one woman testified, Willard appeared and threatened to cut her throat. Abigail Hobbs wanted to confess, but before she did so she was warned by the specters of Sarah Good and "Judah White, a Jersey maid," to defy the court by refusing to confess or by fleeing. Although witchcraft as an extralegal tactic was a fearsome threat, many accusers still felt impelled to go to the court and some even claimed that the bewitched murder victims, as apparitions, had ordered them to "goe and tell these things to the magistrates."[56]

Frightened individuals went to the magistrates for the symbolic and real protection they afforded against a perceived threat. Because many of these men held militia commissions, too, it was easy to see them as an essential—if not primary—element in Samuel Parris's metaphor of a society's safety under siege: "The city of heaven, provided for the saints, is well-walled and well-gated and well-guarded, so that no devils, nor their instruments, shall enter therein."[57] The reassurance that came from knowing that the judges were guarding society from demonic assault, however, could quickly turn to distrust if any of them tried to resist the pressures for prosecution or to prevent the legal system from acting against witchcraft. Judge Nathaniel Saltonstall made this unhappy dis-

---

55. *Mass. Rec.* 4 (pt. ii):196, 216.
56. Upham, *Salem Witchcraft*, 2:323. WRec. 1:94–95, 172, 189, 262–63, 275.
57. Samuel Parris, "Sermons of the Reverend Samuel Parris, 1692–1693," Sept. 1692.

covery when he revealed his firm opposition to the proceedings. When accusations began in his hometown of Haverhill, Saltonstall refused to sign the complaints made there against local women Martha Emerson, Frances Hutchins, and Ruth Wilford. This failed to deter the accusers, however, and townsmen were able to go to Andover and obtain the necessary signature from its resident magistrate, Dudley Bradstreet. Saltonstall also flatly refused to take part in the examinations of the accused at Salem, and he finally left the bench "very much dissatisfied with the proceedings" of the court, according to Thomas Brattle. Not surprisingly, Saltonstall soon was suspected of witchcraft, and it was said that his once-magistratical specter was afflicting people. Personally shaken by the dilemma of abhorring the prosecutions while recognizing that he was being suspected because of his refusal to take part in them, Saltonstall began to drink heavily; after the executions had begun he even appeared at a meeting of the Governor's Council in an obviously drunken state.[58]

Such great demands were placed on the magistrates and the courts to combat witchcraft because the practice of magic, like other forms of extralegal force or authority, was a threat whose danger was magnified at a time of profound insecurity. Those who had joined with the Devil were no longer simply ameliorating a rigid system that required occasional releases of stress. Nor, for that matter, was their use of magic or extralegal force to reimpose the older standards of the mutually dependent community merely an archaically harmless gesture. Rather, they were endangering the very survival of the society, and their use of magic was unacceptably inconsistent with the new social norms and the standards of behavior that had been worked out so laboriously over the course of a generation.

This new attitude toward demonic possession—whether it was claimed credulously or with intent to deceive—can be seen in the behavior associated with many of those persons accused as witches in 1692. One area of everyday life in which witchcraft commonly had been alleged was in household relations, where the practice of witchcraft served to alleviate working conditions. Samuel Wilkins, for example, once had accomplished this by claiming that his loom was bewitched; its cord broke and cut his hand mysteriously, rendering him unable to work. Wilkins was making the claim that he was a *victim* of witchcraft, but it was often suspected that such self-proclaimed victims were actually working in collusion with the Devil in order to subvert authority pat-

58. Upham, *Salem Witchcraft*, 2:455. Samuel Sewell to Nathaniel Saltonstall, 3 Mar. 1693, in *Saltonstall Papers*, 1:211–12. See also ibid., pp. 53–54.

terns. Indeed, they sometimes boasted of such in order to strengthen the force of their resistance. Abigail Hobbs, when asked why she was so disobedient, rude, and "unseemly," asserted that she had "sold herselfe boddy and soule to the old boy" and thus had reason to fear no one.[59] John Bibber's wife Sarah "could fall into fitts as often as she plesed" to avoid taking care of her child, or "when anything crost her humor,"[60] while Tituba, Susannah Martin, Elizabeth How, Elizabeth Paine, Elizabeth Fosdick, and Mary Warren all associated the Devil with interference in work. Warren, significantly, later admitted that she had been drinking "Sider" before her alleged encounter with the Devil.[61] Nevertheless, using the Devil to resist legitimate household authority was a risky matter, and two of these people (How and Martin) were executed.[62]

Similarly, those in subordinate economic positions were suspected in 1692 of using witchcraft to improve their conditions, and in several cases it was alleged that poorer individuals had used magic to cover their thefts: Dorcas Hoar, Mary Parker, and Wilmot Reed were suspected of larceny, but each had covered up her deed by making threats of malefic magical revenge. All of these women were condemned in 1692; except for Hoar, who confessed and was spared, all were executed.[63]

On the other hand, it was also possible for persons in positions of dominance to be accused of witchcraft. But it was not their economic character or status per se that prompted such charges.[64] Rather, witchcraft was identified by the people of Essex as a social tool to be used by anyone—regardless of economic factors—for the purpose of overstepping or challenging established authority patterns. Although this interpretation meant that suspicion was generally directed at those who felt oppressed by such patterns by being in subordinate social or economic positions, suspicions might be directed at dominant persons seen to be exceeding their authority in an extralegal or otherwise unjustified manner. For example, it was contrary to acceptable and legally prescribed rules of behavior to abuse one's position of household dominance by being an excessively harsh husband or master. As a result, several accusations identified satanic artifice as a way of cruelly or unjustly keeping someone

---

59. *WRec.* 1:177–78, 2:3.

60. Ibid., 2:203–5.

61. Ibid., 1:226–27 (Martin), 41 (Tituba); 2:106–7 (Paine and Fosdick), 77–78 (How), 124–25 (Warren).

62. Ibid., 2:69–94 (How); 1:193–233 (Martin).

63. Ibid., 1:245–48 (Hoar); 2:158–60 (Parker). Bailey, *Andover*, p. 221.

64. For a contrary view, see Paul Boyer and Stephen Nissenbaum, *Salem Possessed*, pp. 80–109, where it is suggested that persons of the dominant and more affluent, commercially based Salem Town were the targets of accusation by a resentful community of agrarians at Salem Village.

in subjection. In fact, of the five men executed as witches, four were described as cruel husbands or masters. In the examinations it was alleged that John Proctor "thretend to thrash" his servant Mary Warren. John Willard's wife, it was said, had complained how "cruelly" Willard had beaten her, and a servant of George Jacobs, Sr., related how an apparition of his master stood bearing two barrel staves (often used as clubs in beatings). George Burroughs, although living in Maine, had left behind him the reputation of being a stern husband who scolded his wife for writing to her father or lying in bed too long when ill.[65]

In the same manner, old age was another source of authority or control that might be regarded as unjustified. Many young people were subordinate within the traditional patterns of deference toward their elders and were especially resentful of the deference required toward the aged whose declining powers made such deference seem unwarranted. Youthful accusations against the elderly have been a common feature of witchcraft outbreaks throughout history,[66] and it is possible that in Essex the youthful accusers—such as servants or wives—were attempting to throw off a form of authority they felt unjustifiably onerous. To be sure, the more debilitated a person grew, the less worthy of exercising authority he or she appeared. Accusations by youths of bewitchment by older persons, therefore, identified their authority with the Devil and served to repudiate a resented pattern of fading traditional dominance. Ann Putnam explicitly named her tormentor as "an old gray head man with a great nose" whom "people used to call . . . old father pharoah." Mary Easty (age 58) of Topsfield was named as a witch after rebuking Samuel Smith (age 25), who had been "Rude in discorse" with her. Told that he "might Rue it hereafter," Smith became suspicious of Mary when he allegedly felt a pain in his shoulder while going home, "and the stone wall rattled very much."[67]

The waning authority of the general community to impose its standards of neighborly watchfulness was also reflected in the specific charges made at many Essex witches. The collective discipline of the mutually

65. WRec. 1:63–64 (Proctor), 256 (Jacobs); 2:3 (Willard), 109, 124–25 (Burroughs).

66. For a discussion of this general phenomenon, see A. D. J. Macfarlane, *Witchcraft in Tudor and Stuart England*, pp. 229–32.

67. WRec. 2:201–2, 43. Bailey, *Andover*, p. 207. Youthful accusation against more mature adults therefore should be seen as rooted in the particular social realities and tensions of a specific historical time period (in this case, the age of Filmer's *Patriarcha*) as much as being a largely psychological phenomenon. For an application of a psychological explanation to the events of 1692, see John Demos, "Underlying Themes in the Witchcraft of Seventeenth-Century New England." For other examples in Essex of youthful hostility or resentment toward elders, see Complaint against Bringell [1676], EP 25:90; Complaint against Wilkinson [1679], EP 32:49; and Presentment of Thomas Maule [1682], EP 38:9–13.

dependent community was a traditional ideal of social control to which the earliest Puritan villages had aspired, but in the course of more than half a century's social change this control had lost some of its legitimacy. Like the unquestioned authority of the elderly, community sanction was falling into disfavor and witchcraft accusations—as they did in Essex, England—offered a way of repudiating older ideals and social norms. As a result, meddlesome intervention in, or attention to, the affairs of others was seen as the Devil's activity. Ann Dolliver and Samuel Wardwell, for example, were suspected of having satanic assistance because they seemed to know about matters that were supposed to be private. One of Dolliver's neighbors in Gloucester explicitly equated the two activities, remarking, "I mervalle how much that old witch knowes everything that is done in my house."[68] Sarah Good and Susannah Martin both had unpleasant encounters with neighbors whom they tried to visit, and shortly afterwards each neighbor noticed something mysterious that they ascribed to their unwanted callers.[69]

Adequate fences stood as symbols of local regulation, and statements about menacing spectral livestock were strikingly analogous to neighborly tensions over fences. Trespassing animals were a constant source of irritation between neighbors, and the beasts were frequently chased away by dogs or spoiled by the harsh beatings of bad neighbors. In the spectral antagonism of 1692, animal apparitions would ramble into houses or a spectral pig could reverse normal events and chase away a dog "which at other tymes used to Wory any hog well or Sufficiently." Reference was also made to fence rails that fell apart or, conversely, to a fence that served as protection for a person fleeing a witch's familiar. There were also several allusions to flying witches in Essex, for concern about the violation of fences was ever present. Susannah Sheldon, for instance, explained that witches had pulled her "over the stone walls," and that "she Rid upone a poole."[70]

Other tensions created by intruding animals were apparent, and reports that animals were being harmed mysteriously (and presumably by witches) were common in the accusations of 1692. When Dorcas Hoar's chickens were killed "doing damages" in another person's cornfield, she told the man bringing one of the dead birds back to her "that he

68. WRec. 2:153, 200. On this characteristic in English accusations, see Macfarlane, Witchcraft, p. 172.

69. WRec. 1:26, 224–26.

70. Ibid., 1:155–56, 160–61, 215–16, 219–20, 224–26; 2:87–88, 168–69, 208. Starkey, Devil, p. 174. Bailey, Andover, p. 222. John Hale, "A Modest Inquiry into the Nature of Witchcraft," p. 420. The reports of Essex witches flying contrast suggestively with the relative rarity of such reports in England, where boundary tensions were less acute. On this, see Keith Thomas, Religion and the Decline of Magic, p. 445.

should never be the beter for it before the week was out." Samuel Ward-well, responding to animals on his property, would "bid the devil to take" them, while the widow Sarah Holton believed that Rebecca Nurse had bewitched her husband Benjamin to death "because our piggs gott into hir field."[71]

Mary Easty's elder sister, Rebecca Nurse, has stood as one of the most perplexing examples of those persons accused of witchcraft seemingly for no reason. According to the most recent study of the subject, she was the "very model of Christian piety" and "a respected older woman."[72] But if we accept Sarah Holton's account of an episode that occurred in 1689, Rebecca permitted herself one outburst of bad neighborliness that touched a sensitive chord in Essex: she threatened the use of malicious mischief against the Holton family's pigs that had trespassed on her property. According to Sarah, "Rebekah Nurs . . . came to our house and fell a railing at him [Benjamin Holton] because our piggs gott into hir field, tho our pigs ware sufficiently yoaked and their fence was down in severall places, yet all we could say to hir could no ways passifie hir, but she continewed Railing and scolding a grat while together calling to hir son Benj[amin] Nurs to goe and git a gun and kill our piggs and lett non of them goe out of the field." Shortly afterward Benjamin Holton was "struck blind," and after recurring fits of blindness and weakness throughout the following summer, he died. As in other cases, the link between "spoiling" trespassing animals and the use of malefic magic as related forms of extralegal force was not hard to forge.[73]

Worse still, under examination Rebecca made two mistakes. Her first was to deny the validity of spectral evidence and to assert that "the Devil may appear in my shape." The second was her answer to the question, "Is it not an unaccountable case when you are examined these persons [the accusers] are afflicted?" Like many others who would be sent to their deaths, she implicitly repudiated the authority of the court by replying, "I have got no body to look to but God."[74] It is also noteworthy that her husband Francis was perhaps the most frequently consulted arbitrator in Salem, offering a resolution to disputes that parties did not wish to take to court.[75]

Fencing disputes, however, were only a part of the larger problem of land management in the county, and concern and fear about the actual tenure of land were particularly intense between 1686 and 1692, because

71. WRec. 1:93–94 (Nurse), 249–51 (Hoar); 2:148 (Wardwell).
72. Boyer and Nissenbaum, *Salem Possessed*, pp. 117, 147.
73. WP, 1:22. This episode is also related in Upham, *Salem Witchcraft*, 2:281–83.
74. Upham, *Salem Witchcraft*, 2:68. WP, 1:20.
75. Upham, *Salem Witchcraft*, 1:79.

during the Andros regime land titles were called into question and the system of title certification and boundary determination through litigation was suspended. Even after Andros and company were ousted in 1689, apprehension persisted among New Englanders, and Cotton Mather is said to have expressed his religious concerns by using the interesting metaphor "that the old landlord Satan would arrest the country out of their hands."[76] Not surprisingly, these tensions found their release in witchcraft accusations in relationships where resolution of simmering land conflict had not been attempted in court. Susannah Martin, who was not satisfied with the terms of payment for some land her husband had sold, was suspected of bewitching the buyer's cow to death. Arbitration had been employed to resolve a land controversy between William Hobbs and his neighbors, with whom he was "allways contending." The dispute continued without effective settlement, however, and Hobbs found himself accused of witchcraft in 1692.[77] The most direct connection in the trials between unresolved land rivalry and allegations of malefic magic was demonstrated in Andover, where more people were accused of witchcraft than in any town of the county. The trouble arose in 1691, when Benjamin Abbott was granted land next to the farm of Richard and Martha Carrier. Shortly after this, a neighbor "heard Martha Carrier say that Benjamin Abbutt would wish he had not meddled with that land so near our house." Abbott told the court the rest of the story. Martha, he said, had become "very Angerey, and said she would stick as Closs to Benjamin Abbutt as bark Stooke to the Tree and that I should repent of it afore seven yeares Came to an End and that doctor prescott could never cure me." Magical revenge and mischief were a natural explanation when he developed painful sores on his side and groin, and the affliction lasted until Martha was arrested in 1692—in which case her veiled threats and her challenges to his land were ended. It was also alleged that Giles Corey had bewitched a woman he believed had "caused her master to ask more for a piece of meadow than he [Corey] was willing to give."[78]

Most of the charges brought to the court in 1692, therefore, reflected long-term tensions, uncertainties, and fears. One new problem, however, was the sudden outbreak of war and the imminent threat of Indian raids on the exposed Essex frontier. As the special oyer and terminer court was

76. Joshua Broadbent to Francis Nicholson, 21 June 1692, *CSP* 13:653.
77. *WRec.* 1:185–87 (Hobbs), 218–19 (Martin). Although not explicitly related to land, see the accusations leveled at John and Elizabeth Proctor and at Richard Carrier, in ibid., 1:111–12 (Proctor); 2:198–99 (Carrier).
78. Upham, *Salem Witchcraft*, 2:334 (Corey). *WRec.* 2:59–60 (Carrier).

handling threats of witchcraft with dispatch, it was comforting to be able to identify the military threat as supernatural, too.

Cotton Mather bemoaned the assault then taking place on New England by "an Army of Devils," and many others linked the war and the witchcraft trials. One man, part of a force traveling to relieve the English fort at Casco Bay, recalled strange and demonic goings-on en route. William Barker's confession from prison in 1692 only heightened these fears, for he wrote of the Devil's "app~aring to me like a Black," and of attending a witches' coven at the Salem meetinghouse with "about an hundred five Blades, some with Rapiers by their side."[79]

The fact that George Burroughs lived in Maine when it was ravaged by the French and Indians made him a target of suspicion. Interrogating one confessing witch, the magistrates asked if Burroughs had tried to enlist her aid in killing "the Eastward Souldiers." Ann Putnam, more-over, fed this belief by saying that Burroughs's specter had told her of killing the child of Deodat Lawson because Lawson had served as chaplain in the expedition to Maine. Not only had he murdered the child and Mrs. Lawson, but he was also accused of having "bewitched a grate many souldiers to death at the eastward when Sir Edmon was their."[80]

John Alden was another victim of the war fears gripping Essex County, for he had tried to commandeer Marblehead's cannon in 1690, arousing fears that the town would be left defenseless and easy prey for the French. In 1692 these suspicions reappeared, but further motivations were attributed to what he had done two years earlier. At his examination—after which spectators remarked that he stood outside as "a bold fellow, with his hat on before the judges"—he was accused of selling "powder and shot to the Indians and French." It was also charged that Alden "lies with the Indian squaws, and has Indian papooses."[81]

This charge (in particular, that of having double loyalties) was a very serious one in wartime, and it resulted in witchcraft charges against several others in the Essex community. Although the non-English population was the likely target, no general purge of Jerseymen or Indians resulted. Only Philip English, Tituba, and an Indian slave in Salem by the name of Candy were accused from among those groups, and none of them was executed. Rather, the English population displayed greater

79. Hale, "Modest Inquiry," pp. 419–20.
80. WRec. 1:173, 2:113–14, 123–24. Burroughs, it will be recalled, had been in court before—when he had emphasized the importance of adhering to the spirit of an obligation and not to its strict, legalistic terms. See p. 104 of this volume.
81. Upham, *Salem Witchcraft*, 2:244. On previous suspicions and accusations of arms sales in the county, see Complaint against Littlefield [1690], EP 50:130; and Complaint against Downer [1690], ibid., p. 151.

vigor in accusing English women who had intermarried with other groups. Such people are frequently identified in witch-hunts, because they are viewed as having a dangerously ambiguous status: members of neither the predominant ethnic group nor any clearly defined subgroup, they are distrusted more than the unmistakable outsiders to whom they are married. One anthropologist writes of these "interstitial" persons that they are feared as "intruders" because "their double loyalties and their ambiguous status in the structure where they are concerned makes [sic] them appear as a danger to those belonging fully in it," and the "powers attributed to them symbolize their ambiguous, inarticulate status."[82] In Essex in 1692, Mary English (born Hollingworth) and Mary Derich (or DeRich, born Bassett) were accused women whose marriages to Jersey-men may have rendered them suspicious, while Sarah Osborn (born Warren) had an Irish husband, and Martha Carrier was the wife of a Welshman. Other possible English wives of Jerseymen were Mary De-Riels and a Mrs. White. Both of these accused women were from Salem; the latter was probably Sarah Rumery, who married Zachariah White (formerly LeBlanc) in 1678.[83]

The halt to the witchcraft prosecutions came in early 1693, although the full force of the effort was curbed shortly after the last executions on 22 September 1692. Five days earlier the special court of oyer and terminer had adjourned until the first Tuesday in November, but it was never reconvened. While the first accusations had been made against persons deemed threatening to the social order, later accusations were quite different and endangered the stability they had been initiated to protect. They revealed no pattern at all and were directed at all types of persons, including Lady Phips, the wife of the governor. In addition, the trials were abandoned because a major component of the insecurity pro-pelling them was absent. On 12 October the legislature met to create a new system of justice to preserve order in the province. Laws for such matters as quieting land titles and punishing criminals were enacted at that session, and by 25 November laws appeared for establishing perma-nent courts. Within a month new justices had taken their oaths.[84]

In Andover witchcraft accusations were halted, significantly, by a lawsuit: one accused person went to the court for redress and obtained a writ for the arrest of his accusers in a defamation suit for a thousand

---

82. Mary Douglas, *Purity and Danger*, pp. 123–24.

83. Alonzo Lewis and J. R. Newhall, *History of Lynn, Including Lynnfield, Saugus, Swampscott, and Nahant*, p. 294. Upham, *Salem Witchcraft*, 2:17–18. Bailey, *Andover*, pp. 201–2. Perley, *Salem*, 3:135–36. Winfield S. Nevins, *Witchcraft in Salem Village in 1692*, p. 255.

84. Washburn, *Judicial History*, pp. 141, 144, 151. *Acts and Resolves*, 1:41, 51–55. Samuel Sewall, *The Diary of Samuel Sewall*, 1:302.

pounds in damages.[85] The use of this method was a symbolic turning point in that town and the entire county. With accusations in Andover becoming unpredictable—two sons of Simon Bradstreet were accused—it was growing apparent that the witch-hunt and its accusations had become more of a threat to the legal and social order than a prop. Litigation, moreover, was once again becoming an accessible means of conflict resolution. Samuel Parris, who had done so much to instigate the prosecutions early in 1692, had revealed this aspect of the trials in October, barely two weeks after the provincial legislature began work on a new court system and only six days after the last execution on Gallows Hill. Articulating the desires of the community for order and harmony through the openly determined resolution of conflict, he spoke in a sermon of the need to "sue for kisses."[86] If the residents of Essex County never showered kisses on each other after 1692, they did at least produce a shower of lawsuits. In the process they were regaining the social stability that had been absent for over six years.

85. Bailey, *Andover*, p. 235.
86. Parris, "Sermons," 28 Oct. 1692.

8 Epilogue

A Contentious and Well-Ordered People

The effort to preserve the traditional system of justice in Massachusetts did not end in 1692. Before the Privy Council finally accepted the legislature's judicature plans in 1699, the colony attempted in various ways to reestablish the flexible and efficient legal system it had enjoyed before 1684. In the first plan, sent to London in 1692, the inferior county courts of common pleas were limited to hearing civil cases "tryable at common law," but no such restriction was inserted into the section establishing a superior court. In addition, the legislature barred appeals to the king and the Privy Council in all real property cases; by deftly changing the wording of a clause in the charter, the General Court reserved final jurisdiction in all land causes to the province's judiciary.[1] The Privy Council caught this alteration and disallowed the act, beginning a tug-of-war over the powers of the new provincial judiciary until the bar to real property appeals was finally acknowledged.[2]

Although the provincial court system was quite different from that erected in the 1630s and 1640s, the laws and legal institutions under the second charter served many needs demonstrated under the first. In 1697 Massachusetts lawmakers enacted a law that guaranteed an assured title to anyone holding land without challenge from October 1692 until October 1704, and any legal action to challenge the occupant was "hereby excluded and forever debarred."[3] For every subsequent conveyance, they required a deed "or note in writing" to accompany any land transaction, which was then to be sworn before a magistrate and recorded by the clerk of the county court. The old charter recording law had proved

1. Compare the appeals limitation of the charter (*Acts and Resolves*, 1:15) with the act of 1692 (ibid., p. 76). The former only made reference to permitting appeals in personal actions, while the latter repeated that provision but added the words "and no other."

2. Ibid., pp. 143, 184–85, 283–87, 367–73. The bar generally operated in practice, but it was never explicitly provided by statute, as the approved judicature acts mentioned only appeals to the Privy Council according to the *charter*, where the meaning was not entirely beyond dispute. For a good discussion of this murky but important point, see Joseph H. Smith, *Appeals to the Privy Council from the American Plantations*, pp. 162–63.

3. *Acts and Resolves*, 1:299–301. A law of 1657 had attempted to do the same thing for land held between 1652 and 1662, but it did not have the accompanying legislation of the 1697 law. *Col. Laws 1672–86*, pp. 123–24.

inadequate, of course, but the legislators of the 1690s barred any action at law unless a claimant could produce some sort of written "agreement." If a man giving a deed refused to recognize it, the remedy was simple: he was to be jailed until he made acknowledgment.[4] Similarly, the old law of fencing requirements had been evaded because of its vagueness, and in 1698 strong enforcing provisions were added: the sufficiency of fences was specified in greater detail for all towns, and fence-viewers were to be heavily fined for neglecting their responsibilities.[5]

These specific acts went far to assure certainty in land matters, and in 1698 the General Court enabled the local courts to exercise the broad authority needed in more general problems. The legislature was responding to a need felt in Massachusetts throughout the seventeenth century "for relief in equity in cases not relievable by the rules of common law." Its "Act for Hearing and Determining of Cases in Equity" was an explicit grant to local courts of powers that they had exercised before without statutory authority, and the act applied to contract disagreements as well as to land disputes. The legislators were keenly aware that the need would exist "to moderate the rigour of the law" in the future. They also knew, however, that such "rigour" had "agrieved and oppressed" people during the Dominion regime, and this statute was another attempt to permit such people to seek equitable remedies at the superior or county courts. Unfortunately, it too was disallowed, and equity jurisdiction was finally limited to chancering penalties and to the equity of redemption.[6]

Residents of Essex faced the eighteenth century confident in the ability of their system of local justice to help them regulate their social affairs and impose order. With its powers set out and guaranteed by a relatively friendly Protestant monarchy, they had little fear of future charter removal. They also had less to fear from antinomian challenges from within; and witchcraft, which had represented an ominous threat to the social system, was not the terror it once had seemed. Within three months of the last executions, therefore, the General Court enacted that unless magic was used to commit murder it was punishable only by imprisonment and pillory. The Privy Council disallowed this act as well, but the intent of the legislature's effort is clear: new conditions had made witch-hunts unnecessary in provincial Massachusetts.[7]

Despite the Privy Council's disallowances, the province had obtained a legal system suited to its needs. Law and legal institutions would remain important in the eighteenth century, whether people went to

4. *Acts and Resolves*, 1:46, 298–99.
5. Ibid., pp. 333–34.
6. Ibid., pp. 356–57.
7. Ibid., pp. 90–91.

the justice of the peace, the county courts, or the Superior Court of Judicature. The specific demands on the legal system would change as social realities and necessities changed; the litigation of the second and third generations of the seventeenth century would be as different from that of the revolutionary generation as it had been from the lawsuits of the founders. But litigation would remain an essential facet of New England life, whatever its form.

In contrast to the first years of settlement, legal confrontation no longer drew criticism and opprobrium from the leaders of the province in the 1690s. The founders, who had sought to quell litigiousness, had emphasized local arbitration and the resolution of disputes by town or ecclesiastical mechanisms.[8] At the same time, their English experiences had demonstrated the need for effective judicial institutions, and while trying to reinvigorate communal bodies they were careful to buttress them with a potent county magistracy. The New England experience confirmed this caution and dashed the hopes for effective communalism, as economic growth and the intensified resentments of compact town life forced individuals to turn to the outside authority of extratown institutions like the courts. Litigation not only removed disputes from the emotionally charged arena of the town meeting; confrontation in the courtroom also served to facilitate a social process that had taken place years earlier in parts of England: placing people "far enough apart, so to speak, to be able to hate each other without repercussions on a mystical plane."[9]

Litigation as an agent of orderly social change and economic growth—not just as a final barrier against chaos—had proved vital to Essex society. In a rapidly evolving culture it was essential that people be able to meet and synthesize new ground rules for interaction—in neighborhoods, congregations, and business ventures. The crowded colonial courtroom served more than the litigants, however. Anyone appearing there—formally or merely to watch and listen—learned something about standards of behavior. He gained invaluable social information from listening to a drawn-out lawsuit, and from the court's decision he

8. This frame of mind is described in Darrett Rutman, *Winthrop's Boston*, pp. 43–44, 154, 202, 238.

9. A. D. J. Macfarlane, *Witchcraft in Tudor and Stuart England*, p. 202. It is important to note that this process was not linear and did not occur simultaneously across the Anglo-American world. Rather, these changes should be seen as a morphological process: what occurred in the Essex described by Macfarlane for the Tudor and early Stuart periods could occur half a century later in Essex, Massachusetts. Similarly, these developments could take place later yet in the more isolated parts of Massachusetts and, especially, Connecticut. For a good counterpoint on how different social conditions could create different legal patterns, see John J. Waters, "The Traditional World of the New England Peasants," and William E. Nelson, "The Larger Context of Litigation in Plymouth County, 1725–1825."

learned what his society approved. To Daniel Denison, such disputes were one method of creating the "Fundamentals and Superstructures of Faith and Order, in which we all agree there may be some finishing work, about which we are not altogether like minded, yet no need to pull down the building."¹⁰ The formulas asserted in court were brought back to a community where they were, in turn, communicated. People in Essex would not shun litigation, nor would their leaders try to discourage them from going to court to obtain a satisfactory solution.¹¹

Through that medium the residents of Essex were able to remain a contentious and well-ordered people, and even many who once distrusted the courts came to recognize that the legal system could be a source of their own protection. Thomas Maule revealed this acceptance of the legalist paradigm shortly after the witchcraft trials. Maule, a Salem Quaker, was a merchant who had used the county courts for his business purposes, but as a Quaker he was suspicious of the legal system and once had even been prosecuted for defaming a magistrate, impugning the integrity of the court, and criticizing the "laws of outward man."¹² In 1695 he published *Truth Held Forth and Maintained*, in which he not only articulated the standard Quaker position against oaths and "Persecuting Priests and Rulers," but also took a new and different position— in fact, a legalist one—by saying that the witchcraft trials were "high Rebellion against God and the King" because they had put people to death "without any warrant, precept, command, or example from either."¹³ Linking God and William III was a significant step for an American Quaker, for it joined Quaker concepts—once viewed as the most dangerous doctrine in the colony—with the English liberties that the colony's leaders were insisting upon for themselves after the Glorious Revolution.

Although Maule had had his tract published in what he thought was the safety of New York, he was soon arrested at his house in Salem by a warrant directed to none other than Sheriff George Corwin, who had held that office during the witchcraft trials, and served by Deputy Sheriff Jeremiah Neale, Andros's marshal for Essex County. Thirty-one copies of Maule's pamphlet were confiscated, and he was then indicted by a superior court grand jury at Salem for publishing "divers Slanders against

---

10. Daniel Denison, *Irenicon, or a Salve for New Englands Sore*, pp. 200–201. Oliver Wendell Holmes would refer to litigation as demonstrating the "inarticulate convictions" of a society, as well as its "public policy" (*The Common Law*, p. 32).

11. The Privy Council tried to discourage litigiousness by disallowing the act of 1698 on Massachusetts writs and processes, but the General Court passed it again in 1701. *Acts and Resolves*, 1:316–22, 459. See also the preamble to the 1701 "Act for Review in Civil Causes," ibid., p. 466.

12. Presentment of Thomas Maule [1682], EP 38:9–13.

13. Thomas Maule, *Truth Held Forth and Maintained*, p. 198.

the Churches and Government of the Province," a charge that was drafted, ironically, by King's Attorney Anthony Checkley, who had been prosecutor at the witchcraft trials.[14]

Maule's defense indicated how Quakers could now use the court system to their own advantage. Unlike his coreligionists of 1661 who had railed against the secular authority being used against them and had defied every legal effort to suppress their efforts, Maule claimed the English liberty of a trial by twelve equals in his own county, and as his counsel he secured the services of the skillful Benjamin Bullivant—a former official in the Dominion of New England who had received his legal training in England. Maule did repudiate the authority of the three judges (Thomas Danforth, Elisha Cook, and Samuel Sewall) to "assume . . . the power of the Bishops Court," but he was careful to add that "as you are invested with Magistratical power by Commission from the King, I do respect you." He then pleaded in abatement to the technical insufficiency of the writ, and when that plea was overruled he pleaded that there was "no Evidence in Law against me." Although he acknowledged that there might be erroneous doctrine in the book, he pointed out that in such cases "you may seek to the printer for satisfaction," for "my Name to my Book made by the Printer does not in law evidence to prove the same to be Thomas Maule." This point the jury accepted, for when they returned a verdict of acquittal and the judges demanded to know why, they replied that Maule's name on the book did not prove it to be his work.[15]

Maule's case was an important one, but less for what it presaged in specific terms for freedom of the press than for marking the general acceptance of law in Essex society. As the legalistic consensus was now able to develop unchallenged from within, people would be able to debate their differences and pursue their competing goals within a commonly accepted set of rules and procedures. Maule's legal opponents, after all, had been "Mauld with their own Weapons." Most Essex residents now saw such formal rules as necessary, for the process of emigration to the New World had demonstrated that traditional mechanisms of social control and standards of community behavior could not be transplanted more than ephemerally. Try as they might to duplicate—indeed, to exaggerate—the patterns of communal stability during the first years of colonization, they discovered that they were able to do so only temporarily. Such modes were characteristic of the traditional, interdependent community that had ordered itself by age-old implicit prescriptions en-

14. Thomas Maule, *New Englands Persecutors Mauld with their Own Weapons*, p. 58.
15. Ibid., pp. 61–62.

forced by informal communal pressures. But for persons emigrating to Essex, as for those who would emigrate to any newly settled region of North America, a new system of social control would be necessary. Wherever newcomers met, they might confront each other with competing value systems that would have to be reconciled. As the New World economy developed and became more complex, new and competing interests would collide and require balancing. With no group or interest able to assert unchallengeable control, some type of modus vivendi would have to be synthesized and elevated as a new social ideal. As these realities came to be accepted, so too were the positive possibilities of law admitted. In a New World in which some sector of society would always be witnessing the contests of change, the adaptive functions of law and the legal system would be recognized, for they would be central to the persistent and unremitting transformation of Early American society.

Bibliography

MANUSCRIPT SOURCES

Boston, Massachusetts

MASSACHUSETTS HISTORICAL SOCIETY

Records of the Massachusetts Bay Superior Court of Judicature. Microfilm.

STATE HOUSE

Massachusetts Archives. Vols. 11–129. Microfilm.

Plymouth, Massachusetts

PILGRIM HALL

Recordbook of the Plymouth County Court of General Sessions of the Peace, 1686–1721.

Salem, Massachusetts

COURTHOUSE

File Papers of the Essex County Quarterly and County Court, 1636–1692. 52 vols., arranged chronologically, and vol. 53 of miscellaneous papers.

Minutebook of the Essex Quarterly Court and County Court, terms held at Ipswich and Salem, 1638–1648.

Minutebook of the Essex County Court, terms held at Ipswich and Salem, 1655–1666.

Minutebook of the Essex County Court, terms held at Ipswich, 1646–1666.

Minutebook of the Essex County Court, terms held at Ipswich, 1666–1682.

Minutebook of the Essex County Court, terms held at Ipswich, 1682–1692.

Minutebook of the Norfolk County Court, terms held at Hampton and Salisbury, 1648–1678.

Minutebook of the Norfolk County Court, terms held at Hampton and Salisbury, 1672–1681. Transcript of originals, made by David Pulsifer in 1852.

Minutebook of the Essex Quarterly Court, terms held at Salem, 1636–1641.

Minutebook of the Essex County Court, terms held at Salem, 1667–1679.

Wastebook of material from the Essex County Court, terms held at Ipswich, 1682–1686.

Wastebook of material from the Norfolk County Court, terms held at Hampton and Salisbury, 1650–1680.

ESSEX INSTITUTE

Curwen Family Papers. 4 boxes.
English, Philip. Day Books and Ledgers. 6 vols.
Fiske, John. Notebook, 1636–1675.
Ipswich, Massachusetts. Town Records, 1634 [–1660]. Microfilm.
Parris, Samuel. "Sermons of the Reverend Samuel Parris, 1692–1693." Transcript
   of originals at Connecticut Historical Society.
"Salem Witchcraft—1692." Transcript of original judicial papers, compiled by A.
   N. Frost for the Works Progress Administration, 1938. 3 vols.
Salisbury, Massachusetts. Town Records, 1638–1902. Transcript.

REGISTRY OF DEEDS

Essex County Land Records, 1640–1694. 9 vols. Transcript of originals, made in
   1885.

PUBLISHED RECORDS AND OFFICIAL DOCUMENTS

Allen, D. H., ed. *Essex Quarter Sessions Order Book, 1652–1661*. Chelmsford,
   Eng., 1974.
Bates Harbin, E. H., ed. *Quarter Sessions Records for the County of Somerset*. Vol.
   1, *James I, 1607–1625*. Vol. 2, *Charles I, 1625–1639*. London, 1906–8.
Bennet, J. H. E., and Dewhurst, J. C., eds. *Quarter Sessions Records with Other
   Records of the Justices of the Peace for the County Palatine of Chester, 1559–
   1760*. Chester, Eng., 1940.
Bowden, William H., comp. "Marblehead Town Records, 1648–1683." *Essex In-
   stitute Historical Collections* 69 (1933):207–329.
Chafee, Zechariah, Jr. "Records of the Suffolk County Court, 1671–1680." *Pub-
   lications of the Colonial Society of Massachusetts* 29–30 (*Collections*, Boston,
   1933).
Dalton, Samuel. *Records of the Commissioners Court Held at Hampton by Samuel
   Dalton, 1673–1680*. Abstracted by George F. Dow in *Records and Files of the
   Quarterly Courts of Essex County, Massachusetts*. Vols. 5–8 (Salem, 1916–21).
Dow, George F., ed. *The Probate Records of Essex County, Massachusetts*. 3 vols.
   Salem, 1920.
Elton, G. R., ed. *The Tudor Constitution: Documents and Commentary*. Cam-
   bridge, Eng., 1960.
Farrand, Max, ed. *The Laws and Liberties of Massachusetts. Reprinted from the
   Copy of the 1648 Edition in the Henry E. Huntington Library*. Cambridge,
   Mass., 1929.
Great Britain. Privy Council. *Acts of the Privy Council, Colonial Series*. Vol. 1,
   1613–1680. London, 1908.
Howell James, D. E., ed. *Norfolk Quarter Sessions Order Book, 1650–1657*.
   Norwich, Eng., 1955.
LeHardy, William, ed. *County of Middlesex: Calendar to the Sessions Records*.
   Vol. 1, *1612–1614*. London, 1935.
Libby, Charles Thornton, ed. *Province and Court Records of Maine*. Vols. 1–3.
   Portland, 1929–47.
Manchester, Massachusetts. *Town Records of Manchester, from the Earliest
   Grants of Land, 1636 . . . until 1736*. Salem, 1889.

Massachusetts, Commonwealth of. *Acts and Resolves, Public and Private, of the Province of the Massachusetts Bay.* Vol. 1, *1692–1714.* Boston, 1869.
————. *Historical Data Relating to Counties, Cities, and Towns in Massachusetts.* Boston, 1966.
————. *Laws.* Vol. 13, *Passed at Several Sessions of the General Court, Beginning January, 1834, and Ending April, 1836.* Boston, 1836.
"Massachusetts Royal Commissions, 1681–1774." *Publications of the Colonial Society of Massachusetts* 2 (*Collections*, Boston, 1913).
Mighill, Benjamin P., and Blodgette, George B., eds. *The Early Records of the Town of Rowley, Massachusetts, 1639–1672.* Rowley, 1894.
Moody, Robert E., ed. "Records of the Magistrate's Court at Haverhill, Massachusetts, Kept by Nathaniel Saltonstall, 1682–1695." *Proceedings of the Massachusetts Historical Society* 79 (1967): 151–86.
Morris, Richard B., ed. *Select Cases of the Mayor's Court of New York City, 1674–1784.* Washington, D.C., 1935.
Noble, John, and Cronin, John F., eds. *Records of the Court of Assistants of the Colony of Massachusetts Bay, 1630–1692.* 3 vols. Boston, 1901–28.
O'Callaghan, E. B., ed. *Documents Relative to the Colonial History of the State of New-York.* Vol. 3, *London Documents: I–VIII, 1614–1692.* Albany, 1853.
"Petition from Ipswich" [21 June 1637]. *Proceedings of the Massachusetts Historical Society,* 2d ser. 3 (1886–87): 198–99.
Pierce, Richard D., ed. *Records of the First Church in Salem, Massachusetts, 1629–1736.* Salem, 1974.
Sainsbury, W. N., and Fortescue, J. W. *Calendar of State Papers, Colonial Series, America and West Indies.* Vols. 1–13, *1574–1692.* London, 1860–1902.
Salem, Massachusetts. "Salem Town Records, 1638–1683." *Essex Institute Historical Collections* 9–83 (1868–1947).
————. *Town Records of Salem. October 1, 1634, to November 7, 1659.* Salem, 1868.
Schofield, George A. *The Ancient Records of the Town of Ipswich, 1634–1650.* Ipswich, 1890.
Shurtleff, Nathaniel B., ed. *Records of the Governor and Company of the Massachusetts Bay in New England.* 5 vols. Boston, 1853–54.
Smith, Joseph H., ed. *Colonial Justice in Western Massachusetts (1639–1702): The Pynchon Court Record.* Cambridge, Mass., 1961.
Toppan, Robert N., ed. "Council Records of Massachusetts under the Administration of President Joseph Dudley." *Proceedings of the Massachusetts Historical Society,* 2d ser. 13 (1899):222–86.
Tutle, J. H., ed. "Land Warrants issued under Andros, 1687–1688." *Publications of the Colonial Society of Massachusetts* 21 (*Transactions*, 1919): 292–363.
Upham, W. P., comp. *Wenham Town Records, 1642–1706.* Wenham, 1930.
Weinbaum, Martin, ed. *British Borough Charters, 1307–1660.* London, 1943.
Whitmore, William H., ed. *The Colonial Laws of Massachusetts. Reprinted from the Edition of 1660, with the Supplements to 1672, Containing Also the Body of Liberties of 1641.* Boston, 1889.
————, ed. *The Colonial Laws of Massachusetts. Reprinted from the Edition of 1672, with the Supplements through 1686.* Boston, 1887.
Woodward, William E., ed. *Records of Salem Witchcraft.* 2 vols. Roxbury, Mass., 1864.
Worthley, Harold F., ed. *Records of the Particular (Congregational) Churches of Massachusetts, Gathered 1620–1805.* Cambridge, Mass., 1970.

TRACTS, SERMONS, AND CONTEMPORARY ACCOUNTS

Allen, James. *New-England's Choicest Blessing*. Boston, 1679.

Bradford, William. *Of Plymouth Plantation, 1620–1647* [1650]. Edited by S. E. Morison. New York, 1952.

Brattle, Thomas. "Account of the Witchcraft" [1692]. *Massachusetts Historical Society Collections*, 1st ser. 5 (1798): 61–79.

Bulkeley, Gershom. *Will and Doom, or the Miseries of Connecticut by and Under an Usurped and Arbitrary Power* [1692]. Edited by Charles J. Hoadly. *Collections of the Connecticut Historical Society* 3 (1895): 69–269.

Burr, George L., ed. *Narratives of the Witchcraft Cases, 1648–1706*. 1914. Reprint. New York, 1963.

Calef, Robert. "More Wonders of the Invisible World" [1692]. In *Narratives of the Witchcraft Cases, 1648–1706*, edited by George L. Burr. 1914. Reprint. New York, 1963.

Cotton, John. *The Churches Resurrection, or the Opening of the Fift and Sixt Verses of the 20th Chapter of Revelation*. London, 1642.

Denison, Daniel. *Irenicon, or a Salve for New-Englands Sore*. Boston, 1684.

Falle, Philip. *An Account of the Isle of Jersey, the Greatest of those Islands that are now the Only Remainder of the English Colonial Dominions in France*. London, 1694.

Filmer, Robert. *"Patriarcha" and Other Political Works*. Edited by Peter Laslett. New York, 1949.

Hale, John. "A Modest Inquiry into the Nature of Witchcraft." In *Narratives of the Witchcraft Cases, 1648–1706*, edited by George L. Burr. 1914. Reprint. New York, 1963.

Higginson, John. *Our Dying Saviour's Legacy of Peace to His Disciples in a Troublesome World*. Boston, 1686.

Hooker, Thomas. *The Application of Redemption*. London, 1659.

Hubbard, William. *The Benefit of a Well-Ordered Conversation* [1682]. Boston, 1684.

———. *A General History of New England, from the Discovery to MDCLXXX* [1680]. Boston, 1848.

———. *The Happiness of a People in the Wisdome of their Rulers Directing*. Boston, 1676.

Hutchinson, Thomas, ed. *A Collection of Original Papers Relative to the History of the Colony of Massachusetts Bay* 1769. Reprint. Boston, 1865.

Johnson, Edward. *Wonder-Working Providence* [1653]. Edited by J. F. Jameson. New York, 1910.

Josselyn, John. *An Account of Two Voyages to New England*. London, 1674.

Keayne, Robert. *The Apologia of Robert Keayne* [1653]. Edited by Bernard Bailyn. Boston, 1964.

Lechford, Thomas. *Note-book Kept by Thomas Lechford, Esq., Lawyer, in Boston, Massachusetts Bay, from June 27, 1638 to July 1641*. Cambridge, Mass., 1885.

———. *Plain Dealing, or News from New-England* [1642]. Edited by J. H. Trumbull. Reprint. New York, 1970.

Mather, Cotton. *Detur Dignori. The Righteous Man Described as the Excellent Man*. Boston, 1720.

————. "A Discourse on Witchcraft." In *Memorable Providences, Relating to Witchcraft and Possessions*. Cotton Mather, Boston, 1689.

————. *Magnalia Christi Americana* [1702]. 2 vols. Hartford, Conn., 1853.

————. *Memorable Providences, Relating to Witchcraft and Possessions*. Boston, 1689.

————. *Nunc Dimittis Briefly Descanted On*. Boston, 1709.

————. *The Present State of New England*. Boston, 1690.

————. *Wonders of the Invisible World* [1693]. London, 1862.

Mather, Increase. *Cases of Conscience Concerning Evil Spirits Personating Men*. [1692]. London, 1862.

Maule, Thomas. *New-Englands Persecutors Mauld with Their Own Weapons*. New York, 1697.

————. *Truth Held Forth and Maintained*. New York, 1695.

Moody, Robert E., ed. *The Saltonstall Papers*. Vol. 1, *1607–1789*. *Collections of the Massachusetts Historical Society* 80 (1972).

Randolph, Edward. *Edward Randolph, His Letters and Official Papers from New England, Middle, and Southern Colonies, With Other Documents Relating Chiefly to the Vacating of the Royal Charter of the Colony of Massachusetts Bay, 1676–1703*. Edited by Robert N. Toppan and Alfred T. Goodrick. 7 vols. Boston, 1898–1909.

Sewall, Samuel. *The Diary of Samuel Sewall, 1674–1729*. 2 vols. Edited by M. Halsey Thomas. New York, 1973.

Stoughton, William. *New England's True Interest*. Boston, 1668.

Toppan, Robert N., ed. "Andros Records." *American Antiquarian Proceedings*, new ser. 13 (1899–1900): 237–68.

Whitmore, William H., ed. *The Andros Tracts. Being a Collection of Pamphlets and Official Papers issued during the period between the Overthrow of the Andros Government and the Establishment of the Second Charter of Massachusetts*. 3 vols. Boston, 1868–74.

Winthrop Family. *Correspondence of the Winthrop Family*. In *Collections of the Massachusetts Historical Society*, 4th ser. 6–7 (1863, 1865).

————. *The Winthrop Papers*. Vol. 1, *1498–1628*. Boston, 1929.

Winthrop, John. *The History of New England, from 1630 to 1649*. Edited by James Savage. Boston, 1853.

————. "A Model of Christian Charity" [1630]. In *Puritan Political Ideas, 1558–1794*, edited by Edmund S. Morgan. Indianapolis, Ind., 1965.

————. "A Short History of the Rise, reign, and ruine of the Antinomians, Familists, and Libertines." In *The Antinomian Crisis*, edited by David D. Hall. Middletown, Conn., 1968.

Woodbridge, John. *Severals Relating to a Fund*. Boston, 1682.

LEGAL TREATISES, ABRIDGMENTS, AND REPORTS

Blackstone, William. *Commentaries on the Laws of England. Book the Third*. Oxford, 1768.

Brooke, Sir Robert. *La Graunde Abridgement, Collect and Escrit per le Iudge tresreuerend Syr Robert Brooke*. 2 vols. in 1. London, 1573.

Coke, Sir Edward. *The Fourth Part of the Institutes of the Laws of England* [1642]. London, 1797.

_____. *The Third Part of the Institutes of the Laws of England* [1628]. London, 1797.

Dalton, Michael. *Countrey Justice*. London, 1619.

The English Reports. Vol. 77, *King's Bench Division, Containing Coke, Parts 5–13*. London, 1907.

Finch, Sir Henry. *Law; or, a Discourse Thereof* [1627]. London, 1636.

Greenwood, William. *Curia Comitatus Rediviva, or the Pratique Part of the County-Court Revived*. London, 1657.

Hale, Sir Matthew. "Some Considerations touching the Amendment or Alteration of Lawes." In *A Collection of Tracts Relative to the Laws of England*, edited by Francis Hargrave. Dublin, 1787.

Howe, Mark DeWolfe. *Readings in American Legal History*. Cambridge, Mass., 1949.

Kitchin, John. *Jurisdictions; or, the Lawful Authority of Courts Leet, Courts Baron, Court of Marshalseyes, Court of Pypowder, and Antient Demesne*. London, 1663.

Lambarde, William. *Eirenarcha, or the Office of the Justices of Peace*. London, 1581.

_____. *William Lambarde and Local Government. His "Ephemeris" and Twenty-Nine Charges to Juries and Commissions*. Edited by Conyers Read. Ithaca, N.Y., 1962.

March, John. *Actions for Slaunder . . . to which is added Awards or Arbitrements*. London, 1647.

Peters [*sic*], Hugh. *Good Work for a Good Magistrate. Or, a Short Guide to great quiet*. London, 1651.

St. German, Christopher. *Doctor and Student; or, Dialogues Between a Doctor of Divinity, and A Student in the Laws of England* [1531]. 16th ed. London, 1761.

Sheppard, William. *Of Corporations, Fraternities, and Guilds*. London, 1659.

_____. *The Court-keepers Guide* [1641]. London, 1654.

_____. *England's Balme*. London, 1657.

Tyng, D. A. *Reports of Cases Argued and Determined in the Supreme Judicial Court of the Commonwealth of Massachusetts*. Vol. 14, 1817. Boston, 1864.

Viner, Charles. *A General Abridgment of Law and Equity, Alphabetically Digested under Proper Titles*. 24 vols. London, 1793.

BOOKS AND ARTICLES

Akagi, Roy H. *The Town Proprietors of the New England Colonies: A Study of Their Development, Organization, Activities, and Controversies, 1620–1770*. New York, 1924.

Andrews, Charles McLean. *The Colonial Period of American History*. 4 vols. New Haven, Conn., 1934–38.

_____. *River Towns of Connecticut*. Baltimore, 1889.

_____. "On the Writing of Colonial History." *William and Mary Quarterly*, 3d ser. 1 (1944): 27–48.

Arensberg, Conrad. *The Irish Countryman: An Anthropological Study*. New York, 1937.

Ault, W. O. *Open-Field Farming in Medieval England: A Study of Village By-Laws*. London, 1972.

Axtell, James. "The Vengeful Women of Marblehead. Robert Roules's Deposition of 1677." *William and Mary Quarterly*, 3d ser. 21 (1974): 647–52.

Bailey, Sarah Loring. *Historical Sketches of Andover*. Boston, 1880.

Bailyn, Bernard. *Ideological Origins of the American Revolution*. Cambridge, Mass., 1967.

————. *The New England Merchants in the Seventeenth Century*. Cambridge, Mass., 1955.

————. "Politics and Social Structure in Virginia." In *Seventeenth-Century America*, edited by James Morton Smith. Chapel Hill, N.C., 1959.

————, and Bailyn, Lotte. *Massachusetts Shipping, 1697–1714*. Cambridge, Mass., 1959.

Barnes, Thomas G. "Law and Liberty (and Order) in Early Massachusetts." In *Papers Read at a Clark Library Seminar, November 3, 1973*. Los Angeles, 1975.

————. *Somerset, 1625–1640: A County's Government during the "Personal Rule."* Cambridge, Mass., 1961.

Barnes, Viola F. *The Dominion of New England: A Study in British Colonial Policy*. New Haven, Conn., 1923.

Belknap, Henry W. "Philip English, Commerce Builder." *American Antiquarian Society Proceedings*, new ser. 41 (1931): 17–24.

Bennett, H. S. *Life on the English Manor: A Study of Peasant Conditions, 1150–1400*. Cambridge, Mass., 1960.

Berthoff, Rowland T. "The American Social Order: A Conservative Hypothesis." *American Historical Review* 69 (1960): 495–514.

Bidwell, Percy, and Falconer, John I. *History of Agriculture in the Northern United States*. Washington, D.C., 1925.

Black, Barbara A. "The Judicial Power and the General Court in Early Massachusetts (1634–1686)." Ph.D. dissertation, Yale University, 1975.

Bloch, Marc. *Feudal Society*. 2 vols. Translated by L. A. Manyon. Chicago, 1961.

Bond, Carroll T. "Introduction to the Legal Procedure." In *Proceedings of the Court of Chancery of Maryland, 1669–1679*, edited by J. Hall Pleasants. *Maryland Archives*, vol. 51. Baltimore, 1934.

Boyer, Paul, and Nissenbaum, Stephen. *Salem Possessed: The Social Origins of Witchcraft*. Cambridge, Mass., 1974.

Breen, Timothy H. *The Character of the Good Ruler: A Study of Puritan Political Ideas in New England, 1630–1730*. New Haven, Conn., 1970.

————, and Foster, Stephen. "The Puritans' Greatest Achievement: A Study of Social Cohesion in Seventeenth-Century Massachusetts." *Journal of American History* 60 (1973): 5–22.

Bruchey, Stuart. *The Roots of American Economic Growth, 1607–1861*. New York, 1965.

Bushman, Richard. *From Puritan to Yankee: Character and the Social Order in Connecticut, 1690–1715*.

Carroll, Peter N. *Puritanism and the Wilderness: The Intellectual Significance of the New England Frontier, 1629–1700*. New York, 1969.

Cockburn, J. S. *A History of English Assizes, 1558–1714*. Cambridge, Eng., 1972.

Collinson, Patrick. *The Elizabethan Puritan Movement*. Berkeley, 1967.

Cook, George Allan. *John Wise, Early American Democrat*. New York, 1952.

Coser, Lewis A. *The Functions of Social Conflict*. 1956. Reprint. New York, 1969.

Davies, M. G. *The Enforcement of English Apprenticeship*. Cambridge, Mass., 1956.

Davis, Andrew M. "Corporations in the Days of the Colony." *Publications of The Colonial Society of Massachusetts* 1 (1892–94): 183–214.

Davisson, William I. "Essex County Price Trends: Money and Markets in Seventeenth-Century Massachusetts." *Essex Institute Historical Collections* 103 (1967): 291–342.

Dawson, John P. *A History of Lay Judges*. Cambridge, Mass., 1960.

Demos, John. "John Godfrey and His Neighbors: Witchcraft and the Social Web in Colonial Massachusetts." *William and Mary Quarterly*, 3d ser. 33 (1976): 242–65.

———. *A Little Commonwealth: Family Life in Plymouth Colony*. New York, 1970.

———. "Underlying Themes in the Witchcraft of Seventeenth-Century New England." *American Historical Review* 75 (1970): 1311–26.

Douglas, Mary. *Purity and Danger*. London, 1965.

Durkheim, Emile. *Emile Durkheim on the Division of Labor in Society*. Translated by George Simpson. New York, 1933.

Evans-Pritchard, E. E. *Witchcraft, Oracles, and Magic among the Azande*. Oxford, 1937.

Ewen, C. L'Estrange. *Witch Hunting and Witch Trials: The Indictments for Witchcraft from the Records of 1373 Assizes Held for the Home Circuit, 1559–1763*. London, 1929.

Firth, Raymond. *Elements of Social Organization*. 3d ed. Boston, 1961.

Flaherty, David H., ed. *Essays in the History of Early American Law*. Chapel Hill, N.C., 1969.

———. *Privacy in Colonial New England*. Charlottesville, Va., 1972.

Ford, A. C. *Colonial Precedents of our National Land System as it Existed in 1800*. Madison, Wis., 1910.

Forster, G. C. F. *The East Riding Justices of the Peace in the Seventeenth Century*. East Yorkshire Local History Series, no. 30. York, Eng., 1973.

Foster, Stephen. *Their Solitary Way: The Puritan Social Ethic in the First Century of Settlement in New England*. New Haven, Conn., 1971.

Geertz, Clifford. "Ideology as a Cultural System." In *Ideology and Discontent*, edited by D. E. Apter. New York, 1964.

Gildrie, Richard. *Salem, Massachusetts, 1626–1683, A Covenant Community*. Charlottesville, Va., 1975.

Gleason, J. H. *The Justices of the Peace in England, 1558–1640*. Oxford, 1969.

Gluckman, Max. *Custom and Conflict in Africa*. Oxford, 1965.

Goebel, Julius G. "King's Law and Local Custom in Seventeenth-Century New England." *Columbia Law Review* 31 (1931): 416–48.

Goodell, A. C. "The Origins of Towns in Massachusetts." *Proceedings of the Massachusetts Historical Society*, 2d ser. 5 (1890): 320–31.

Greene, Evarts B., and Harrington, Virginia D. *American Population before the Federal Census of 1790*. New York, 1932.

Greven, Philip. *Four Generations. Population, Land, and Family, in Colonial Andover, Massachusetts*. Ithaca, N.Y., 1970.

Hagood, Margaret. *Statistics for Sociologists*. New York. 1941.

Hall, David D. *The Faithful Shepherd: A History of the Puritan Ministry in the Seventeenth Century*. Chapel Hill, N.C., 1972.

Hall, Michael G. *Edward Randolph and the American Colonies, 1676–1703.* 1960. Paperback ed. New York, 1969.

Hansen, Chadwick. *Witchcraft at Salem.* Paperback ed. New York, 1970.

Harris, Ralph Bartram. "Philip English." *Essex Institute Historical Collections* 66 (1930): 273–90.

Haskins, George Lee. "The Beginnings of the Recording System in Massachusetts." *Boston University Law Review* 21 (1941): 281–304.

————. "Ecclesiastical Antecedents of Criminal Punishment in Early Massachusetts." *Proceedings of the Massachusetts Historical Society* 72 (1957–60): 21–35.

————. *Law and Authority in Early Massachusetts: A Study in Tradition and Design.* New York, 1960.

Hill, Christopher. *The Century of Revolution, 1603–1714.* New York, 1961.

————. *Society and Puritanism in Prerevolutionary England.* New York, 1964.

Hirst, Derek. *The Representative of the People?: Voters and Voting in England under the Early Stuarts.* Cambridge, Eng., 1975.

Holdsworth, W. S. *A History of English Law.* 16 vols. London, 1903–66.

Holmes, Clive. *The Eastern Association in the English Civil War.* Cambridge, Eng., 1974.

Holmes, Oliver Wendell. *The Common Law* [1881]. Edited by Mark DeWolfe Howe. Boston, 1963.

Howe, Mark DeWolfe. "The Recording of Deeds in the Colony of Massachusetts Bay." *Boston University Law Review* 28 (1948): 1–6.

————. "The Sources of Law in Colonial Massachusetts." In *Law and Authority in Colonial America,* edited by George A. Billias. Barre, Mass., 1965.

Hurst, J. Willard. "Legal Elements in United States History." *Perspectives in American History* 5 (1971): 3–92.

Hutchinson, Thomas. *History of the Colony and Province of Massachusetts Bay.* 3 vols. Edited by Lawrence Shaw Mayo. Cambridge, Mass., 1936.

Ingram, M. J. "Law and Disorder in Early Seventeenth-Century Wiltshire." In *Crime in England, 1550–1800,* edited by J. S. Cockburn. Princeton, N. J., 1977.

Innes, Stephen. "Land Tenancy and Social Order in Springfield, Massachusetts. 1652–1702." *William and Mary Quarterly,* 3d ser. 35 (1978): 33–56.

Key, V. O., Jr. *A Primer of Statistics for Political Scientists.* New York, 1954.

Kittredge, George L. *Witchcraft in Old and New England.* Cambridge, Mass., 1929.

Knappen, M. M. *Tudor Puritanism: A Chapter in the History of Idealism.* Paperback ed. Chicago, 1965.

Konig, David T. "A New Look at the Essex 'French': Ethnic Frictions and Community Tensions in Seventeenth-Century Essex County, Massachusetts." *Essex Institute Historical Collections* 110 (1974): 167–80.

Kuhn, Thomas S. *The Structure of Scientific Revolutions.* Chicago, 1962.

Laslett, Peter. *The World We Have Lost.* New York, 1965.

Laswell, Harold, and Arens, Richard. "The Role of Sanction in Conflict Resolution." *Journal of Conflict Resolution* 11 (1967): 27–39.

Lewis, Alonzo. *The History of Lynn.* Boston, 1829.

————, and Newhall, J. R. *History of Lynn, Including Lynnfield, Saugus, Swampscott, and Nahant.* 2 vols. Boston, 1865.

Lewis, I. M. "A Structural Approach to Witchcraft and Spirit Possession." In

Witchcraft Confessions and Accusations, edited by Mary Douglas. London, 1970.

Little, David B. *Religion, Order, and Law: A Study in Prerevolutionary England.* New York, 1968.

Lockridge, Kenneth A. *A New England Town, The First Hundred Years: Dedham, Massachusetts, 1636–1736.* New York, 1970.

McFarland, Raymond. *A History of the New England Fisheries.* Philadelphia, 1911.

Macfarlane, A. D. J. *Witchcraft in Tudor and Stuart England: A Regional and Comparative Study.* London, 1970.

―――――. "Witchcraft in Tudor and Stuart England." In *Crime in England, 1550–1800*, edited by J. S. Cockburn. Princeton, N. J., 1977.

Mayo, Lawrence Shaw. *John Endecott: A Biography.* Cambridge, Mass., 1936.

Middlekauff, Robert. *The Mathers: Three Generations of Puritan Intellectuals, 1596–1728.* New York, 1971.

Miller, Perry. "Errand into the Wilderness." In *Errand into the Wilderness*, edited by Perry Miller. New York, 1956.

―――――. *The New England Mind.* 2 vols. Vol. 1, *The Seventeenth Century.* Vol. 2, *From Colony to Province.* Boston, 1939–53.

Moore, G. H. *Final Notes on Witchcraft in Massachusetts.* New York, 1885.

Moore, Sally Falk. "Selection for Failure in a Small Social Field. Ritual Concord and Fraternal Strife among the Chagga, Kilimanjaro, 1968–1969." In *Symbol and Politics in Communal Ideology: Cases and Questions*, edited by Sally Falk Moore and Barbara C. Myerhoff. Ithaca, N.Y., 1975.

Morgan, Edmund S. *The Puritan Dilemma: The Story of John Winthrop.* Boston, 1958.

―――――. *The Puritan Family.* Rev. ed. New York, 1966.

―――――. "The Puritans and Sex." *New England Quarterly* 15 (1942): 591–607.

―――――. *Visible Saints: The History of a Puritan Idea.* New York, 1963.

Morris, Richard B. *Studies in the History of American Law.* New York, 1930.

Murdock, Kenneth B. *Increase Mather, the Foremost American Puritan.* Cambridge, Mass., 1925.

Nelson, William E. "The Larger Context of Litigation in Plymouth, 1725–1825." In *The Plymouth Court Records*, edited by David Thomas Konig. Wilmington, Del., 1978.

Nevins, Winfield S. *Witchcraft in Salem Village in 1692.* Salem, 1916.

Oberholzer, Emil, Jr. *Delinquent Saints: Disciplinary Action in the Early Congregational Churches of Massachusetts.* New York, 1952.

Palfrey, John Gorham. *History of New England.* 4 vols. Boston, 1875.

Perley, Sidney. *The History of Salem, Massachusetts.* 3 vols. Salem, 1924–28.

Perzel, Edward S. "Landholding in Ipswich." *Essex Institute Historical Collections* 104 (1968): 303–28.

Phillips, James Duncan. *Salem in the Seventeenth Century.* Boston, 1933.

Phythian-Adams, Charles. "The Communal Year at Coventry, 1450–1550." In *Crisis and Order in English Towns, 1500–1700*, edited by Peter Clark and Paul Slack. London, 1972.

Pope, Robert G. "New England versus the New England Mind: The Myth of Declension." *Journal of Social History* 3 (1969): 95–108.

Pospisil, Leo. "Legal Levels and the Multiplicity of Legal Systems in Human Societies." *Journal of Conflict Resolution* 11 (1967): 2–26.

Postan, M. M. *The Medieval Economy and Society: An Economic History of Britain in the Middle Ages*. London, 1972.

Powers, Edwin. *Crime and Punishment in Early Massachusetts, 1620–1692*. Boston, 1966.

Raftis, J. Ambrose. *Tenure and Mobility: Studies in the Social History of the Medieval English Village*. Toronto, 1964.

Rife, Clarence W. "Land Tenure in New Netherlands." In *Essays in Colonial History Presented to Charles McLean Andrews*. New Haven, Conn., 1931.

Roads, Samuel, Jr. *History and Traditions of Marblehead*. Boston, 1880.

Rutman, Darrett B. *Winthrop's Boston: Portrait of a Puritan Town*. 1965. Paperback ed. New York, 1972.

Sabine, Lorenzo. *Report on the Principal Fisheries of the American Seas*. Washington, D.C., 1853.

Saunders, A. C. *Jersey before and after the Norman Conquest of England*. Jersey, 1935.

_____. *Jersey in the Fifteenth and Sixteenth Centuries*. Jersey, 1933.

Savage, James. *A Genealogical Dictionary of the First Settlers of New England*. 4 vols. Boston, 1860–62.

Scott, William R. *The Constitution and Finance of English, Scottish, and Irish Joint-Stock Companies to 1720*. Vol. 2, *Companies for Foreign Trade, Colonization, Fishing, and Mining*. Cambridge, Eng., 1910.

Sears, John Humphrey. *The Physical Geography, Geology, Mineralogy, and Paleontology of Essex County, Massachusetts*. Salem, 1905.

Sibley, John Langdon. *Biographical Sketches of Graduates of Harvard University in Cambridge, Massachusetts*. 17 vols. Cambridge, Mass., 1873–85.

Simpson, A. W. B. *An Introduction to the History of the Land Law*. Oxford, 1961.

Slade, Daniel Denison. *Major Daniel Denison*. Boston, 1869.

Smith, A. Hassell. *County and Court: Government and Politics in Norfolk, 1558–1603*. Oxford, 1974.

Smith, Joseph H. *Appeals to the Privy Council from the American Plantations*. New York, 1950.

Starkey, Marion. *The Devil in Massachusetts*. 1949. Paperback ed. New York, 1969.

Tawney, R. H. *The Agrarian Problem in the Sixteenth Century*. New York, 1912.

Thomas, Keith. "History and Anthropology." *Past and Present*, no. 24 (1963): 3–24.

_____. *Religion and the Decline of Magic*. New York, 1971.

Thorne, Samuel E. "Dr. Bonham's Case." *Law Quarterly Review* 54 (1938): 543–52.

Trevelyan, G. M. *English Social History*. London, 1941.

Trotter, Eleanor M. *Seventeenth-Century Life in the Country Parish, with Special Reference to Local Government*. Cambridge, Eng., 1909.

Upham, Charles W. *Salem Witchcraft*. 2 vols. Boston, 1867.

Usher, R. G., ed. *The Presbyterian Movement in the Reign of Queen Elizabeth as Illustrated by the Minute Book of the Dedham Classis*. London, 1905.

Veall, Donald. *The Popular Movement for Law Reform, 1640–1660*. Oxford, 1970.

Wall, Robert E. *Massachusetts Bay: The Crucial Decade, 1640–1650*. New Haven, Conn., 1972.

Walzer, Michael. "Puritanism as a Revolutionary Ideology." *History and Theory* 3 (1960): 59–90.

———. *The Revolution of the Saints: A Study in the Origins of Radical Politics.* Cambridge, Mass., 1965.

Washburn, Emory. *Sketches in the Judicial History of Massachusetts.* Boston, 1840.

Waters, John J. "The Traditional World of the New England Peasants: A View from Seventeenth-Century Barnstable." *New England Historical and Genealogical Register* 130 (1976): 3–22.

Webb, Sidney, and Webb, Beatrice. *English Local Government.* Vol. 1, *The Parish and the County.* Vol 2, *The Manor and the Borough.* London, 1906–8.

Weber, Max. *Economy and Society.* Edited by Guenther Roth and Claus Wittich. 3 vols. New York, 1968.

Weeden, William B. *Economic and Social History of New England.* 2 vols. 1890. Reprint. New York, 1963.

Weis, Frederick Lewis. *The Colonial Clergy and the Colonial Churches of New England.* Lancaster, Mass., 1936.

Woodruff, Edwin H. "Chancery in Massachusetts." *Law Quarterly Review* 5 (1889): 370–86.

Wright, Carroll D. *Report on the Custody and Condition of the Public Records of Parishes, Towns, and Counties.* Boston, 1889.

Wrightson, Keith E. "The Puritan Reformation of Manners, with special reference to the Counties of Lancashire and Essex, 1640–1660." Ph.D. dissertation, University of Cambridge, 1973.

Index

The Author

David Thomas Konig is assistant professor of history at
Washington University in St. Louis.

The Book

Typeface: Stempel V-I-P Sabon

Design and composition: The University of North Carolina Press

Paper: Sixty pound 1854 by S. D. Warren Company

Binding cloth: Roxite B 53561 by The Holliston Mills, Incorporated

Printer and binder: Braun-Brumfield, Incorporated

Published by The University of North Carolina Press